# BEST

# PLAYS

## Middle Level

## 7 Plays for Young People

*with Lessons for Teaching the Basic Elements of Literature*

JAMESTOWN PUBLISHERS

*a division of* NTC/CONTEMPORARY PUBLISHING GROUP
Lincolnwood, Illinois USA

**Editorial Development:** Patricia Opaskar, Mary Ann Trost
**Cover Design:** Steve Straus
**Cover Illustration:** Lori Lohstoeter
**Interior Design:** Steve Straus
**Interior Illustration:** Jude Macaren

ISBN: 0-89061-896-8 (hardbound)
ISBN: 0-89061-876-3 (softbound)

Published by Jamestown Publishers,
a division of NTC/Contemporary Publishing Group, Inc.,
4255 West Touhy Avenue,
Lincolnwood (Chicago), Illinois 60712-1975 U.S.A.

01 02 03 04 05 06 MV 10 9 8 7 6 5 4 3

# ACKNOWLEDGMENTS

Acknowledgment is gratefully made to the following publishers, authors, and agents for permission to reprint these works. Every effort has been made to determine copyright owners. In the case of any omissions, the Publisher will be pleased to make suitable acknowledgments in future editions.

*Charley's Aunt: A Play in Three Acts* by Brandon Thomas. Used by permission of Samuel French, Inc.

*Trifles* by Susan Glaspell. Reprinted by permission of G. P. Putnam's Sons from *Plays* by Susan Glaspell, copyright 1920 by Dodd, Mead & Company, Inc., copyright renewed 1948 by Susan Glaspell.

*Driving Miss Daisy* by Alfred Uhry. Copyright © 1986 by Alfred Uhry. Used by permission of Flora Roberts, Inc.

*The Devil and Daniel Webster* by Stephen Vincent Benét. Copyright © 1938, 1939, Stephen Vincent Benét. Copyright renewed 1966 by Thomas C. Benet, Rachel Benet Lewis, Stephanie Benet Mahin. CAUTION: The reprinting of *The Devil and Daniel Webster* included in this volume is reprinted by permission of the author and Dramatists Play Service, Inc. The amateur performance rights in this play are controlled exclusively by Dramatists Play Service, Inc., 440 Park Avenue South, New York, NY 10016. No nonprofessional production of the play may be given without obtaining in advance the written permission of the Dramatists Play Service, Inc., and paying the requisite fee. Inquiries regarding all other rights should be addressed to Robert A. Friedman Dramatic Agency, Inc., 1501 Broadway, Suite 2310, New York, NY 10023.

*The Marriage Proposal* by Anton Chekhov. Copyright © 1967 by Joachim Neugroschel, translator. Reprinted by permission of the translator.

*Sorry, Wrong Number* by Lucille Fletcher. Copyright © 1948, 1952 by Lucille Fletcher.

*The Trouble with Tribbles* by David Gerrold. Copyright © 1973 by David Gerrold. Reprinted by permission of the author.

# CONTENTS

# TO THE STUDENT

How would you like to spend time with one of the greatest speakers in American history, one of the greatest detectives of all time, or the crew of a starship? Well, all of these experiences and more are possible through the plays in this book.

Plays, like short stories and novels, can take you into whole new worlds. They can introduce you to people and situations that you could never meet in real life but that can help you see real life in new and clearer ways. Like other forms of fiction, the plays in this book all contain characters, plots, and themes. Unlike short stories and novels, however, plays are intended to be performed and shared with many people at once.

To get the full effect of most plays, you need to see them performed by skilled actors and with all the costumes, scenery, and special effects that the playwright has in mind. With a little help from your imagination, however, you can come close to that experience by reading the plays. One of the advantages of reading plays rather than watching them is that you can reread certain parts to understand them better or to enjoy them more than once.

The plays you are about to read include some of the most successful dramas of American stage and television, as well as a translation of a work by a well-known Russian author. The plays include thrillers, comedies, and science fiction. They also include stories about everyday life. You are sure to find some people and plots you can enjoy and remember for years.

As you read this book you will learn about the elements of a play, and you will study the techniques that playwrights used to create them. You also will have a chance to try some of these techniques in your own writing.

## UNIT FORMAT AND ACTIVITIES

- Each unit begins with an illustration of a scene from the play you will read. This illustration will help you understand or make predictions about the play.
- The Introduction begins with information about the play and its author. It then presents an important literary concept and gives you an opportunity to develop this concept in your own writing. Finally, it contains questions for you to consider as you read.
- The text of the play makes up the next section. In a few cases, the selection consists of only one act or a sequence of scenes from a longer play.
- Following each play are questions that test your comprehension of events and other elements of the play, as well as your critical thinking skills. Your answers to these questions and to other exercises in the unit should be recorded in a personal literature notebook. Check your answers with your teacher.
- Your teacher may provide you with charts to record your progress in developing your comprehension skills: The Comprehension Skills Graph *records* your scores and the Comprehension Skills Profile *analyzes* your scores—providing you with information about the skills on which you need to focus. You can talk with your teacher about ways to work on those comprehension skills.
- The next section contains three lessons, which begin with a discussion of the literary concept that is the unit's focus. Each lesson illustrates a technique that the author uses to develop the concept. For example, you will see how a playwright uses stage directions, dialogue, and action to create characters.
- Short-answer exercises test your understanding of the author's techniques, as illustrated by short excerpts from the play. You can check your answers to the exercises with your teacher and determine what you need to review.
- Each lesson also includes a writing exercise that guides you in creating your own original work using the techniques you have just studied.

Discussion guides and a final writing activity round out each unit in the book. These activities will help sharpen your reading, thinking, speaking, and writing skills.

Reading the plays in this book will enable you to recognize and appreciate the skills it takes to write an entertaining play. When you understand what makes a play good, you become a better reader and viewer. The writing exercises and assignments will help you become a better writer by giving you practice in using the authors' techniques to make your own plays interesting.

# How to Read a Play

# Charley's Aunt

by Brandon Thomas

## INTRODUCTION

*ABOUT THE SELECTION*

From the time it hit the stage, *Charley's Aunt* has been an exceptionally popular comedy. Its first production opened in London in 1892, when the costumes described in the performance notes were fashionable. The play was so popular that the theater was officially ordered not to "cause a nuisance through the assembly of crowds." Midway through its four-year London run, it opened in New York, where it enjoyed similar success. The play was translated into many languages and, almost nonstop until the mid-1930s, some production of it was running somewhere in the world.

The play became a silent movie in 1925. It was filmed with sound in 1930 and again in 1941, this time with Jack Benny as the star. In 1949, a musical version was a hit on Broadway. There have been two television productions of the farce. Even today, more than 100 years later, the original play is performed practically every year by some regional theater.

For modern audiences much of the appeal of this play lies in its old-fashioned and elegant setting, and in its charming characters. But its primary appeal is the humor of a situation shared with such modern comedies as *Some Like It Hot* and *Tootsie*: a man awkwardly pretending to be a woman is trusted by women and courted by other men. In the passage that you will read, from the middle of Act I, the fun begins as an Oxford student is unwillingly drawn into impersonating a friend's rich aunt.

The play is set in an era when college was almost exclusively for rich young men, and when respectable single women were never in a man's rooms without an older woman as chaperone. Act I starts in the rooms of Oxford student Jack Chesney. Jack and his friend Charley Wykeham confess to each other that they are madly in love with Kitty and Amy, the ward and the niece of pompous and domineering Stephen Spettigue. Spettigue plans to take the young women to Scotland the next day, and the young men are about to leave Oxford as the school term ends. The students are desperate to find a way to have private talks with the women immediately.

Charley tells Jack that he expects the arrival, at any minute, of a rich aunt who has been in Brazil his whole life but who has been paying for his education. Jack proposes to invite Kitty and Amy to a luncheon in honor of the aunt, Donna Lucia d'Alvadorez. Jack sends invitations by messenger to the young women. Then he sends his manservant, Brassett, to invite a third student, Lord Fancourt Babberley, called Babbs, so that this "jolly, cheerful little chap" can keep Donna Lucia amused while Jack and Charley pair off with Kitty and Amy.

Babbs sends back word that he is busy with a luncheon of his own. When he comes to Jack's rooms a few minutes later to get refreshments for his expected guests. Jack and Charley explain their situation to him and appeal to him to stay. Babbs insists that he must meet that afternoon with other students involved in an amateur theatrical production he has joined. Before the others arrive, he wants to try on his costume. He explains that he is to play the role of an old lady. Unwilling to let Lord Fancourt slip out of his hands, Jack sends his manservant, Brassett, to Lord Fancourt's rooms to get the costume. Soon Babbs discovers he has been drawn into the starring role of an unplanned theatrical production.

**ABOUT THE AUTHOR**

Brandon Thomas (1856–1914) was a British actor and dramatist who is noted for his one spectacularly successful play, the farce *Charley's Aunt*. When *Charley's Aunt* was first performed in London in 1892, Thomas played the role of Sir Francis Chesney.

**ABOUT THE LESSONS**

The lessons that follow *Charley's Aunt* focus on the written form of a play and how it differs from other written forms of fiction. The lessons explain how playwrights use stage directions to establish mood and pacing; to explain how objects and actors should be positioned on stage; and to communicate how the actors should speak, move, and act.

## WRITING: STAGING A DAY IN YOUR LIFE

Realistic plays—and even farces like *Charley's Aunt*—try to make what happens on the stage seem as if it were happening in real life. At the end of this unit, you will transform a few minutes of your own life into the form of a play. The following activities will help you find material for your "slice-of-life" playlet:

- At random moments over the next few days, observe your surroundings carefully. Make a mental list of objects you see. In a classroom, what is on the walls? What pieces of equipment are visible? At home, where is the television set? How large is it? What else is in that room? If you wanted to transfer one of the rooms to the stage, what scenery would you need? what objects? Look for a room that you think would present itself well enough on stage for others to recognize it. Prepare by listing the characteristics of at least three different rooms.
- During conversations, be aware of gestures and movements that you and others make. For example, if you are arguing,

do you tend to speak loudly and use hand gestures, or do you act stiff and cold? When you talk on the phone, do you twist the cord or pace? When you're excited, does your voice get high-pitched, or do you repeat yourself? Keep a list of mannerisms that you see in yourself and your friends, particularly those that indicate different attitudes and emotions.

* Continue to add to your two lists. At the end of the unit, you will decide which of your details will help to present a realistic setting and a natural-looking conversation.

**AS YOU READ**

*Charley's Aunt* involves a great deal of visual humor, for which its author provided very specific directions. You will be able to follow the action better if you relate page-by-page stage directions to the stage diagram on page 6. Note the location of these abbreviations on the diagram: R. (right), R.C. (right of center), C. (center), L.C. (left of center), and L. (left). Note also that the two doors on stage left (the right side as the audience sees the stage) are identified by the abbreviations L.I.E. (the door downstage, that is, closer to the audience) and L.U.E. (the door upstage, that is, farther from the audience).

The questions below will help you think about some of the ways in which plays are different from other types of fiction. As you read this excerpt from *Charley's Aunt*, keep these questions in mind:

* How does the form of a play differ from the form of a short story or novel? Why does it take this form?
* How does the playwright help readers imagine the arrangement of things on stage?
* How does the playwright help readers imagine the actions, attitudes, and movements of the people on stage?

# *from*
# Charley's Aunt

⊖

by Brandon Thomas

## ACT III

Drawing Room at Spettigue's House. (Evening)

"Dinner lubricates business."—*Boswell*

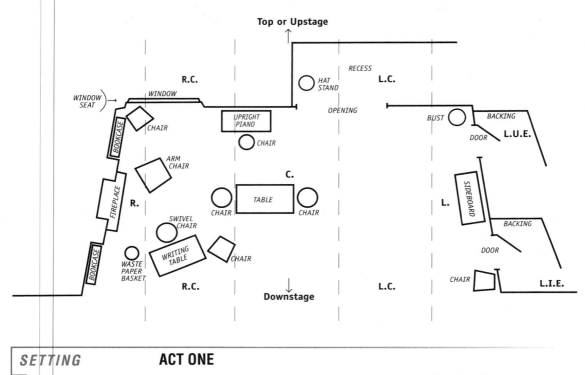

## ACT ONE

"When pious frauds—are dispensations."—*Hudibras*

**SCENE:** *Interior of* **Jack Chesney***'s Rooms, St. Olde's College, Oxford. Morning.*

*The walls are oak panelled or half-panelled or plain cream-washed walls with beautiful, low heraldic ceiling in cream, picked out in colour and dull gold. Door opening off, with passage backing, leading to outer door* L.I.E. *Door opening off to bedroom, with light backing,* L.U.E. *Between doors an oak sideboard with cupboard underneath. Large opening and recess with curtain to draw* L.C. *Long bay window* R.C. *with view of quad,*[1] *window seat with four cushions and one*

---

[1] quadrangle, such as a square formed by several buildings on a college campus

*magazine. Long red curtains. Upright piano* C. *with pile of music on top between window and recess. Fireplace* R., *looking-glass, etc., on mantel, low bookcases* R. *and* L. *of it. Saddle back armchair by fire. Table* C. *with ashtray and books and table cover in dark material on it, with two single chairs* R. *and* L. *of it, with sweater over back of* L. *chair. Writing table down* R.C. *by fire, with A.B.C. time table, magazine, and "Corona" cigar box. Circular hat stand inside corner of recess with boxing gloves, single sticks, etc., on it. Plaster bust of Plato on pedestal* L. *corner of room—angle. Clock and photographs of chorus girls and flowers on mantel shelf, more photographs and books on top of bookcases, pipes, tobacco jars, etc. Prints on walls above. Above on wall* L. *groups of Rowing Eights,[2] football teams. Six dining-room chairs arranged as follows: two* R. *and* L. *of* C. *table, one below door* L.I.E., *one at piano, one* L. *side of writing table, one top* R. *corner by window. Antique furniture, well-worn comfortable chairs. Quad is seen through window, and sunlight streams in through window.*

**Note:** This excerpt begins as Jack and Charley are persuading Lord Fancourt to stay for luncheon. They want him to keep Charley's visiting aunt, Donna Lucia, occupied while they talk privately with the other guests, Kitty and Amy. Lord Fancourt has plans to meet fellow student actors involved in a theatrical production in which he is to play the part of an old lady. Before the meeting, he wants to try on his costume. Jack insists that Lord Fancourt (nicknamed Babbs) try on the costume at Jack's rooms and stay for the luncheon. Jack sends his manservant, Brassett, to Lord Fancourt's rooms to get the costume. As the excerpt begins, all three students are standing around the table in the center of the room.

---

[2] rowing teams

*(Re-enter **Brassett** with dress box, L.I.E.— a large brown cardboard box with gilt edges, like an exaggerated chocolate box.)*

**Brassett.**    Your things, m'lord.

*(**Charley** goes down R., sits chair side of writing table. **Jack** goes R.C. front of C. table.)*

**Lord Fancourt.**    *(taking box from **Brassett**)* Thank you, Brassett. You're an awfully good chap. *(crosses to **Jack**; aside)* I say, Jack, could you lend me half a crown?[3] *(turns upstage and puts box on window seat at back)*

*(**Brassett** at sideboard)*

**Jack.**    *(feels in pockets, then aside to **Charley**)* Charley! Have you half a crown?

**Charley.**    *(pulling out linings of trouser pockets)* No, Jack, I haven't.

**Jack.**    *(crossing L., aside to **Brassett**)* Brassett! Give me half a crown, will you?

**Brassett.**    Yes, sir. *(takes out handful of money—gives half a crown)*

**Jack.**    *(comes C.)* Babbs!

*(**Lord Fancourt** comes down R.C.)*

**Jack.**    *(aside to **Lord Fancourt**)* Here you are. *(gives half-crown and crosses to **Charley** R.)*

**Lord Fancourt.**    Thanks. *(crosses to **Brassett**, L.)* Brassett, here you are.

*(**Jack** and **Charley** see half-crown given back to **Brassett** and laugh. **Charley** collapsed in chair L. of writing table. **Jack** ditto into chair R. of table C. Lord Fancourt turns, puzzled, crosses to **Jack**. **Jack** whispers to him, points to **Brassett**, then twice to himself, then to **Lord Fancourt**, and then to **Brassett** again. **Lord Fancourt** joins in laughter and goes up to window seat and picks up dress box. **Brassett**, during this action, exits L.U.E.)*

---

[3] a silver coin formerly used in Great Britain, worth two and a half shillings, or two shillings sixpence

**Jack.**   (*to* **Lord Fancourt**, *pointing to box*) What have you got there?

**Lord Fancourt.**   Chocolates.

**Charley.**   Chocolates? (*still seated in chair*)

**Jack.**   Let's have a look!

**Lord Fancourt.**   No, I'll tell you what I'll do. I'll try them on after lunch while you're all in the garden.

**Jack.**   You can't do that; we shall want you with us. Try them on now; won't take long, will it?

**Lord Fancourt.**   Only a minute or two. (*lifts box on to his* L. *shoulder, crossing upstage to* L.) I've lost an awful lot of time over these theatricals. (*at door*) But next term I mean to work.

(*Exits* L.U.E. **Jack** *goes up to front of fireplace.*)

**Kitty.**   (*off*) Oh yes, here it is; here's the name!

**Amy.**   (*off*) Oh, so it is! "Mr. Chesney." I wonder if they're in.

(*Knock*)

**Jack.**   (*to* **Charley** *at chair*) Here they are, and your aunt's not come yet. (*rushes to mantelpiece to see the time, notices photographs, slams them face down, arranges tie, smoothes hair all in a hurry, returns below table* C.)

**Charley.**   (*rises, getting behind* **Jack**) Good gracious! What shall we do? (*also trying to see in mirror*)

(*Re-enter* **Brassett**, L.U.E., *goes to door* L.I.E.)

**Jack.**   Oh, let them come in. We can explain. (*crossing* L.C. *below table* C.) Show them in, **Brassett**.

(**Brassett** *opens door, showing in* **Kitty** *and* **Amy**, *closes door and goes up back, and then exits* L.U.E.)

**Jack.**   (*shaking hands with* **Kitty**) How do you do? (*shaking hands with* **Amy**) So kind of you to come!

**Kitty.**   Oh, we were very pleased to be able to come. Weren't we, Amy?

(*They both cross to table* R. **Charley** *joins* **Amy** L.)

**Amy.**   Oh, yes. (*to* **Charley**) Mr. Wykeham, are we too early?

**Charley.**    Oh no, no!

(*They shake hands and move up to C. table together.* **Charley**, *in his nervousness, backs into the chair, then offers it to* **Amy**; *she sits in chair L. of C. table.*)

**Kitty.**    Yes, Mr. Chesney, you didn't mention any time.

(**Jack** *gives chair;* **Kitty** *sits L. of writing table.*)

**Jack.**    Oh, not at all, not at all! We're delighted! (*going to fireplace to look at clock; aside*) She'll be here soon.

(*Enter* **Lord Fancourt** L.U.E., *in his shirt-sleeves—to C. upstage, sees girls, and bolts[4] back L.U.E. in terror the girls may see him.* **Brassett** *takes tray from table C. and off through recess up L.C.*)

**Kitty.**    (*sitting*) And this is where you think and study and do all your work and everything?

**Jack.**    Oh yes, we do a lot of that sort of thing here. (*sits*)

**Kitty.**    You've jolly quarters here.

(**Jack** *and* **Kitty** *continue to talk aside.*)

**Charley.**    (*to Amy*) I'm so glad you were able come here today. You're off to Scotland tomorrow and we shall miss you so much.

**Amy.**    Yes, Uncle always takes us to some dreadful remote place at this time of the year, where we never see a soul, and it's *so* dreary.

**Charley.**    Why does he?

**Amy.**    I don't know.

**Charley.**    It's a shame!

**Amy.**    Why, are you sorry we're going?

**Charley.**    Sorry? Why, it's put me—and Jack—into a perfect fever; that's why we were so anxious to see you here today.

**Amy.**    It's lucky Uncle is away in town, or I don't think we could have come.

**Charley.**    Why?

---

[4] to start suddenly and run away

**Amy.**   I don't know, but he raises such odd objections, and then you know he's so peculiar about Kitty.

**Charley.**   Why?

**Amy.**   She's an heiress, you know, and he's her guardian.

(*They talk aside.*)

**Jack.**   (*ardently*) Miss Verdun, have you forgotten that dance the other night? I *never* shall.

**Kitty.**   No.

**Jack.**   No! Those stolen moments in the garden by ourselves were the very happiest of all my life, and out there in the moonlight—ah, moonlight is the true atmosphere for—for sentiment.

**Kitty.**   I wonder how many people have said that?

**Jack.**   (*let down a little*) Kitty, I know when you like you can be an awful plague,[5] but today you are quite cynical.

**Kitty.**   I know I am; I'm thinking of that man.

**Jack.**   Of what man?

**Kitty.**   Of my guardian—Mr. Spettigue, who hurries us away from all our best friends directly we get to know anyone really well, for fear of—

**Jack.**   For fear of what?

**Kitty.**   (*evasively*). Oh, I don't know!

**Jack.**   Why *does* he?

**Kitty.**   (*looking up and smiling*) Because he's a selfish, wicked old man.

**Jack.**   Are you—really—so sorry to go away?

**Kitty.**   No, I am angry. But don't speak about it any more, or, as Amy says, "I shall cry."

**Amy.**   (*rising and speaking to* **Charley** *as they come down* L. *a little*) What a dear—sweet—old lady your aunt must be, Mr.

---

[5] slang of the day intended as a compliment

Wykeham! I am longing to know her. Where is she?

**Charley.** *(aside)* Jack! *(rapidly, in agonized aside and beckoning* **Jack**, *who goes* R.C. *to him)* Where's my aunt?

**(Jack** *whispers something in his ear and turns away.)*

**Charley.** *(not catching it)* What?

**(Jack** *shrugs shoulders hopelessly and returns to* **Kitty**. **Kitty** *and* **Amy** *see nothing of this last scene, which must be played rapidly.)*

**Charley.** *(to* **Amy**, *hesitatingly)* Oh, why, she's hardly arrived yet.

**Amy.** *(surprised)* No, oh! *(crosses to* **Kitty***)* Kitty, Mr. Wykeham's aunt hasn't come yet.

**Kitty.** *(rising)* Hasn't come? *(crossing to* C.*)* Oh—*(turning to* **Jack***)* Then we must—we'll—run and do some shopping— and come back. Shan't be long. Good-bye!

**(Kitty** *crosses* **Amy** *to* L.I.E. **Charley** *has worked round to door, which he opens.* **Jack** *follows)*

**Amy.** *(to* **Jack***)* Good-bye.

**Jack.** Good-bye.

**Kitty.** *(to* **Charley** *at door)* Good-bye.

**Amy.** *(to* **Charley** *at door—rather sadly)* Good-bye.

*(Exit* L.I.E., **Kitty** *first, then* **Amy***)*

**Charley.** *(at door* L.I.E.*)* Good-bye! *(unconsciously taking the same tone)*

*(Slight pause.* **Jack** *and* **Charley** *look at each other blankly; both sit on* C. *table and shake hands.)*

**Jack.** See that? Off like a shot when they found your aunt wasn't here.

**Charley.** Makes an awful difference, doesn't it?

**Jack.** *(hurrying* **Charley** *off* L.I.E.*)* Now look here, you cut off to the station and bundle the old girl here in a fly.[6]

**(Charley** *picks up his hat from* C. *table.)*

---

[6] a one-horse carriage, particularly one for hire

**Charley.** (*turning at door* L.I.E.) The old girl! What do you mean?

**Jack.** Well, your aunt—and I'll see after the lunch and keep an eye on Babbs.

**Charley.** (*going*) All right! (*returning*) I say, Jack, I feel happier since I've seen them, don't you?

**Jack.** (*impatiently*) Yes. Be off! (*going towards writing table*)

(*Exit* **Charley**, L.I.E. *Enter* **Lord Fancourt** *in shirt-sleeves and waist-coat*, L.U.E., *comes down* L. *of* **Jack** *cautiously.* **Jack** *turns and sees* **Lord Fancourt**.)

**Lord Fancourt.** I say, old chap, have you got any hairpins?

(*Enter* **Brassett**, L.U.E., *coming down* L. *to sideboard*)

**Jack.** Hairpins? Great Scot, no!

**Lord Fancourt.** May I send your man for some?

**Jack.** Yes, certainly.

**Lord Fancourt.** (*aside to* **Jack**). I say, have you got sixpence?

**Jack.** (*feeling hurriedly and impatiently in pockets*) No—afraid not.

**Lord Fancourt.** Why, you haven't got anything! (*aside to* **Brassett**) I say, Brassett, I gave you half a crown just now; do you mind making it two shillings[7] and getting me sixpennyworth of hairpins?

**Brassett.** (*with a look*) Certainly, m'lord.

**Lord Fancourt.** You can keep the change. (*exit* **Brassett**, L.I.E.) I say, Jack, were those the girls?

(*Both* C.)

**Jack.** Yes. But what the deuce made you jump out like that? They might have seen you!

**Lord Fancourt.** I didn't know they were here.

(*Knock at outer door,* L.I.E.)

**Jack.** Look out! There's somebody else. (**Lord Fancourt** *bolts and*

---

[7] a coin used in Great Britain; at the time of the play it was worth 12 pence

*exits door* L.U.E.*)* By George! There was a lot of hope in what Kitty said; in another minute I'd have told her that I— *(going to table* R.*, back turned to door* L.I.E.*)* But never mind, everything's going on splendidly. *(knock repeated)* Come in!

*(Enter* **Sir Francis Chesney** L.I.E.*)*

*(**Colonel Sir Francis Chesney, Bart.**, late Indian Service.[8] Tall, good-looking, smart in appearance and manners, wearing small military moustache, actually fifty-one but looking nearer forty, very smart, cheery and young in manner. Wears brown lounge suit, bowler hat, and carries gloves and Malacca walking-stick. He has just arrived from London.)*

**Sir Francis.**    Jack!

**Jack.**    *(turning, surprised, and delighted)* Dad! *(Going* C.*)*

**Sir Francis.**    My dear boy!

*(They shake hands* C.*)*

**Jack.**    Dear old Dad! What brings you here! Wherever have you come from?

**Sir Francis.**    From town, my lad. To have a chat with you and to bring you your check. *(puts hat, stick, and gloves on sideboard)*

**Jack.**    Thanks, Dad; you're a brick![9]

**Sir Francis.**    *(smiling)* A bit over-baked, my boy, after all my years in India. *(coming* C. *below table)*

**Jack.**    A bit crisped, Dad, but a humbug pictorially.[10]

**Sir Francis.**    Am I? How do you make that out?

**Jack.**    How old are you?

**Sir Francis.**    What do you say to fifty—

**Jack.**    Fifty?

**Sir Francis.**    *One!*

**Jack.**    Who'd believe it?

---

[8] formerly a member of the British armed forces in India

[9] slang term meaning a solid, reliable person

[10] slang of the day intended as a compliment

**Sir Francis.**    (*cheerfully and unconcernedly*) Well, we all grow old. (*sits on C. table*)

(**Sir Francis** *takes out pocketbook containing check already made out to* **Jack** *and bundle of bills pinned together.*)

**Jack.**    And as presentably as possible. Why, dear old Dad, even you at fifty—

**Sir Francis.**    *One!*

**Jack.**    Fifty years ago would have been a stout, white-haired— or bald—top-booted, domineering old boy! And instead, here you are, a smart, bang up-to-date sort of chap one can talk to like a chum! Now how have you done it?

**Sir Francis.**    Don't know.

**Jack.**    Do you drink?

**Sir Francis.**    All I want.

**Jack.**    Eat well?

**Sir Francis.**    Never noticed.

**Jack.**    There you are! Consequently health good, temper perfect—we're going to be great pals, Dad.

**Sir Francis.**    (*handing check*) Here you are, my boy. There's your check to go on with. (*gives check; looking at bills*)

**Jack.**    Thanks, Dad! (*sees amount of check—smiles to* **Sir Francis**) I haven't seen half enough of you.

**Sir Francis.**    (*holding up bills*) I see your hospitality—

**Jack.**    I hope, Dad—

**Sir Francis.**    Never mind; same when I was a lad. (*They laugh.* **Sir Francis** *rises; they both move towards table* R. **Jack** *back of table.* **Sir Francis** L. *of it.*) I'm very satisfied with you. It's something to go down from college with a record like yours. (*picks up cigar box and opens it*) I say, my boy, where the deuce did you get these cigars?

**Jack.**    (*casually*) Those, Dad?

**Sir Francis.**    (*putting box down, sits* L. *by writing table*) Ah! That accounts for the bills. And now, my lad, we must begin to think.

**Jack.**   (*sits at writing table*) Think?

**Sir Francis.**   Now that I have come into the family title, as you know, I have also—which you don't know—come into the family debts and difficulties.

**Jack.**   Debts!

**Sir Francis.**   Which are far more than I expected, with the result that all the money I've been saving for you in India goes to pay them. And in short, Jack, you and I, for the next few years—will be, comparatively speaking, *poor men.*

**Jack.**   (*rises and crosses behind desk to* C) Poor men! (*aside*) This settles me with old Spettigue!

**Sir Francis.**   (*rising*) However, I'm in hopes of a small appointment for you—(**Jack** *turns hopefully*)—in Bengal. (*goes to fireplace*)

(*Re-enter* **Brassett**, L.I.E.)

**Jack.**   Bengal! What a horrible place! (*turns, sees* **Brassett** *as he passes upstage* L., *to him, irritably*) What is it, Brassett?

**Brassett.**   (*holding up, by a fine string loop, a tiny brown paper packet; to* **Jack**) His lordship's hairpins, sir.

**Jack.**   Confound his hairpins!

(**Brassett** *exits* L.U.E.)

**Jack.**   (*aside, recollecting*) By George! The dad'll be an odd one. I must get rid of Babbs somehow if the dad stays. (*suddenly*) Stays! Why not? (*aloud*) Dad, I've an idea. (**Sir Francis** *turns and comes* C. *to* **Jack.**) Couldn't this matter be settled by a wealthy marriage?

**Sir Francis.**   No, that's the sort of thing I rather deprecate.[11] I don't think, Jack, I'd—

**Jack.**   Listen. My chum—that is Charley Wykeham's aunt,

---

[11] express disapproval of

Donna Lucia d'Alvadorez—is coming here to lunch today.
She's a widow—

**Sir Francis.**    (*dubiously*) A widow?

**Jack.**    And a millionaire.

**Sir Francis.**    (*more hopefully*) And a millionaire?

**Jack.**    And a *charming* woman.

**Sir Francis.**    No, Jack, I don't think I'd advise you to do a
thing of this kind merely for the sake of money.

**Jack.**    No, not me, Dad—*you.*

**Sir Francis.**    Me! You young rascal. (*Attempts to punch* **Jack.**
**Jack** *dodges under his upraised arm to fireplace* R.) No, no! I
shall never marry again. (*goes towards sideboard*)

**Jack.**    (*bringing him back again* C. *by the arm*) Don't be rash,
Dad. Think it over. Where are your things?

**Sir Francis.**    At the hotel.

**Jack.**    Go and change. Make yourself look as nice as possible,
come back to lunch at one o'clock; and Dad, put a flower
in your buttonhole—

**Charley.**    (*shouting off, excitedly*) I say, Jack!

(*Enter* **Charley**, L.I.E., *hurriedly, with telegram. Almost runs into*
**Sir Francis**)

**Jack.**    (*introducing*) Oh, Dad, Charley Wykeham. Charley, my
father.

**Sir Francis.**    (*shakes hands with* **Charley**) Glad to know you, my
boy, glad to know you.

**Jack.**    (*to* **Sir Francis**, *aside*) Her nephew—nice boy, you'll like
him.

**Sir Francis.**    (*laughing to* **Charley**) I thought it was the fire brigade.

(**Charley** *laughs, goes up* L. *behind table* C. *to fireplace.*)

**Jack.**    Now, don't forget. Put a flower in your buttonhole,
takes years off a man, a flower in his buttonhole.

**Sir Francis.** *(turning and taking hat, stick, and gloves from side-board)* No, Jack, you come and lunch with me at the Mitre. *(at door* L.I.E.*)*

**Jack.** (C.) Now, don't be rash, Dad! See her first, see her *first!*

**Sir Francis.** *(putting his hat on jauntily)* All right, **Jack.** I'll have a look at her. *(smiling)* I'll have a look at her. *(exits,* L.I.E.*)*

**Jack.** (C., *to* **Charley**) Well, what is it?

**Charley.** *(comes down* R. *of* **Jack**, C.; *excited and anxious; gives telegram)* Read that.

**Jack.** *(reads)* "Important business, don't expect me for a few days. Lucia d'Alvadorez." *(excitedly)* No!

**Charley.** *(nervously)* She's not coming!

**Jack.** But she must! Go—wire—telegraph—

**Charley.** No use. There's no time. *(goes up to window* R.*)*

**Jack.** *(in front of* C. *table)* But hang it! The girls won't remain without a chaperone. What are we to do?

**Charley.** Couldn't we ask the proctor's wife, old Mrs.— *(looks out of window)*

**Jack.** *(gloomily)* Who'd sit and stare like an owl.

**Charley.** *(turning to* **Jack**) Here they are! *They're* coming! *(again looking out of window)*

**Jack.** *(sitting on table* C.*)* What on earth are we to do?

**Lord Fancourt.** *(off* L.U.E.*)* I say, Jack, come and look at me!

**Jack.** *(irritably, turning upstage and going* L.U.E.*)* What the deuce is it? *(opens door, looks off, starts back a step in amazement)* By George! Splendid! *(to* **Charley**) Charley, come here quickly! Do you know what a pious fraud[12] is?

**(Charley** *crosses to Jack up* C.*)*

**Charley.** *(surprised and puzzled)* Pious fraud?

---

[12] act of trickery marked by false devoutness

**Jack.**   First cousin to a miracle! (*pushes* **Charley** *across him*) Look!

**Charley.**   (*looks off* L.U.E.) What is it?

**Jack.**   Babbs—*your aunt!*

**Charley.** Babbs! (*turning upon* **Jack**) My aunt!

**Jack.**   It's the only one you've got, so you'll have to make the best of her. (*pushes* **Charley** *down to* R.; *drops down* L.)

**Lord Fancourt.** (*off*) I say—look here—

(*Enter* **Lord Fancourt**, *dressed as an old lady*, L.U.E., *in black satin, fichu,*[13] *wig, cap, etc. Stands up* L.C., *smiling.*)

**Lord Fancourt.** How's this? (*then walks down* L., *smiling benignly*[14])

(**Charley** *looks on in amazement.* **Jack** *with determined satisfaction. As laughter subsides,* **Jack** *speaks.*)

**Jack.**   Splendid!

(*Loud knock, outer door,* L.I.E.)

**Lord Fancourt.**   (*looking at door in affright*) Who's that? (*offers to bolt*)

**Jack.**   (*seizing him by the shoulders* L.) The girls!

(**Charley**, R. *of* **Lord Fancourt**)

**Lord Fancourt.**   (*looking at* **Jack**) The girls?

**Jack.**   Charley's aunt can't come.

**Lord Fancourt.**   Can't she? I'll go and take these things off. (*Turns to bolt up* L.U.E.)

(**Jack** *grabs him, assisted by* **Charley.**)

**Jack.**   No, they won't stop if you do.

**Lord Fancourt.**   Won't stop! What do you mean?

**Jack.**   You must be Charley's aunt!

---

[13] a woman's triangular scarf or cape, worn over the shoulders and crossed or tied at the breast

[14] in a kind and gentle manner

**Lord Fancourt.** *(in dismay) Me? No!!!!*

*(Charley seizes* **Lord Fancourt** *by* R. *arm,* **Jack** *holding his* L. *arm.* **Lord Fancourt** *backs a little and sinks down. They then slide him across to chair* L. *of writing table.* **Lord Fancourt** *rises twice and each time is pushed down again by* **Charley**, *who then gives chair a kick backwards with the heel of his* R. *foot, careful to kick chair while it appears to audience as if he had kicked* **Lord Fancourt**, *who writhes.* **Jack** *leaves him and goes* C. *to meet girls.* **Charley** *stands* L. *of the chair so as to hide* **Lord Fancourt** *from door* L.I.E. **Brassett** *enters,* L.U.E.)

**Jack.**    Show them in, Brassett.

(**Brassett** *opens door* L.I.E. *Enter* **Kitty** *and* **Amy**, L.I.E., **Amy** *carrying bunch of flowers in tissue paper.* **Jack** *joins them.* **Lord Fancourt** *makes an arch of* **Charley**'s *right arm and looks through it to see what girls are like, much to* **Charley**'s *annoyance.* **Charley**, *furious, smacks* **Lord Fancourt**'s *face (he actually hits his own arm).* **Lord Fancourt** *draws back as though his face had been hit, clamping his hand over his nose and mouth.)*

**Jack.**    Ah! You've got back. So glad!

(**Brassett** *exits,* L.U.E.)

**Kitty.**    Yes; we've been longer than we intended, but Amy wanted to get some flowers for Charley's aunt. Has she come?

**Amy.**    Yes. Has she? I hope she's come!

**Jack.**    Oh yes, she's come.

(**Jack** *crosses* R.C. **Kitty** *and* **Amy** *follow—***Charley** *moves upstage to clear* **Lord Fancourt**.)

**Jack.**    *(introducing)* Donna Lucia, Miss Spettigue, Miss Verdun. *(to girls)* Donna Lucia d'Alvadorez, Charley's aunt!

# REVIEWING AND INTERPRETING

Record your answers to these questions in your personal literature notebook. Follow the directions for each part.

**REVIEWING**   Try to complete each of these sentences without looking back at the play.

*Recalling Facts*

**1.** When talking with his father, Jack suggests that the family's money problems might be solved by his
   a. marrying Donna Lucia.
   b. father's marrying Donna Lucia.
   c. marrying Kitty.
   d. cutting back on expenses.

*Undertsanding Main Ideas*

**2.** The scene between Jack and his father indicates that the two
   a. have little in common.
   b. try to hide things from each other.
   c. sincerely like and respect each other.
   d. have as little to do with each other as possible.

*Identifying Cause and Effect*

**3.** Jack and Charley insist that Babbs impersonate Charley's aunt because
   a. he has never acted before, and this experience will give him needed practice in acting.
   b. he is so handsome that Kitty and Amy won't pay attention to them when he is around.
   c. they simply want to play a trick on Kitty and Amy.
   d. Kitty and Amy will leave if they discover Donna Lucia is not present.

*Identifying Sequence*

**4.** Jack doesn't think of having Babbs impersonate Charley's aunt until
   a. he sees Babbs in the costume of an old lady.
   b. his father, Sir Francis, gives him the idea.
   c. Kitty and Amy come back.
   d. Charley receives a telegram from Donna Lucia.

*Recognizing Literary Elements (Conflict)*

**5.** As this passage ends, the biggest concern that Jack, Charley, and Babbs face is
   a. what grades they are getting in the college courses they just completed.
   b. whether Jack and Charley are dressed correctly for a luncheon.
   c. how old the real Donna Lucia is.
   d. whether the impostor Donna Lucia will be found out.

**INTERPRETING**

To complete these sentences, you may look back at the play if you'd like.

*Making Inferences*

**6.** After Jack sends his manservant Brassett to Lord Fancourt's rooms to fetch his costume, Fancourt borrows money to tip Brassett. The only inference you *cannot* draw from this episode is that
   a. Lord Fancourt appreciates what others do for him.
   b. Brassett depends totally on tips to make a living.
   c. Fancourt is short of cash at the moment.
   d. Brassett knows where Lord Fancourt's rooms are, perhaps because of previous errands there.

*Analyzing*

**7.** The passage you have read indicates that the author's purpose in writing *Charley's Aunt* was to
   a. express personal emotions.
   b. protest against rigid social rules.
   c. inform the audience about life at Oxford.
   d. make the audience laugh.

*Predicting Outcomes*

**8.** From the scene between Jack and his father, Sir Francis, you probably can expect that
   a. Jack's father will try to romance the impostor Donna Lucia.
   b. Jack and his father will get into a fight and harm each other physically later in the play.
   c. Sir Francis will begin to criticize his son for spending money, for some reason.
   d. Sir Francis will bring a new girlfriend to the luncheon.

*Making Generalizations*

**9.** The fact that his friends found nothing unusual in Jack's life style at Oxford suggests that, at that time,
   a. many students at the college had private suites and personal servants.
   b. most students at the college had even grander living quarters than Jack.
   c. Jack's rooms were the finest at the college.
   d. Jack was attending the college on a needs-based scholarship.

*Understanding Literary Elements (Character)*

**10.** Some qualities that make audiences sympathetic to the three students are their
   a. out-of-date slang and their wealth.
   b. wealth and their lack of concern about studies.
   c. friendship and their worries about expressing their feelings to their girlfriends.
   d. out-of-date slang and their lack of concern about studies.

Now check your answers with your teacher. Study the questions you answered incorrectly. What types of questions were they? Talk with your teacher about ways to work on those skills.

# How to Read a Play

In almost all cases, plays are written to be performed in front of audiences. Unlike a novelist, the typical playwright does not intend for his or her words to tell a complete, detailed story to one reader at a time. Rather, the playwright expects actors to contribute their talents to the play to create a complete experience for the audience.

The nature of plays leads to the special form in which they are written. The most important element of a play is its dialogue—the words spoken by the actors. Also important are the stage directions, which give suggestions for how the play should be performed, staged, and lit. The playwright expects the director, the actors, and the production crew to start with those basic stage directions and turn them into a memorable event.

As the reader of a play, you must fill in for all the missing contributors. You begin, like every production company, with the words. You read the same directions that the director and cast do. You imagine the setting, lighting, and sound effects that the playwright has instructed the crews to create. To do all of these jobs effectively, you need to know where to find and how to interpret all the information that the playwright provides.

In the lessons that follow, you will look at some of the methods that playwright Brandon Thomas uses to let readers know what is happening on stage:

1. He uses a special format to introduce the characters and their dialogue.

2. He describes the appearance of the stage and where the actors should position themselves on it.

3. He indicates the movements and gestures that the actors should make, as well as the attitudes they should convey as they speak and move.

## LESSON 1    CHARACTERS, SETTING, AND DIALOGUE

While reading a play, remember that a playwright is speaking not only to the reader but to the director and actors as well. The first things that the director and actors need to know about a play are what characters are in it, and when and where the action occurs. A typical play begins with that vital information. A description of what is required on stage at the beginning of the play follows. Only after all this background information is provided does the playwright begin the story.

*Characters*    The list of characters at the beginning of a play is called the *cast of characters*. Sometimes the playwright lists each character's name and briefly describes him or her. Such a list is a useful reference tool. When you come across lines for a character you don't recognize, you can refer to the cast list for help. In addition, the descriptions of the characters help you imagine the people or actors you would like to see in each role. Not all playwrights provide descriptions of the characters at the beginning of the play, however. Instead, they may describe the character within stage directions at his or her first entrance. Here, for example, is the description of Sir Francis Chesney provided at his entrance.

> (**Colonel Sir Francis Chesney, Bart.**, *late Indian Service. Tall, good-looking, smart in appearance and manners, wearing small military moustache, actually fifty-one but looking nearer forty, very smart, cheery and young in manner. Wears brown lounge suit, bowler hat, and carries gloves and Malacca walking-stick. He has just arrived from London.*)

Playwrights may choose not to add any character descriptions at all. Instead, they may use only dialogue to establish the characters, as Thomas does in the passage where Kitty and Amy enter, beginning on page 9.

*Scenes and Acts*  The action in a play is organized according to scenes and acts. All the events occurring in one place and time make up a single *scene*. Sometimes a change in scene involves a new place, and new scenery may be brought on stage. At other times a scene change simply involves a new time. In such cases the playwright may simply ask for the lights to go down briefly. Then when the lights come up on the same scenery, the audience knows that time has passed. Scenes can range in length from just a few lines to hundreds of lines.

An *act* is usually made up of several short scenes. Many plays consist of only one act. Most full-length plays today have two or three acts, separated by an intermission. Below is the *synopsis*, or brief summary, of the organization of *Charley's Aunt*. How many acts are in this play? How much time does the play cover? Where is each act set?

SYNOPSIS OF SCENES

ACT I

Jack Chesney's Rooms in College. (Morning)

"When pious frauds—are dispensations."—*Hudibras*

ACT II

Garden outside Jack Chesney's Rooms. (Afternoon)

"While there's tea, there's hope."—*Pinero*

ACT III

Drawing Room at Spettigue's House. (Evening)

"Dinner lubricates business."—*Boswell*

There are three acts, each in a different setting. The time covered is less than one day—from one morning until that evening. In this synopsis playwright Thomas has matched each act with a quotation to suggest its theme. Thomas has also described each act with a quotation. Think about how the quotation for Act I applies to the play. *Pious frauds* are acts of trickery marked by false devoutness, and dispensations are special releases, or exemptions from a general rule; the phrase suggests that there are times when the usual rules against tricking someone don't apply.

A director looking at this synopsis will realize how important it is to present each setting effectively. Any mistake in the set will be in front of the audience for an entire act. Readers also will realize that they need to visualize each setting clearly. If they don't have a good mental picture of the room, much of the action will be hard to follow.

*Setting*   At the beginning of the play, and again when the scenery is changed, the playwright describes the *setting*—the background scenery and movable objects that establish the surroundings and atmosphere. Review the description of Jack Chesney's rooms on pages 6–7. Also refer to the stage diagram accompanying it. Notice how the furnishings are a combination of refinement (piano, bookcases, writing table, and bust of Plato) and of informality (photographs of chorus girls, prints of sports teams, boxing gloves, and well-worn comfortable chairs). The rooms reflect their occupant, a young, stylish, and sports-loving single man who does a good deal of casual entertaining.

*Dialogue*   The playwright shows who is speaking by writing the name of the character before his or her speech, or lines of *dialogue*. As each new speech begins, a new character's name appears at the beginning of his or her lines.

When a play is published, each character's name usually is printed in special type. For example, a name may be printed in all capital letters or in a darker print called boldface. As you have seen, this book uses boldfacing. In a handwritten script, the name, in dialogue, is often followed by a period or a colon. The consistent position of the speaker's name and its special style set it off from the words that the speaker says. This makes it easier for readers to follow along and for the actors to spot their lines as they read the play aloud.

EXERCISE ①

Read the following conversation from the passage. Then use what you have learned in this lesson to answer the questions that follow it.

**Amy.**    (*rising and speaking to* **Charley** *as they come down* L. *a little*) What a dear—sweet—old lady your aunt must be, Mr. Wykeham! I am longing to know her. Where is she?

**Charley.**    (*aside*) Jack! (*rapidly, in agonized aside and beckoning* **Jack**, *who goes* R.C. *to him.*) Where's my aunt?

(**Jack** *whispers something in his ear and turns away.*)

**Charley.**    (*not catching it*) What?

(**Jack** *shrugs shoulders hopelessly and returns to* **Kitty**. **Kitty** *and* **Amy** *see nothing of this last scene, which must be played rapidly.*)

**Charley.**    (*to* **Amy**, *hesitatingly*) Oh, why, she's hardly arrived yet.

**Amy.**    (*surprised*) No, oh! (*crosses to* **Kitty**) Kitty, Mr. Wykeham's aunt hasn't come yet.

**Kitty.** (*rising*) Hasn't come? (*crossing to* C.) Oh—(*turning to* **Jack**) Then we must—we'll—run and do some shopping—and come back. Shan't be long. Good-bye!

(**Kitty** *crosses* **Amy** *to* L.I.E. **Charley** *has worked round to door, which he opens.* **Jack** *follows.*)

**Amy.**    (*to* **Jack**) Good-bye.

**Jack.**    Good-bye.

**Kitty.**    (*to* **Charley** *at door*) Good-bye.

**Amy.**    (*to* **Charley** *at door—rather sadly*) Good-bye.

(*Exit* L.I.E., **Kitty** *first, then* **Amy**.)

**Charley.**    (*at door* L.I.E.) Good-bye! (*unconsciously taking the same tone*)

(*Slight pause.* **Jack** *and* **Charley** *look at each other blankly; both sit on* C. *table and shake hands.*)

**Jack.**    See that? Off like a shot when they found your aunt wasn't here.

**Charley.** Makes an awful difference, doesn't it?

**Jack.** (*hurrying* **Charley** *off* L.I.E.) Now look here, you cut off to the station and bundle the old girl here in a fly.

1. How many characters take part in this conversation? Who are they?

2. Which of the young men is in charge? How does the playwright show that he is the leader and that the other young man is his follower?

3. Identify some statements and actions in the scene that reflect the period of 1892 rather than today.

Now check your answers with your teacher. Review this part of the lesson if you don't understand why an answer was incorrect.

## WRITING ON YOUR OWN ①

A comedy or dramatic series on television usually has a small number of characters who are part of the story every week. In this exercise you will use what you have learned in the lesson to draw up a cast of characters for a show that you watch regularly. Follow these steps:

- On your paper, identify the show for which you will list a cast of characters. Then list the characters in their approximate order of importance. List only the characters who appear regularly.
- For each character on the cast list, write no more than two sentences describing him or her. Be sure to mention the character's most striking characteristics—both good and bad.
- Exchange your cast list with a classmate who watches the same show. Ask if your classmate agrees with your choice of characters and their descriptions. If not, work together to decide how to improve your list.

## LESSON ②  SETTING AND STAGE DIRECTIONS

As a playwright creates a play, he or she imagines where the scenery and properties, or *props* (movable objects such as chairs, coats, dishes), will be on the stage. The playwright also imagines how the actors will enter and exit each scene and how they will move around while in the scene. To communicate where things and people should be on stage, playwrights use a shorthand set of directions. Interpreting the shorthand is simple as long as you remember that the directions describe the stage from the actors' point of view, not the audience's. For example, the term *downstage* (D. or D.S.) refers to the section of the stage closest to the audience; *upstage* (U. or U.S.) is the section farthest from the audience. *Stage right* (R.) is to the actors' right (and the audience's left). *Stage left* (L.) is to the actors' left (and the audience's right). *Center stage* (C.) is in the middle of the stage. Examine the stage diagram below. All of its labels are combinations of these directions.

**Chart of a Stage**

**Backstage**

| Upstage Right (U.R.) | Upstage, R.C. | Upstage Center (U.C.) | Upstage, L.C. | Upstage Left (U.L.) |
|---|---|---|---|---|
| Right (R.) | Right of Center (R. C.) | Center (C.) | Left of Center (L. of C.) | Left (L.) |
| Downstage Right (D.R.) | Downstage, R.C. | Downstage Center (D.L.) | Downstage, L.C. | Downstage Left (D.L.) |

(Offstage Right)        (Offstage Left)

**Audience**

Sometimes the publisher of a script includes one or more diagrams of different scenes. This was true with *Charley's Aunt*. For example, the diagram that appears at the beginning of the play, on page 6, is the scene design of Act I, the interior of Jack's rooms.

Compare the diagram on the opposite page with the scene diagram and stage directions on pages 6–7. You will note that in this particular play, the writer uses two additional abbreviations not often seen: L.I.E. and L.U.E. They indicate the positions of two doors (exits) at the extreme left of the stage setting. L.U.E. refers to the position of the upstage door, and L.I.E. refers to the door closer to the audience, downstage.

As the play progresses, the playwright inserts other directions about movements of people and things on stage. These directions are always set off from the dialogue by parentheses. In addition, in most printed plays, stage directions are set in italic type. For example, at the beginning of this excerpt, Jack, Charley, and Lord Fancourt are standing together behind the table in the center of the room.

> (*Re-enter* **Brassett** *with dress box, L.I.E., a large brown cardboard box with gilt edges, like an exaggerated chocolate box.*)
> **Brassett.** Your things, m'lord.
> (**Charley** *goes down R., sits chair side of writing table.* **Jack** *goes R.C. front of C. table.*)
> **Lord Fancourt.** (*taking box from* **Brassett**) Thank you, Brassett.

The stage directions in this passage dictate how the three actors standing next to the center table are to scatter around the stage: Charley goes to sit beside the writing table, Jack moves to the front of the center table, and Lord Fancourt goes left to join Brassett at the downstage door.

## EXERCISE ②

Do this exercise with a partner. Copy the scene design from page 6 onto a sheet of paper. Then read this passage, which continues the scene discussed on page 31. Use what you have learned to complete the exercises that follow it.

> **Lord Fancourt.**    (*taking box from* **Brassett**) Thank you, Brassett. You're an awfully good chap. (*crosses to* **Jack**; *aside*) I say, Jack, could you lend me half a crown? (*turns upstage and puts box on window seat at back*)

1. Determine where the four characters are when Lord Fancourt begins this speech. On your copy of the scene design, draw a circle near the downstage door to represent Brassett; label it *B*. Draw one triangle labeled *C* to show where Charley sits. Draw another triangle labeled *J* to show Jack's position. Draw a square at Lord Fancourt's position. Label the square *LF–1*.

2. Beginning at the square that shows Lord Fancourt's first position, draw a dotted line that traces movement after the words "You're an awfully good chap." Draw a second square to show where he is when he delivers his aside to Jack. Label his second position *LF–2*.

3. From Lord Fancourt's second square *(LF–2)*, continue the dotted line to show the rest of his route. Draw a third square to show where he stands at the end of this speech, and label it *LF-3.*

4. In one or two sentences, describe Lord Fancourt's position changes. Use abbreviations for the relevant stage directions, for example, *from* D.C. *to* U.C.

Now check your answers with your teacher. Review this part of the lesson if you don't understand why an answer was incorrect.

## WRITING ON YOUR OWN  (2)

Just as a television comedy series has regular characters, it also has regular settings. For example, much of the action may happen in the main character's living room, school, or office.

In this exercise you will use what you have learned to write stage directions for a regular setting in a show that you watch. Follow these steps:

- Choose the program you will work with. Review the settings you see every week and choose one of them.
- Where are the openings for doors and hallways? Are there windows? If so, where are they? Are there posters, bookcases, or other large decorations on the walls? Write a stage direction that describes the setting.
- What large pieces of furniture are in the room? What do they look like? How are they arranged? What small appliances or decorations are there? Write a stage direction that describes the props in this setting.
- How does this scene help set the tone of the program? For example, a kitchen strewn with toys might suggest the importance of children and a casual tone. An elegant dining room would suggest a more sophisticated tone. Write a sentence or two describing how the setting of your chosen show contributes to its overall tone.

## LESSON 3    ACTIONS AND ATTITUDES

Some playwrights choose to keep their stage directions very brief. When Shakespeare wrote, for example, he probably didn't even write down all the entrances and exits. After all, he was working directly with the company that would perform his work, so he could discuss their movements and expressions with them personally. Most modern playwrights, however, don't have the luxury of speaking directly to the actors in their plays. Therefore, they must insert stage directions that tell actors not only when and how to take certain actions but also what feelings and attitudes the actors should convey as they take those actions and say their lines.

To see how important stage directions are, read this version of Kitty and Amy's first entrance. The stage directions have been deleted. Then go back and reread Thomas's version on pages 9–10. What is lost by the deletion of Thomas's stage directions?

**Jack.** How do you do? So kind of you to come!

**Kitty.** Oh, we were very pleased to be able to come. Weren't we, Amy?

**Amy.** Oh, yes. Mr. Wykeham, are we too early?

**Charley.** Oh no, no!

**Kitty.** Yes, Mr. Chesney, you didn't mention any time.

**Jack.** Oh, not at all, not at all! We're delighted! She'll be here soon.

**Kitty.** And this is where you think and study and do all your work and everything?

**Jack.** Oh yes, we do a lot of that sort of thing here.

Without stage directions, readers have no idea of Jack's and Charley's anxieties, or of Lord Fancourt's accidental entrance. From the words alone, the four people in the conversation could be having a very pleasant, but also very dull, exchange. All of the humor of the scene has dropped out.

## EXERCISE ③

Reread the first page of the selection (page 8) through the stage direction quoted below. Then use what you have learned in this lesson to answer the following questions.

> (**Jack** and **Charley** see half-crown given back to **Brassett** and laugh. **Charley** collapsed in chair L. of writing table. **Jack** ditto into chair R. of table C. **Lord Fancourt** turns, puzzled, crosses to **Jack**. **Jack** whispers to him, points to **Brassett**, then twice to himself, then to **Lord Fancourt** and then to **Brassett**

*again.* **Lord Fancourt** *joins in laughter and goes up to window seat and picks up dress box.* **Brassett,** *during this action, exits L.U.E.)*

1. Why does Lord Fancourt want the half-crown? Who, in the end, provides the half-crown?

2. What does the stage direction above reveal about Jack and Charley's reaction to this business that is not known from the dialogue?

3. How does Lord Fancourt respond to Jack and Charley's reaction? What does this stage direction suggest about the relationships among the students? What does it suggest about the relationship between them and Brassett?

Now check your answers with your teacher. Review this part of the lesson if you don't understand why an answer was incorrect.

## WRITING ON YOUR OWN ③

Playwrights like to provide directions where they think the meaning or attitude of lines can be misunderstood. In this exercise you will see for yourself how changing the way lines are delivered can change their meaning. Follow these steps:

- Read this scene. How should the lines be read if the scene is from a comedy about workers in an insurance office? Rewrite the lines, adding stage directions to give Debbie laughs. Use props if you wish.

### CAST OF CHARACTERS
**Mr. West**—*an inspector from the home office*
**Debbie Eastman**—*an insurance agent at East Northern Life*
**Mandy Fellows**—*Debbie's eager young assistant*

**Mr. West.**    I've come to see the files on Jack Grabowski.

**Debbie.**    Jack Grabowski? Hmmm. I can't find them under *J*.

**Mandy.**    Ms. Eastman, I think I filed them under G.

**Debbie.**    Mandy, you'll have to learn the systems in this office if you want to get ahead.

**Mandy.**    Yes, Ms. Eastman. I'm sorry, Ms. Eastman.

**Debbie.**    Oh, look, Mr. West. Here are those files, after all.

**Mr. West.**    Thank you. This folder seems quite thick. How odd! How did this get in here?

- Now imagine how the lines should be read if the scene is from a suspenseful murder mystery. Rewrite the lines once more, inserting new stage directions to arouse suspicion about Debbie.

## DISCUSSION GUIDES

1. How have the attitudes toward college and dating changed since the times depicted in *Charley's Aunt*? What advantages and disadvantages do you see in the system that was accepted in the 1890s? Would you personally prefer to live a century ago? Why or why not? Discuss these questions with the rest of your class. Create charts recording answers to the first two questions and take an informal poll of responses to the third.

2. Only five men and two women appear in this excerpt from *Charley's Aunt*, and two of the male characters (Brassett and Sir Francis) could be read by one person. Team up with five or six other classmates and read the excerpt aloud. Afterwards, compare your favorite parts. Be prepared to explain your choices.

3. By the end of this excerpt, the three young men are becoming involved in a questionable course of action. Lord Fancourt's friends are forcing him to impersonate a rich woman. What possible developments might arise from this deception? With a small group, list several plot complications that you might include if you were writing the play. Compare your possible plot developments with those that other groups come up with.

   If possible, one or more class members should read the complete play and report back to the class about which ideas, if any, were used by playwright Brandon Thomas and how the deception is finally ended.

# WRITE THE BEGINNING OF A PLAY ABOUT YOUR LIFE

In this exercise you will use what you have learned in this unit to write the introductory material and first few lines of a play about a day in your life.

If you have questions about the writing process, refer to Using the Writing Process on page 300.

- Assemble the writing that you did for this unit, including: *1)* lists describing familiar settings and gestures, *2)* a cast list describing major characters in a television series, *3)* stage directions for the set of a television series, *4)* two versions of the same dialogue with different stage directions that produce different moods.

- After reviewing your assignments, write the introductory material and a very brief passage from a possible play about a day in your life. Begin with the cast of characters. List yourself and a few other people with whom you interact on a regular basis. Write a one- or two-sentence description of each character. Provide information that would help a director cast each character.

- Next, list the scenes for a three-act play about your day. Include only those settings where something of interest would occur. Describe each scene in a phrase, such as "Later that afternoon at the gym."

- Write stage directions for one interior scene on your list. Describe the room in detail, stating the location of doorways, windows, and major props. If you wish, draw a scene design as well.

- Write the first few speeches of the dialogue in that scene. At least two speakers must take part in the scene. Insert stage directions describing actions. Set off the speakers' names and the stage directions clearly.
- Proofread your work for spelling, grammar, punctuation, capitalization, and formatting errors. Make a final copy and save it in your writing portfolio.

# Trifles

○

## by Susan Glaspell

## INTRODUCTION

*ABOUT THE
SELECTION*

John Wright, the owner of a lonely farmhouse, has been found strangled in his bed. It seems to be a clear case of murder, but the only suspect is his quiet, timid wife who has no obvious motive for killing her husband. Three men—the sheriff, the County Attorney, and Wright's neighbor—have come to the house to search for evidence in the case. Accompanying the men are the sheriff's wife and the neighbor's wife. While the men search the house for clues to solve the murder, the women busy themselves in the kitchen, gathering a few of Mrs. Wright's possessions to take to her in jail. Will anyone find the evidence needed to crack the case?

*Trifles* is Susan Glaspell's best-known and most often produced play. It is an unusual play in many ways. It doesn't have much action, there is a great deal of dialogue, and the main character never appears on stage. However, Glaspell raises a number of issues in the play: the isolation of women in Midwestern farm towns, how to handle feelings of guilt, and the moral question of whether it is right to speak out or to remain silent. Glaspell aimed to produce drama that was not timid but challenging. As you read, you can decide for yourself if she reached her goal with *Trifles*.

**ABOUT THE AUTHOR**

Susan Glaspell was born in 1882 in Davenport, Iowa. After graduating from Drake University in Des Moines, she became a reporter for the *Des Moines Daily News*. In 1901, she returned to Davenport and became a successful writer of short stories for women's magazines.

In 1913, she married George Cram Cook, another author, and they moved to Greenwich Village in New York City. In 1915, Glaspell and her husband collaborated on a one-act play. They submitted it to a theatrical group in New York, but it was rejected. The following summer in Provincetown, Massachusetts, they presented that play along with another play written by a friend. The plays were so well received that Glaspell and Cook began the Provincetown Players, a theatrical group that had a major effect on American theater. The group introduced new American writers, particularly those working with experimental techniques and unconventional ideas. It is best remembered for producing the first plays of Eugene O'Neill, one of the most important playwrights of the twentieth century.

At the end of the first summer at Provincetown, Cook announced that more plays would be presented the following summer, one of which would be written by his wife, Susan Glaspell. Glaspell had not written any play, but as she described later, she sat in the theater, staring at the small stage until she imagined a kitchen and then some characters entering. The setting reminded her of an incident she had known about as a reporter. The result was *Trifles*.

Glaspell also tried her hand at writing novels, but she is best known for her plays. In 1930, she wrote *Alison's House*, a play based on the life of poet Emily Dickinson. For this effort, she was awarded the Pulitzer Prize for drama.

**ABOUT THE LESSONS**

The lessons that follow *Trifles* focus on plot. The *plot* of a story or a play is its connected sequence of events. A typical plot begins with the *exposition*, or introduction, during which the author introduces the characters and the setting. Soon, a *conflict*, or problem, develops. Throughout the next part of the plot—known as the *rising action*—the conflict becomes more complicated and tension builds. The point of highest excitement is called the *climax*, which is also known as the turning point. After the climax, the tension eases and the action slows down. This is referred to as *falling action*. The story or play ends with the *resolution*, during which problems are solved and the plot draws to a close.

**WRITING:** ANALYZING A PLOT

At the end of this unit, you will write a plot summary for a play, movie, or television show that you remember well. The suggestions below will help you begin thinking about the events in the plot:

- Think of several plays, movies, or television shows that you have seen recently and list their titles. Picture one important scene from each title on your list and write a sentence to describe it. Tell who is in the scene, where it takes place, and what the characters are doing. Leave a space next to each sentence so you have space to write your answers for the next step.
- Decide whether each scene you have described is part of the exposition, the rising action, the climax, the falling action, or the resolution. Label the scene with the part of the plot it represents.
- Review your list as you work through the lessons in this unit. As you learn more about each part of the plot, you may want to change the labels for your scenes.

AS YOU READ

The questions below will help you think about the plot of *Trifles*. Try to answer these questions as you read the play.

- How does the playwright introduce the characters and the setting? What conflict do the main characters face?
- What further complications are introduced during the rising action? How is the climax the turning point of the play?
- What happens after the climax? How does the play end?

# Trifles

⊜

by Susan Glaspell

CAST

**Sheriff Peters**

**County Attorney Henderson**

**Mr. Hale**

**Mrs. Peters,** *the sheriff's wife*

**Mrs. Hale**

SCENE

*The kitchen in the now abandoned farmhouse of **John Wright**, a gloomy kitchen, and left without having been put in order—the walls covered with a faded wall paper. D.R. is a door leading to the parlor. On the R. wall above this door is a built-in kitchen cupboard with shelves in the upper portion and drawers below. In the rear wall at R., up two steps is a door opening onto stairs leading to the second floor. In the rear wall at L. is a door to the shed and from there to the outside. Between these two doors is an old-fashioned black iron stove. Running along the L. wall from the shed door is an old iron sink and sink shelf, in which is set a hand pump. Downstage of the sink is an uncurtained window. Near the window is an old wooden rocker. Center stage is an unpainted wooden* *kitchen table with straight chairs on either side. There is a small chair* D.R. *Unwashed pans under the sink, a loaf of bread outside the breadbox, a dish towel on the table—other signs of incompleted work. At the rear the shed door opens and the* **Sheriff** *comes in followed by the* **County Attorney** *and* **Hale.** *The* **Sheriff** *and* **Hale** *are men in middle life, the* **County Attorney** *is a young man; all are much bundled up and go at once to the stove. They are followed by the two women—the Sheriff's wife,* **Mrs. Peters,** *first; she is a slight wiry woman, a thin nervous face.* **Mrs. Hale** *is larger and would ordinarily be called more comfortable looking, but she is disturbed now and looks fearfully about as she enters. The women have come in slowly, and stand close together near the door.*

---

**County Attorney.** *(at stove rubbing his hands)* This feels good. Come up to the fire, ladies.

**Mrs. Peters.** *(after taking a step forward)* I'm not—cold.

**Sheriff.** *(unbuttoning his overcoat and stepping away from the stove to right of table as if to mark the beginning of official business)* Now, Mr. Hale, before we move things about, you explain to Mr. Henderson just what you saw when you came here yesterday morning.

**County Attorney.** *(crossing down to left of the table)* By the way, has anything been moved? Are things just as you left them yesterday?

**Sheriff.** *(looking about)* It's just the same. When it dropped below zero last night I thought I'd better send Frank out this morning to make a fire for us— *(sits right of center table)* no use getting pneumonia with a big case on, but I told him not to touch anything except the stove—and you know Frank.

**County Attorney.** Somebody should have been left here yesterday.

**Sheriff.** Oh—yesterday. When I had to send Frank to Morris Center for that man who went crazy—I want you to know I had my hands full yesterday. I knew you could get back from Omaha by today and as long as I went over everything here myself—

**County Attorney.** Well, Mr. Hale, tell just what happened when you came here yesterday morning.

**Hale.** *(crossing down to above table)* Harry and I had started to town with a load of potatoes. We came along the road from my place and as I got here I said, "I'm going to see if I can't get John Wright to go in with me on a party telephone." I spoke to Wright about it once before and he put me off, saying folks talked too much anyway, and all he asked was peace and quiet—I guess you know about how much he talked himself; but I thought maybe if I went to the house and talked about it before his wife, though I said to Harry that I didn't know as what his wife wanted made much difference to John—

**County Attorney.** Let's talk about that later, Mr. Hale. I do want to talk about that, but tell now just what happened when you got to the house.

**Hale.** I didn't hear or see anything; I knocked at the door, and still it was all quiet inside. I knew they must be up, it was past eight o'clock. So I knocked again, and I thought I heard somebody say, "Come in." I wasn't sure, I'm not sure yet, but I opened the door—this door *(indicating the door by which the two women are still standing)* and there in that rocker— *(pointing to it)* sat Mrs. Wright. *(They all look at the rocker* D.L.*)*

**County Attorney.** What—was she doing?

**Hale.** She was rockin' back and forth. She had her apron in her hand and was kind of—pleating it.

**County Attorney.** And how did she—look?

**Hale.** Well, she looked queer.

**County Attorney.**    How do you mean—queer?

**Hale.**    Well, as if she didn't know what she was going to do next. And kind of done up.

**County Attorney.**    *(takes out notebook and pencil and sits left of center table)* How did she seem to feel about your coming?

**Hale.**    Why, I don't think she minded—one way or other. She didn't pay much attention. I said, "How do, Mrs. Wright, it's cold, ain't it?" And she said, "Is it?"—and went on kind of pleating at her apron. Well, I was surprised; she didn't ask me to come up to the stove, or to set down, but just sat there, not even looking at me, so I said, "I want to see John." And then she—laughed. I guess you would call it a laugh. I thought of Harry and the team outside, so I said a little sharp: "Can't I see John?" "No," she says, kind o' dull like. "Ain't he home?" says I. "Yes," says she, "he's home." "Then why can't I see him?" I asked her, out of patience. " 'Cause he's dead," says she. *"Dead?"* says I. She just nodded her head, not getting a bit excited, but rockin' back and forth. "Why—where is he?" says I, not knowing what to say. She just pointed upstairs—like that. *(Himself pointing to the room above.)* I started for the stairs, with the idea of going up there. I walked from there to here—then I says, "Why, what did he die of?" "He died of a rope around his neck," says she, and just went on pleatin' at her apron. Well, I went out and called Harry. I thought I might— need help. We went upstairs and there he was lyin'—

**County Attorney.**    I think I'd rather have you go into that upstairs, where you can point it all out. Just go on now with the rest of the story.

**Hale.**    Well, my first thought was to get that rope off. It looked . . . *(stops, his face twitches)* . . . but Harry, he went up to him, and he said, "No, he's dead all right, and we'd better not touch anything." So we went back downstairs. She was still sitting that same way. "Has anybody been notified?" I asked. "No," says she, unconcerned. "Who did this, Mrs.

Wright?" said Harry. He said it business-like—and she stopped pleatin' of her apron. "I don't know," she says. "You don't *know*?" says Harry. "No," says she. "Weren't you sleepin' in the bed with him?" says Harry. "Yes," says she, "but I was on the inside." "Somebody slipped a rope round his neck and strangled him and you didn't wake up?" says Harry. "I didn't wake up," she said after him. We must 'a' looked as if we didn't see how that could be, for after a minute she said, "I sleep sound." Harry was going to ask her more questions but I said maybe we ought to let her tell her story first to the coroner,[1] or the sheriff, so Harry went fast as he could to Rivers' place, where there's a telephone.

**County Attorney.**    And what did Mrs. Wright do when she knew that you had gone for the coroner?

**Hale.**    She moved from the rocker to that chair over there (*pointing to a small chair in the* D.R. *corner*) and just sat there with her hands held together and looking down. I got a feeling that I ought to make some conversation, so I said I had come in to see if John wanted to put in a telephone, and at that she started to laugh, and then she stopped and looked at me—scared. (*The* **County Attorney,** *who has had his notebook out, makes a note.*) I dunno, maybe it wasn't scared. I wouldn't like to say it was. Soon Harry got back, and then Dr. Lloyd came, and you, Mr. Peters, and so I guess that's all I know that you don't.

**County Attorney.**    (*rising and looking around*) I guess we'll go upstairs first—and then out to the barn and around there. (*to the* **Sheriff**) You're convinced that there was nothing important here—nothing that would point to any motive?

**Sheriff.**    Nothing here but kitchen things. (*The* **County Attorney,** *after again looking around the kitchen, opens the door of a cupboard closet in* R. *wall. He brings a small chair from* R.—*gets up on it and looks on a shelf. Pulls his hand away, sticky.*)

---

[1] offical who investigates the cause of death that may not be due to natural causes

**County Attorney.**    Here's a nice mess. (*The women draw nearer* U.C.)

**Mrs. Peters.**    (*to the other woman*) Oh, her fruit; it did freeze. (*to the* **Lawyer**) She worried about that when it turned so cold. She said the fire'd go out and her jars would break.

**Sheriff.**    (*rises*) Well, can you beat the women! Held for murder and worryin' about her preserves.

**County Attorney.**    (*getting down from chair*) I guess before we're through she may have something more serious than preserves to worry about. (*crosses down* R.C.)

**Hale.**    Well, women are used to worrying over trifles.[2] (*The two women move a little closer together.*)

**County Attorney.**    (*with the gallantry[3] of a young politician*) And yet, for all their worries, what would we do without the ladies? (*The women do not unbend. He goes below the center table to the sink, takes a dipperful of water from the pail and pouring it into a basin, washes his hands. While he is doing this the* **Sheriff** *and* **Hale** *cross to cupboard, which they inspect. The* **County Attorney** *starts to wipe his hands on the roller towel, turns it for a cleaner place*). Dirty towels! (*Kicks his foot against the pans under the sink.*) Not much of a housekeeper, would you say, ladies?

**Mrs. Hale.**    (*stiffly*) There's a great deal of work to be done on a farm.

**County Attorney.**    To be sure. And yet (*with a little bow to her*) I know there are some Dickson County farmhouses which do not have such roller towels. (*He gives it a pull to expose its full length again.*)

**Mrs. Hale.**    Those towels get dirty awful quick. Men's hands aren't always as clean as they might be.

**County Attorney.**    Ah, loyal to your sex, I see. But you and Mrs. Wright were neighbors. I suppose you were friends, too.

---

[2]something of very little importance or value

[3]courtesy, especially to ladies

**Mrs. Hale.** (*shaking her head*) I've not seen much of her of late years. I've not been in this house—it's more than a year.

**County Attorney.** (*crossing to women U.C.*) And why was that? You didn't like her?

**Mrs. Hale.** I liked her all well enough. Farmers' wives have their hands full, Mr. Henderson. And then—

**County Attorney.** Yes—?

**Mrs. Hale.** (*looking about*) It never seemed a very cheerful place.

**County Attorney.** No—it's not cheerful. I shouldn't say she had the homemaking instinct.

**Mrs. Hale.** Well, I don't know as Wright had, either.

**County Attorney.** You mean that they didn't get on very well?

**Mrs. Hale.** No, I don't mean anything. But I don't think a place'd be any cheerfuller for John Wright's being in it.

**County Attorney.** I'd like to talk more of that a little later. I want to get the lay of things upstairs now. (*He goes past the women to U.R. where steps lead to a stair door.*)

**Sheriff.** I suppose anything Mrs. Peters does'll be all right. She was to take in some clothes for her, you know, and a few little things. We left in such a hurry yesterday.

**County Attorney.** Yes, but I would like to see what you take, Mrs. Peters, and keep an eye out for anything that might be of use to us.

**Mrs. Peters.** Yes, Mr. Henderson. (*The men leave by U.R. door to stairs. The women listen to the men's steps on the stairs, then look about the kitchen.*)

**Mrs. Hale.** (*crossing L. to sink*) I'd hate to have men coming into my kitchen, snooping around and criticizing. (*She arranges the pans under sink which the* **Lawyer** *had shoved out of place.*)

**Mrs. Peters.** Of course it's no more than their duty. (*crosses to cupboard U.R.*)

**Mrs. Hale.**    Duty's all right, but I guess that deputy sheriff that came out to make the fire might have got a little of this on. (*gives the roller towel a pull*) Wish I'd thought of that sooner. Seems mean to talk about her for not having things slicked up when she had to come away in such a hurry. (*crosses* R. *to* **Mrs. Peters** *at cupboard*)

**Mrs. Peters.**    (*who has been looking through cupboard, lifts one end of a towel that covers a pan*) She had bread set. (*stands still*)

**Mrs. Hale.**    (*eyes fixed on a loaf of bread beside the breadbox, which is on a low shelf of the cupboard*) She was going to put this in there. (*Picks up loaf, then abruptly drops it. In a manner of returning to familiar things.*) It's a shame about her fruit. I wonder if it's all gone. (*gets up on the chair and looks*) I think there's some here that's all right, Mrs. Peters. Yes—here; (*holding it toward the window*) this is cherries, too. (*looking again*) I declare I believe that's the only one. (*Gets down, jar in her hand. Goes to the sink and wipes it off on the outside.*) She'll feel awful bad after all her hard work in the hot weather. I remember the afternoon I put up my cherries last summer. (*She puts the jar on the big kitchen table, center of the room. With a sigh, is about to sit down in the rocking chair. Before she is seated realizes what chair it is; with a slow look at it, steps back. The chair which she has touched rocks back and forth.* **Mrs. Peters** *moves to center table and they both watch the chair rock for a moment or two.*)

**Mrs. Peters.**    (*Shaking off the mood which the empty rocking chair has evoked. Now in a businesslike manner she speaks*) Well, I must get those things from the front room closet. (*She goes to the door at the* R., *but, after looking into the other room, steps back.*) You coming with me, Mrs. Hale? You could help me carry them. (*They go in the other room; reappear,* **Mrs. Peters** *carrying a dress, petticoat and skirt,* **Mrs. Hale** *following with a pair of shoes.*) My, it's cold in there. (*She puts the clothes on the big table, and hurries to the stove.*)

**Mrs. Hale.** *(right of center table examining the skirt)* Wright was close.[4] I think maybe that's why she kept so much to herself. She didn't even belong to the Ladies' Aid. I suppose she felt she couldn't do her part, and then you don't enjoy things when you feel shabby. I heard she used to wear pretty clothes and be lively, when she was Minnie Foster, one of the town girls singing in the choir. But that—oh, that was thirty years ago. This all you was to take in?

**Mrs. Peters.** She said she wanted an apron. Funny thing to want, for there isn't much to get you dirty in jail, goodness knows. But I suppose just to make her feel more natural. *(crosses to cupboard)* She said they was in the top drawer in this cupboard. Yes, here. And then her little shawl that always hung behind the door. *(opens stair door and looks)* Yes, here it is. *(quickly shuts door leading upstairs)*

**Mrs. Hale.** *(abruptly moving toward her)* Mrs. Peters?

**Mrs. Peters.** Yes, Mrs. Hale? *(at U.R. door)*

**Mrs. Hale.** Do you think she did it?

**Mrs. Peters.** *(in a frightened voice)* Oh, I don't know.

**Mrs. Hale.** Well, I don't think she did. Asking for an apron and her little shawl. Worrying about her fruit.

**Mrs. Peters.** *(Starts to speak, glances up, where footsteps are heard in the room above. In a low voice)* Mr. Peters says it looks bad for her. Mr. Henderson is awful sarcastic in a speech and he'll make fun of her sayin' she didn't wake up.

**Mrs. Hale.** Well, I guess John Wright didn't wake when they was slipping that rope under his neck.

**Mrs. Peters.** *(crossing slowly to table and placing shawl and apron on table with other clothing)* No, it's strange. It must have been done awful crafty and still. They say it was such a— funny way to kill a man, rigging it all up like that.

---

[4] miserly or stingy

**Mrs. Hale.** *(crossing to left of* **Mrs. Peters** *at table)* That's just what Mr. Hale said. There was a gun in the house. He says that's what he can't understand.

**Mrs. Peters.** Mr. Henderson said coming out that what was needed for the case was a motive; something to show anger, or—sudden feeling.

**Mrs. Hale.** *(who is standing by the table)* Well, I don't see any signs of anger around here. *(She puts her hand on the dish towel which lies on the table, stands looking down at table, one-half of which is clean, the other half messy)* It's wiped to here. *(Makes a move as if to finish work, then turns and looks at loaf of bread outside the breadbox. Drops towel. In that voice of coming back to familiar things)* Wonder how they are finding things upstairs. *(crossing below table to* D.R.*)* I hope she had it a little more red-up up there. You know, it seems kind of *sneaking.* Locking her up in town and then coming out here and trying to get her own house to turn against her!

**Mrs. Peters.** But, Mrs. Hale, the law is the law.

**Mrs. Hale.** I s'pose 'tis. *(unbuttoning her coat)* Better loosen up your things, Mrs. Peters. You won't feel them when you go out. (**Mrs. Peters** *takes off her fur tippet, goes to hang it on chair back left of table, stands looking at the workbasket on floor near* D.L. *window.)*

**Mrs. Peters.** She was piecing a quilt. *(She brings the large sewing basket to the center table and they look at the bright pieces,* **Mrs. Hale** *above the table and* **Mrs. Peters** *left of it.)*

**Mrs. Hale.** It's a log cabin pattern. Pretty, isn't it? I wonder if she was goin' to quilt it or just knot it? *(Footsteps have been heard coming down the stairs. The* **Sheriff** *enters followed by* **Hale** *and the* **County Attorney.***)*

**Sheriff.** They wonder if she was going to quilt it or just knot it! *(The men laugh, the women look abashed.)*

**County Attorney.** *(rubbing his hands over the stove)* Frank's fire didn't do much up there, did it? Well, let's go out to the barn and get that cleared up. (*The men go outside by* U.L. *door.*)

**Mrs. Hale.** (*resentfully*) I don't know as there's anything so strange, our takin' up our time with little things while we're waiting for them to get the evidence. (*She sits in chair right of table smoothing out a block with decision.*) I don't see as it's anything to laugh about.

**Mrs. Peters.** (*apologetically*) Of course they've got awful important things on their minds. (*pulls up a chair and joins* **Mrs. Hale** *at the left of the table*)

**Mrs. Hale.** (*examining another block*) Mrs. Peters, look at this one. Here, this is the one she was working on, and look at the sewing! All the rest of it has been so nice and even. And look at this! It's all over the place! Why, it looks as if she didn't know what she was about! (*After she has said this they look at each other, then start to glance back at the door. After an instant* **Mrs. Hale** *has pulled at a knot and ripped the sewing.*)

**Mrs. Peters.** Oh, what are you doing, Mrs. Hale?

**Mrs. Hale.** (*mildly*) Just pulling out a stitch or two that's not sewed very good. (*threading a needle*) Bad sewing always made me fidgety.

**Mrs. Peters.** (*with a glance at door, nervously*) I don't think we ought to touch things.

**Mrs. Hale.** I'll just finish up this end. (*suddenly stopping and leaning forward*) Mrs. Peters?

**Mrs. Peters.** Yes, Mrs. Hale?

**Mrs. Hale.** What do you suppose she was so nervous about?

**Mrs. Peters.** Oh—I don't know. I don't know as she was nervous. I sometimes sew awful queer when I'm just tired. (**Mrs. Hale** *starts to say something, looks at* **Mrs. Peters**, *then goes on sewing.*) Well, I must get these things wrapped up. They may be through sooner than we think. (*putting apron and other things together*) I wonder where I can find a piece of paper, and string. (*rises*)

**Mrs. Hale.**   In that cupboard, maybe.

**Mrs. Peters.**   (*crosses* R. *looking in cupboard*) Why, here's a bird-cage. (*holds it up*) Did she have a bird, Mrs. Hale?

**Mrs. Hale.**   Why, I don't know whether she did or not—I've not been here for so long. There was a man around last year selling canaries cheap, but I don't know as she took one; maybe she did. She used to sing real pretty herself.

**Mrs. Peters.**   (*glancing around*) Seems funny to think of a bird here. But she must have had one, or why would she have a cage? I wonder what happened to it?

**Mrs. Hale.**   I s'pose maybe the cat got it.

**Mrs. Peters.**   No, she didn't have a cat. She's got that feeling some people have about cats—being afraid of them. My cat got in her room and she was real upset and asked me to take it out.

**Mrs. Hale.**   My sister Bessie was like that. Queer, ain't it?

**Mrs. Peters.**   (*examining the cage*) Why, look at this door. It's broke. One hinge is pulled apart. (*takes a step down to* **Mrs. Hale**'s *right*)

**Mrs. Hale.**   (*looking too*) Looks as if someone must have been rough with it.

**Mrs. Peters.**   Why, yes. (*She brings the cage forward and puts it on the table.*)

**Mrs. Hale.**   (*glancing toward* U.L. *door*) I wish if they're going to find any evidence they'd be about it. I don't like this place.

**Mrs. Peters.**   But I'm awful glad you came with me, Mrs. Hale. It would be lonesome for me sitting here alone.

**Mrs. Hale.**   It would, wouldn't it? (*dropping her sewing*) But I tell you what I do wish, Mrs. Peters. I wish I had come over sometimes when *she* was here. I— (*looking around the room*) —wish I had.

**Mrs. Peters.**   But of course you were awful busy, Mrs. Hale— your house and your children.

**Mrs. Hale.** *(rises and crosses* L.*)* I could've come. I stayed away because it weren't cheerful—and that's why I ought to have come. I— *(looking out* L. *window)* —I've never liked this place. Maybe because it's down in a hollow and you don't see the road. I dunno what it is, but it's a lonesome place and always was. I wish I had come over to see Minnie Foster sometimes. I can see now— *(shakes her head)*

**Mrs. Peters.** *(left of table and above it)* Well, you mustn't reproach[5] yourself, Mrs. Hale. Somehow we just don't see how it is with other folks until—something turns up.

**Mrs. Hale.** Not having children makes less work—but it makes a quiet house, and Wright out to work all day, and no company when he did come in. *(turning from window)* Did you know John Wright, Mrs. Peters?

**Mrs. Peters.** Not to know him; I've seen him in town. They say he was a good man.

**Mrs. Hale.** Yes—good; he didn't drink, and kept his word as well as most, I guess, and paid his debts. But he was a hard man, Mrs. Peters. Just to pass the time of day with him— *(shivers)* Like a raw wind that gets to the bone. *(pauses, her eye falling on the cage)* I should think she would 'a' wanted a bird. But what do you suppose went with it?

**Mrs. Peters.** I don't know, unless it got sick and died. *(She reaches over and swings the broken door, swings it again, both women watch it.)*

**Mrs. Hale.** You weren't raised round here, were you? (**Mrs. Peters** *shakes her head.)* You didn't know—her?

**Mrs. Peters.** Not till they brought her yesterday.

**Mrs. Hale.** She—come to think of it, she was kind of like a bird herself—real sweet and pretty, but kind of timid and—fluttery. How—she—did—change. *(Silence; then as if struck by a happy thought and relieved to get back to everyday*

---

[5] blame

*things. Crosses* R. *above* **Mrs. Peters** *to cupboard, replaces small chair used to stand on to its original place* D.R.) Tell you what, Mrs. Peters, why don't you take the quilt in with you? It might take up her mind.

**Mrs. Peters.**    Why, I think that's a real nice idea, Mrs. Hale. There couldn't possibly be any objection to it, could there? Now, just what would I take? I wonder if her patches are in here—and her things. *(They look in the sewing basket.)*

**Mrs. Hale.**    *(crosses to right of table)* Here's some red. I expect this has got sewing things in it. *(brings out a fancy box)* What a pretty box. Looks like something somebody would give you. Maybe her scissors are in here. *(Opens box. Suddenly puts her hand to her nose.)* Why— **(Mrs. Peters** *bends nearer, then turns her face away.)* There's something wrapped up in this piece of silk.

**Mrs. Peters.**    Why, this isn't her scissors.

**Mrs. Hale.**    *(lifting the silk)* Oh, Mrs. Peters—it's— **(Mrs. Peters** *bends closer.)*

**Mrs. Peters.**    It's the bird.

**Mrs. Hale.**    But, Mrs. Peters—look at it! Its neck! Look at its neck! It's all—other side *to.*

**Mrs. Peters.**    Somebody—wrung—its—neck. *(Their eyes meet. A look of growing comprehension, of horror. Steps are heard outside.* **Mrs. Hale slips box under quilt pieces, and sinks into her chair. Enter Sheriff** *and* **County Attorney. Mrs. Peters** *steps* D.L. *and stands looking out of window.)*

**County Attorney.**    *(as one turning from serious things to little pleasantries)* Well, ladies have you decided whether she was going to quilt it or knot it? *(crosses to* C. *above table)*

**Mrs. Peters.**    We think she was going to—knot it. **(Sheriff** *crosses to right of stove, lifts stove lid and glances at fire, then stands warming hands at stove.)*

**County Attorney.**    Well, that's interesting, I'm sure. *(seeing the bird-cage)* Has the bird flown?

**Mrs. Hale.** (*putting more quilt pieces over the box*) We think the—cat got it.

**County Attorney.** (*preoccupied*) Is there a cat? (**Mrs. Hale** *glances in a quick covert[6] way at* **Mrs. Peters**.)

**Mrs. Peters.** (*turning from window, takes a step in*) Well, not now. They're superstitious, you know. They leave.

**County Attorney.** (*to* **Sheriff Peters** *continuing an interrupted conversation*) No sign at all of anyone having come from the outside. Their own rope. Now let's go up again and go over it piece by piece. (*They start upstairs.*) It would have to have been someone who knew just the— (**Mrs. Peters** *sits down left of table. The two women sit there not looking at one another, but as if peering into something and at the same time holding back. When they talk now it is in the manner of feeling their way over strange ground, as if afraid of what they are saying, but as if they cannot help saying it.*)

**Mrs. Hale.** (*hesitantly and in hushed voice*) She liked the bird. She was going to bury it in that pretty box.

**Mrs. Peters.** (*in a whisper*) When I was a girl—my kitten—there was a boy took a hatchet, and before my eyes—and before I could get there— (*covers her face an instant*) If they hadn't held me back I would have— (*catches herself, looks upstairs where steps are heard, falters weakly*) —hurt him.

**Mrs. Hale.** (*with a slow look around her*) I wonder how it would seem never to have had any children around. (*pause*) No, Wright wouldn't like the bird—a thing that sang. She used to sing. He killed that, too.

**Mrs. Peters.** (*moving uneasily*) We don't know who killed the bird.

**Mrs. Hale.** I knew John Wright.

**Mrs. Peters.** It was an awful thing was done in this house that night, Mrs. Hale. Killing a man while he slept, slipping a rope around his neck that choked the life out of him.

---

[6]secretive; not open

**Mrs. Hale.**   His neck. Choked the life out of him. (*Her hand goes out and rests on the bird-cage.*)

**Mrs. Peters.**   (*with rising voice*) We don't know who killed him. We don't *know.*

**Mrs. Hale.**   (*her own feeling not interrupted*) If there'd been years and years of nothing, then a bird to sing to you, it would be awful—still, after the bird was still.

**Mrs. Peters.**   (*something within her speaking*) I know what stillness is. When we homesteaded in Dakota, and my first baby died—after he was two years old, and me with no other then—

**Mrs. Hale.**   (*moving*) How soon do you suppose they'll be through looking for the evidence?

**Mrs. Peters.**   I know what stillness is. (*pulling herself back*) The law has got to punish crime, Mrs. Hale.

**Mrs. Hale.**   (*not as if answering that*) I wish you'd seen Minnie Foster when she wore a white dress with blue ribbons and stood up there in the choir and sang. (*a look around the room*) Oh, I *wish* I'd come here once in a while! That was a crime! That was a crime! Who's going to punish that?

**Mrs. Peters.**   (*looking upstairs*) We mustn't—take on.

**Mrs. Hale.**   I might have known she needed help! I know how things can be—for women. I tell you, it's queer, Mrs. Peters. We live close together and we live far apart. We all go through the same things—it's all just a different kind of the same thing. (*brushes her eyes, noticing the jar of fruit, reaches out for it*) If I was you I wouldn't tell her her fruit was gone. Ter her it *ain't*. Tell her it's all right. Take this in to prove it to her. She—she may never know whether it was broke or not.

**Mrs. Peters.**   (*Takes the jar, looks about for something to wrap it in; takes petticoat from the clothes brought from the other room, very nervously begins winding this around the jar. In a false* *voice)* My, it's a good thing the men couldn't hear us. Wouldn't they just laugh! Getting all stirred up over a little thing like a—dead canary. As if that could have anything to do with—with—wouldn't they *laugh!* (*The men are heard coming downstairs.*)

**Mrs. Hale.** (*under her breath*) Maybe they would—maybe they wouldn't.

**County Attorney.** No, Peters, it's all perfectly clear except a reason for doing it. But you know juries when it comes to women. If there was some definite thing. (*Crosses slowly to above table.* **Sheriff** *crosses* D.R. **Mrs. Hale** *and* **Mrs. Peters** *remain seated at either side of table.*) Something to show—something to make a story about—a thing that would connect up with the strange way of doing it— (*The women's eyes meet for an instant. Enter* **Hale** *from outer door.*)

**Hale.** (*remaining* U.L. *by door*) Well, I've got the team around. Pretty cold out there.

**County Attorney.** I'm going to stay awhile by myself. (*to the* **Sheriff**) You can send Frank out for me, can't you? I want to go over everything. I'm not satisfied that we can't do better.

**Sheriff.** Do you want to see what Mrs. Peters is going to take in? (*The* **Lawyer** *picks up the apron, laughs.*)

**County Attorney.** Oh, I guess they're not very dangerous things the ladies have picked up. (*Moves a few things about, disturbing the quilt pieces which cover the box. Steps back.*) No, Mrs. Peters doesn't need supervising. For that matter a sheriff's wife is married to the law. Ever think of it that way, Mrs. Peters?

**Mrs. Peters.** Not—just that way.

**Sheriff.** (*chuckling*) Married to the law. (*moves to* D.R. *door to the other room*) I just want you to come in here a minute, George. We ought to take a look at these windows.

**County Attorney.** (*scoffingly*) Oh, windows!

**Sheriff.**    We'll be right out, Mr. Hale. (**Hale** *goes outside. The* **Sheriff** *follows the* **County Attorney** *into the other room. Then* **Mrs. Hale** *rises, hands tight together, looking intensely at* **Mrs. Peters***, whose eyes make a slow turn, finally meeting* **Mrs. Hale***'s. A moment* **Mrs. Hale** *holds her, then her own eyes point the way to where the box is concealed. Suddenly,* **Mrs. Peters** *throws back quilt pieces and tries to put the box in the bag she is carrying. It is too big. She opens box, starts to take bird out, cannot touch it, goes to pieces, stands there helpless. Sound of a knob turning in the other room.* **Mrs.Hale** *snatches the box and puts it in the pocket of her big coat. Enter* **County Attorney** *and* **Sheriff***, who remains D.R.*)

**County Attorney.**    (*crosses to U.L. door, facetiously[7]*) Well, Henry, at least we found out that she was not going to quilt it. She was going to—what is it you call it, ladies?

**Mrs. Hale.**    (*standing C. below table facing front, her hand against her pocket*) We call it—knot it, Mr. Henderson.

---

⊙

---

[7]humorously; in a joking way

# REVIEWING AND INTERPRETING

Record your answers to these questions in your personal literature notebook. Follow the directions for each part.

*REVIEWING*    Try to complete each of these sentences without looking back at the play.

*Recalling Facts*

1. Mr. Wright has been murdered by someone who
   a. shot him with the gun that he kept in his house.
   b. tied a rope around his neck and strangled him.
   c. poisoned him with cherry preserves.
   d. stabbed him with a sewing scissors.

*Identifying Sequence*

2. The women find the dead canary
   a. before the sheriff finds the broken preserve jars.
   b. before Mrs. Hale rips away the careless quilt stitching.
   c. after Mrs. Peters finds the bird cage.
   d. before Mr. Hale describes the scene of the crime.

*Identifying Cause and Effect*

3. The women think that Mrs. Wright may have killed her husband because he
   a. was too quiet.
   b. was so stingy.
   c. never let her see her friends.
   d. broke her canary's neck.

*Understanding Main Ideas*

4. The men are trying to find
   a. why Mrs. Wright would want to kill her husband.
   b. evidence that Mr. Wright committed suicide.
   c. the murder weapon.
   d. evidence that someone else killed Mr. Wright.

*Recognizing Literary Elements (Setting)*

**5.** This play is set around the year
   a. 1700.
   b. 1800.
   c. 1900.
   d. 1950.

**INTERPRETING**

To complete these sentences, you may look back at the play if you'd like.

*Making Inferences*

**6.** Because Mr. Wright was a cold, humorless man, the women guess that
   a. the Wright home had been depressing and lonely.
   b. Mr. Wright had wanted to kill himself.
   c. Mr. Wright had threatened to kill Mrs. Wright.
   d. Mrs. Wright encouraged people to visit her often.

*Analyzing*

**7.** The men's attitude toward the women is
   a. suspicious.
   b. nasty.
   c. admiring.
   d. condescending.

*Predicting Outcomes*

**8.** When the women return to town, they probably will
   a. tell their husbands all they learned.
   b. force Mrs. Wright to confess to her crime.
   c. continue to keep their findings secret.
   d. report their findings to the judge.

*Making Generalizations*

**9.** The following statement best expresses what the women realize as they glimpse details from Mrs. Wright's life:
   a. "We all go through the same things—it's all just a different kind of the same thing."
   b. " . . . you don't enjoy things when you feel shabby."
   c. "Men's hands aren't always as clean as they might be."
   d. "There's a great deal of work to be done on a farm."

*Understanding*
*Literary Elements*
*(Theme)*

**10.** The theme of this play is that
  a. men are not able to see trifles, or small details.
  b. women are the best detectives because they worry about trifles.
  c. women can focus only on trifles.
  d. little details are often more important than big events.

Now check your answers with your teacher. Study the questions you answered incorrectly. What types of questions were they? Talk with your teacher about ways to work on those skills.

# *Understanding Plot*

As you know, the sequence of events in a story or play is called the *plot*. Unlike the author of a novel, a playwright doesn't have the luxury of including a lot of details in the play. Therefore, he or she plans the plot carefully, making every word and action count.

Whether they are part of a short story, a novel, or a play, plots are usually divided into five parts, as shown in the following diagram:

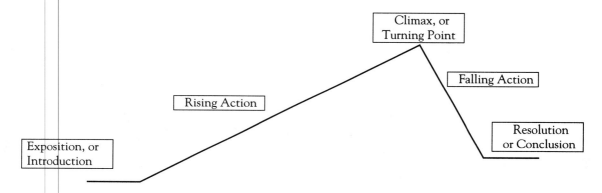

Diagram of a Plot

*Exposition*    During the exposition—which is also known as the introduction—the author describes the setting and the main characters. The exposition prepares the reader or audience for the action that is to come. The problem, or *conflict*, that the characters will face is also introduced during the exposition.

*Rising Action*    During the rising action, the plot thickens. The problem is explained, the conflict becomes more complicated, and the tension builds.

*Climax*    The climax is the most exciting part of the plot. Usually, it is also the turning point of the story.

*Falling Action*    During the falling action, readers find out how the characters react to events that occurred or decisions that were made. Readers' questions are also answered and loose ends are tied up.

*Resolution*    The last part of the plot is the resolution. This is the conclusion of the story; it brings things to a satisfying close.

In the lessons that follow, you will look at the ways in which playwright Susan Glaspell develops the plot of *Trifles*:

1. She uses stage directions and dialogue to introduce the setting, the characters, and the conflict.

2. She has the tension build as the evidence accumulates and a climax is reached.

3. She ends the play with falling action and a conclusion.

## LESSON ① EXPOSITION AND RISING ACTION

Remember, during the *exposition*, the playwright introduces the setting and the main characters. When the curtain rises on a play, the audience is transported to a different time and place. Although readers can't see the stage, they can visualize the opening setting by reading the stage directions that come before the play. For example, what do you learn about the setting of *Trifles* from these opening stage directions?

**SCENE:** *The kitchen in the now abandoned farmhouse of* **John Wright,** *a gloomy kitchen, and left without having been put in order—the walls covered with a faded wall paper.* D.R. *is a door leading to the parlor. On the* R. *wall above this door is a built-in kitchen cupboard with shelves in the upper portion and drawers below. In the rear wall at* R., *up two steps is a door opening onto stairs leading to the second floor. In the rear wall at* L. *is a door to the shed and from there to the outside. Between these two doors is an* *old-fashioned black iron stove. Running along the* L. *wall from the shed door is an old iron sink and sink shelf, in which is set a hand pump. Downstage of the sink is an uncurtained window.*

These stage directions help form a dismal picture in the reader's mind. The farmhouse is described as "now abandoned." The kitchen's walls are covered with faded wallpaper—a sign that the house is probably owned by someone either without much money or without any interest in keeping the room up-to-date. The kitchen is gloomy and untidy. The old-fashioned iron stove and the hand pump suggest that the play is set in the past, before running water was common in kitchens.

The stage directions also describe all five of the play's characters as they enter the stage. However, though three men and two women enter, only the men carry on a conversation for quite a while. Neither woman joins the conversation until several pages into the play, and even then this woman first speaks only to the other woman.

> **County Attorney.**    Here's a nice mess. (*The women draw nearer* U.C.)
>
> **Mrs. Peters.**    (*to the other woman*) Oh, her fruit; it did freeze. (*to the* **Lawyer**) She worried about that when it turned so cold. She said the fire'd go out and her jars would break.
>
> **Sheriff.**    (*rises*) Well, can you beat the women! Held for murder and worryin' about her preserves.

Because they do not speak for such a long time, it seems that the women do not feel comfortable expressing themselves here. When the sheriff ridicules Mrs. Peters's words and doesn't even respond to her directly, it becomes obvious that their perception of their situation is accurate—their opinions are not valued by the men.

Besides introducing the setting and the characters, the exposition also introduces the *conflict*, or problem, that the characters face. The men's dialogue explains the situation in which the characters find themselves. They have come to the house to look for a motive in the killing of its owner, Mr. Wright. Finding evidence about the murder seems to be the characters' main problem. However, as the play continues you see that there is more than one conflict at work. There is also a tension between the women and the men about what each one considers important details. The men recede into the background, entering and exiting excitedly in their search for obvious clues. The women, on the other hand, find small clues that begin to pile up and make them wonder about Mrs. Wright's innocence.

EXERCISE ① 

Read this passage in which the women discover the dead bird. Then use what you have learned in this lesson to answer the questions that follow the passage.

> **Mrs. Hale.** *(crosses to right of table)* Here's some red. I expect this has got sewing things in it. *(brings out a fancy box)* What a pretty box. Looks like something somebody would give you. Maybe her scissors are in here. *(Opens box. Suddenly puts her hand to her nose.)* Why— (**Mrs. Peters** *bends nearer, then turns her face away.*) There's something wrapped up in this piece of silk.
>
> **Mrs. Peters.** Why, this isn't her scissors.
>
> **Mrs. Hale.** *(lifting the silk)* Oh, Mrs. Peters—it's— (**Mrs. Peters** *bends closer.*)
>
> **Mrs. Peters.** It's the bird.
>
> **Mrs. Hale.** But, Mrs. Peters—look at it! Its neck! Look at its neck! It's all—other side *to.*
>
> **Mrs. Peters.** Somebody—wrung—its—neck. *(Their eyes meet. A look of growing comprehension, of horror. Steps are heard outside.* **Mrs. Hale** *slips box under quilt pieces, and*

*sinks into her chair. Enter* **Sheriff** *and* **County Attorney. Mrs. Peters** *steps* D.L. *and stands looking out of window.)*

**1.** Who do the women suspect has wrung the bird's neck? Why is this a significant find? How does it raise the tension in the story?

**2.** Why do you think the women decide not to mention this evidence to the sheriff?

Now check your answers with your teacher. Review this part of the lesson if you don't understand why an answer was incorrect.

## WRITING ON YOUR OWN ①

In an earlier writing exercise, you described and labeled scenes from several different plays, movies, or television shows. Now you will focus on one of those scenes as you explore its plot. Follow these steps:

- Choose one of the plays, movies, or television shows on your list and write a short paragraph describing what you saw as the curtain went up or after the opening credits ended.
- Think about the characters in the story. What was each character doing the first time he or she appeared on stage or screen? Write a sentence describing your first glimpse of each character.
- How did the author introduce the conflict? Write a few sentences telling how you first came to realize the nature of the problem that the characters would have to face.
- List about five events that helped create rising tension. Do not include the climax—the most exciting event—at this time.
- Save your description. You will refer to it again later in the unit.

## LESSON ② CLIMAX, OR TURNING POINT

At a certain point in a story, a turning point is reached. Perhaps the characters can no longer avoid making a decision. Or perhaps a situation becomes so impossible that some sort of action must be taken. That point in the plot is called the *climax*.

The climax is a crucial part of any story. If the plot has been planned well, readers and audiences should feel a sense of relief that the problem is finally being faced. Whether the outcome is perceived as positive or negative, the characters have looked at the problem and will now have to deal with the consequences of their actions.

Read this passage to see how Susan Glaspell created the exciting climax in *Trifles*:

> **Sheriff.** We'll be right out, Mr. Hale. (**Hale** *goes outside. The* **Sheriff** *follows the* **County Attorney** *into the other room. Then* **Mrs. Hale** *rises, hands tight together, looking intensely at* **Mrs. Peters**, *whose eyes make a slow turn, finally meeting* **Mrs. Hale**'s. *A moment* **Mrs. Hale** *holds her, then her own eyes point the way to where the box is concealed. Suddenly* **Mrs. Peters** *throws back quilt pieces and tries to put the box in the bag she is carrying. It is too big. She opens box, starts to take bird out, cannot touch it, goes to pieces, stands there helpless. Sound of a knob turning in the other room.* **Mrs. Hale** *snatches the box and puts it in the pocket of her big coat. Enter* **County Attorney** *and* **Sheriff**, *who remains* D.R.)

The women are both convinced that the dead canary gives Mrs. Wright a motive for killing her husband. Although Mrs. Peters fails in her attempt to make off with the box containing the evidence, Mrs. Hale succeeds. Together they willingly accept that they have become judge and jury, deciding Mrs. Wright's guilt or innocence. From this moment on, they can no longer consider themselves just onlookers but must realize that they are participants—if not in the crime, then at least in the cover-up.

EXERCISE ②

Read the following passage. Then use what you have learned in this lesson to answer the questions.

**Mrs. Peters.** (*Takes the jar, looks about for something to wrap it in; takes petticoat from the clothes brought from the other room, very nervously begins winding this around the jar. In a false voice*) My, it's a good thing the men couldn't hear us. Wouldn't they just laugh! Getting all stirred up over a little thing like a—dead canary. As if that could have anything to do with—with—wouldn't they *laugh!* (*The men are heard coming downstairs.*)

**Mrs. Hale.** (*under her breath*) Maybe they would—maybe they wouldn't.

**County Attorney.** No, Peters, it's all perfectly clear except a reason for doing it. But you know juries when it comes to women. If there was some definite thing. (*Crosses slowly to above table.* **Sheriff** *crosses* D.R. **Mrs. Hale** *and* **Mrs. Peters** *remain seated at either side of table.*) Something to show—something to make a story about—a thing that would connect up with this strange way of doing it— (*The women's eyes meet for an instant. Enter* **Hale** *from outer door.*)

1. In this passage just before the climax, the tension is building rapidly. Why is Mrs. Peters so nervous? Why does the playwright describe Mrs. Hale as speaking under her breath?

2. The County Attorney explains that he is searching for "something to make a story about." How do his words increase the tension and force the women to make their climactic decision?

Now check your answers with your teacher. Review this part of the lesson if you don't understand why an answer was incorrect.

## WRITING ON YOUR OWN ②

Review what you wrote for the previous writing exercise. Then do the following:

- Try to remember the climax of the plot you are analyzing. Make some notes about it. Who was present? Where did it take place? Why was it so exciting? What was changed or decided upon at the climax?
- Use the notes you just made to recreate the scene in which the climax took place. Don't try to remember the exact words that the actors said. Just convey the intent of the scene as closely as possible. Write it as if it were a play, with dialogue and stage directions about the setting and the placement of the characters. Follow the format that you see in this book. Be sure to show how this moment is the turning point of the story.

## LESSON ③   FALLING ACTION AND RESOLUTION

After the excitement of the climax, tensions ease and the action slows down. The part of the play that follows the climax is called the *falling action*. The major conflict has been faced and dealt with. At this point, the characters realize the changes that have taken place. The urgency of the rising action is gone, and now the author has time to answer any lingering questions about the results of the characters' decisions and actions.

In some plays, the falling action is lengthy. Several events may follow the climax. Sometimes, the falling action may even feature a surprise ending. In other plays, however, this part of the play is extremely short or may be missing altogether. Look back at the ending of *Trifles*. What happens after the climax?

**Sheriff.** We'll be right out, Mr. Hale. (**Hale** *goes outside. The* **Sheriff** *follows the* **County Attorney** *into the other room. Then* **Mrs. Hale** *rises, hands tight together, looking intensely at* **Mrs. Peters**, *whose eyes make a slow turn, finally meeting* **Mrs. Hale**'s. *A moment* **Mrs. Hale** *holds her, then her own eyes point the way to where the box is concealed. Suddenly* **Mrs. Peters** *throws back quilt pieces and tries to put the box in the bag she is carrying. It is too big. She opens box, starts to take bird out, cannot touch it, goes to pieces, stands there helpless. Sound of a knob turning in the other room.* **Mrs. Hale** *snatches the box and puts it in the pocket of her big coat. Enter* **County Attorney** *and* **Sheriff**, *who remain* D.R.)

**County Attorney.** (*crosses to* U.L. *door, facetiously*) Well, Henry, at least we found out that she was not going to quilt it. She was going to—what is it you call it, ladies?

**Mrs. Hale.** (*standing* C. *below table facing front, her hand against her pocket*) We call it—knot it, Mr. Henderson.

Mrs. Hale is barely able to hide the box containing the dead bird before the County Attorney and the sheriff enter the room. Their entrance is the only event that takes place after the climax. Therefore, in this play, there is almost no falling action.

The falling action is not the last part of a plot. To show that the story is complete, the author finishes with a *resolution*, or conclusion. The conclusion to a story is like the last bite of a good meal. It should give the whole presentation a satisfying, unmistakable finish. In a play, the last lines often give audiences something to think about as they leave the theater.

## EXERCISE ③

Reread the passage containing the falling action and resolution. Take note, especially, of the last conversation between the County Attorney and Mrs. Hale. Then use what you have learned in this lesson to answer the questions below.

1. What detail in the conclusion makes it seem unlikely that Mrs. Hale will change her mind?

2. What effect does the County Attorney's attitude probably have on the women's determination to protect Mrs. Wright?

3. Mrs. Hale seems to be having a little private fun with the County Attorney's joking words. She replies emphatically that Mrs. Wright was going to "knot it." What else did Mrs. Wright knot besides the quilt? Why is this line a fitting end to the play?

Now check your answers with your teacher. Review this part of the lesson if you don't understand why an answer was incorrect.

### WRITING ON YOUR OWN ③

In this exercise you will analyze the falling action and resolution of your chosen play, movie, or television show. Follow these steps:

- Jot down notes about everything that happened after the climax of the play, movie, or show.
- Then describe the resolution, or final scene. Tell who was there, where it took place, and what was said.
- Was there anything left undone or unanswered at the end of the play, movie, or show? If so, write down the questions that you would have liked answered during the falling action or the resolution.

## DISCUSSION GUIDES

1.  At the end of the play, Mrs. Hale and Mrs. Peters decide to withhold the evidence that they have uncovered about a possible motive for Mr. Wright's murder. With a small group of classmates, discuss their decision. Why do you think they cover up for Mrs. Wright? How do they justify their actions? Would you have done the same thing in their position if you were aware that withholding evidence is illegal? After your discussion, poll the members of your group. How many would have hidden the evidence? How many would have revealed it to the authorities? What is the reasoning behind each answer?

2.  Suppose the women had immediately reported the evidence that they found to the sheriff and the County Attorney. Do you think the men would have changed their attitudes toward the women, considering they uncovered the possible motive for the crime? Or do you think the men would have continued to belittle the women's intelligence and abilities? Work with a partner to find clues in the play that support your answer. Then present your opinion and your evidence to the class.

3.  How does the playwright bring the audience over to the women's side in the conflict between the men and the women? Work with a small group to review the play, looking for particular events or lines of dialogue that put the men in a bad light. Find passages that cause you to sympathize with the women. Make a list of these events and lines of dialogue. Then compare your group's list with that of other groups in your class.

# WRITE A PLOT SUMMARY

In this unit you have seen how authors develop the plots of their plays. Now you will summarize the plot of a familiar play, movie, or television show. Follow the steps below to complete your summary.

If you have any questions about the writing process, refer to Using the Writing Process beginning on page 300.

- Assemble the writing you did for all the exercises in this unit, including: *1)* a paragraph describing the opening setting of your chosen show, sentences telling how the characters were introduced, sentences explaining how the conflict was introduced, and a list of rising action events; *2)* the climactic scene from the show, recreated in play form; *3)* a description of the last scene and questions that should have been answered.
- Begin your summary by naming the play, movie, or TV show you will be focusing on and telling when and where you saw it.
- Use these subtitles: *Exposition, Rising Action, Climax, Falling Action,* and *Resolution*. Under each subtitle, write sentences or paragraphs summarizing the events that can be matched with those parts of the plot. For example, under *Exposition*, you might write the following:

  The show begins with a picture of a small bungalow on a residential street in present-day America. We see the living room of the house, with an easy chair, a TV, and a sofa. Two children, about 10 and 13 years old, are watching TV and eating popcorn. Their father comes in the front door, turns off the TV, and says, "I thought I gave you a job to do!"

- When you finish your summary, read it over. Do you agree with your placement of each event? Have you thought of more events? If you want to add events or change their categories, do so before you write your final summary.
- Proofread your summary for spelling, grammar, punctuation, and capitalization errors. Then make a final copy and save it in your writing portfolio.

# Characters

# Driving Miss Daisy

by Alfred Uhry

## INTRODUCTION

ABOUT THE
SELECTION

Seventy-two-year-old Daisy Werthan, a Jewish widow, can no
longer operate a car safely. In her last driving outing, she
demolished her new car, a garage, and a shed. Her son Boolie
decides that Daisy needs a chauffeur to drive her around her
hometown of Atlanta, Georgia. Daisy disagrees violently, saying that she is capable of driving herself. Ignoring his mother's
protests, Boolie hires a 60-year-old African-American driver
named Hoke Coleburn to be Daisy's chauffeur. *Driving Miss
Daisy* is the story of how Daisy and Hoke learn to get along
and value each other over a 25-year period. Their relationship grows to the point where, near the end of the play, Daisy
can say to Hoke, "You're my best friend."

Playwright Alfred Uhry based the main characters, Daisy
and Hoke, on his grandmother and her African-American
chauffeur, Will Coleman. The play was originally performed
in the spring of 1987 at a small New York theater that seated
only 74 people. Uhry thought that was the right size for a little play that would appeal only to him, his family, and a few
other Southerners. He was amazed to find out that its appeal
was much broader. In one of the glowing reviews of the play,
critic Mel Gussow of the *New York Times* wrote, "The author

and his actors repeatedly embellish the story with strokes of humanity and humor, as the two people come to realize they have far more in common than they ever publicly admit."

*Driving Miss Daisy* won the Pulitzer Prize in 1988, and in 1989 Uhry wrote the screenplay for the movie version. The film, starring Morgan Freeman as Hoke, Jessica Tandy as Daisy, and Dan Ackroyd as Boolie, won four Academy Awards.

## ABOUT THE AUTHOR

Alfred Uhry, the son of a social worker and a furniture salesman, was born in Atlanta, Georgia, in 1936. Although he and his family were Jewish, he was not raised in a strict Jewish home and remembers celebrating Christmas and Easter along with his non-Jewish friends. Mr. Uhry graduated from Brown University and then moved to New York City to write lyrics for musicals. For several years, he worked with composer Robert Waldman and taught playwrighting part-time. Frustrated with his limited success, Uhry had decided to return to teaching full-time when his interest in writing his own play was renewed, and he completed *Driving Miss Daisy*. The success of this play was probably responsible for his continued efforts at playwrighting.

In 1996, Uhry's play *The Last Night of Ballyhoo* premiered in Atlanta. That play, like *Driving Miss Daisy*, is set in Atlanta and features characters based on people Uhry knew as a child. *The Last Night of Ballyhoo* won the 1997 Tony Award for Best Play and was a finalist for the 1997 Pulitzer Prize for Drama.

## ABOUT THE LESSONS

The lessons that follow *Driving Miss Daisy* focus on characters. The characters in a story or play are the people or animals who perform the action. If a character in a play is truly effective and unique, you will remember him or her long after you leave the theater. The challenge for a playwright is to create characters who have as much genuine personality as the people you meet every day. When the playwright does his or her job well, you begin to feel as if you know the characters on stage as well as you know your own family and friends.

## WRITING: DESCRIBING A CHARACTER

At the end of this unit, you will write a character sketch. The suggestions below will help you start thinking about the character you will describe:

- When you write about a character, it's a good idea to have a clear picture of him or her in mind. One way to do this is to base your character on someone you know. Begin by making a list of elderly family members or friends you know well. For each person on your list, jot down a few notes about how the person looks, moves, and sounds.
- Then think of one or two adjectives that you would use to describe the personality of each person. List the adjectives under each name.
- Save your lists. You will use them again later in the unit.

## AS YOU READ

As you read this excerpt from *Driving Miss Daisy*, think about these questions:

- How has the playwright used stage directions to reveal the characters of Daisy, Boolie, and Hoke?
- How do the characters' words and actions help them reveal their own personalities, as well as the personalities of the other characters?
- How does the playwright show the change that takes place in the characters and in their relationships to each other?

# Driving Miss Daisy

by Alfred Uhry

**CAST**

**Daisy Werthan**, *a widow*
**Hoke Coleburn**, *her chauffeur*
**Boolie Werthan**, *her son*

**SCENE**

*In the dark we hear a car ignition turn on, and then a horrible crash. Bangs and booms and wood splintering. When the noise is very loud, it stops suddenly and the lights come up on* **Daisy Werthan***'s living room, or a portion thereof.* **Daisy***, age 72, is wearing a summer dress and high heeled shoes. Her hair, her clothes, her walk, everything about her suggests bristle and feist[1] and high energy. She appears to be in excellent health. Her son,* **Boolie Werthan***, 40, is a businessman, Junior Chamber of Commerce style. He has a strong, capable air. The Werthans are Jewish, but they have strong Atlanta accents.*

**Daisy.** No!
**Boolie.** Mama!

---

[1] excitability and spirit

**Daisy.** No!

**Boolie.** Mama!

**Daisy.** I said no, Boolie, and that's the end of it.

**Boolie.** It's a miracle you're not laying in Emory Hospital—or decked out at the funeral home. Look at you! You didn't even break your glasses.

**Daisy.** It was the car's fault.

**Boolie.** Mama, the car didn't just back over the driveway and land on the Pollard's garage all by itself. You had it in the wrong gear.

**Daisy.** I did not!

**Boolie.** You put it in reverse instead of drive. The police report shows that.

**Daisy.** You should have let me keep my La Salle.

**Boolie.** Your La Salle was eight years old.

**Daisy.** I don't care. It never would have behaved this way. And you know it.

**Boolie.** Mama, cars, don't behave. They are behaved upon. The fact is you, all by yourself, demolished that Packard.

**Daisy.** Think what you want. I know the truth.

**Boolie.** The truth is you shouldn't be allowed to drive a car any more.

**Daisy.** No.

**Boolie.** Mama, we are just going to have to hire somebody to drive you.

**Daisy.** No *we* are not. This is my business.

**Boolie.** Your insurance policy is written so that they are going to have to give you a brand new car.

**Daisy.** Not another Packard, I hope.

**Boolie.** Lord Almighty! Don't you see what I'm saying?

**Daisy.** Quit talking so ugly to your mother.

**Boolie.** Mama, you are seventy-two years old and you just cost the insurance company twenty-seven hundred dollars. You are a terrible risk. Nobody is going to issue you a policy after this.

**Daisy.** You're just saying that to be hateful.

**Boolie.** O.K. Yes. Yes I am. I'm making it all up. Every insurance company in America is lined up in the driveway waving their fountain pens and falling all over themselves to get you to sign on. Everybody wants Daisy Werthan, the only woman in the history of driving to demolish a three week old Packard, a two car garage and a free standing tool shed in one fell swoop!

**Daisy.** You talk so foolish sometimes, Boolie.

**Boolie.** And even if you could get a policy somewhere, it wouldn't be safe. I'd worry all the time. Look at how many of your friends have men to drive them. Miss Ida Jacobs, Miss Ethel Hess, Aunt Nonie—

**Daisy.** They're all rich.

**Boolie.** Daddy left you plenty enough for this. I'll do the interviewing at the plant. Oscar in the freight elevator knows every colored man in Atlanta worth talking about. I'm sure in two weeks time I can find you somebody perfectly—

**Daisy.** No!

**Boolie.** You won't even have to do anything, Mama. I told you. I'll do all the interviewing, all the reference checking, all the—

**Daisy.** No. Now stop running your mouth! I am seventy-two years old as you so gallantly reminded me and I am a widow, but unless they rewrote the Constitution and didn't tell me, I still have rights. And one of my rights is the right to invite who I want—not who you want—into my house. You do accept the fact that this is my house? What I do not want—and absolutely will not have is some— *(She gropes for a bad enough word.)* some chauffeur sitting in my kitchen, gobbling my food, running up my phone bill. Oh, I hate all that in my house!

**Boolie.** You have Idella.

**Daisy.** Idella is different. She's been coming to me three times a week since you were in the eighth grade and we know how to stay out of each other's way. And even so there are nicks and chips in most of my wedding china and I've seen her throw silver forks in the garbage more than once.

**Boolie.** Do you think Idella has a vendetta[2] against your silverware?

**Daisy.** Stop being sassy. You know what I mean. I was brought up to do for myself. On Forsyth Street we couldn't afford them and we did for ourselves. That's still the best way, if you ask me.

**Boolie.** Them! You sound like Governor Talmadge.

**Daisy.** Why, Boolie! What a thing to say! I'm not prejudiced! Aren't you ashamed?

**Boolie.** I've got to go home. Florine'll be having a fit.

**Daisy.** Y'all must have plans tonight.

**Boolie.** Going to the Ansleys for a dinner party.

**Daisy.** I see.

**Boolie.** You see what?

**Daisy.** The Ansleys. I'm sure Florine bought another new dress. This is her idea of heaven on earth, isn't it?

**Boolie.** What?

**Daisy.** Socializing with Episcopalians.

**Boolie.** You're a doodle, Mama. I guess Aunt Nonie can run you anywhere you need to go for the time being.

**Daisy.** I'll be fine.

**Boolie.** I'll stop by tomorrow evening.

**Daisy.** How do you know I'll be here? I'm certainly not dependent on you for company.

---

[2]act of vengeance, often motivated by a long-term feud

**Boolie.**   Fine. I'll call first. And I still intend to interview colored men.

**Daisy.**   No!

**Boolie.**   Mama!

**Daisy.**   (*singing to end discussion*)

After the ball is over

After the break of morn

After the dancers leaving

After the stars are gone

Many a heart is aching

If you could read them all—

(*Lights fade on her as she sings and come up on* **Boolie** *at his desk at the Werthan Company. He sits at a desk piled with papers, and speaks into an intercom.*)

**Boolie.**   O. K., Miss McClatchey. Send him on in. (*He continues working at his desk.* **Hoke Coleburn** *enters, a black man of about 60, dressed in a somewhat shiny suit and carrying a fedora, a man clearly down on his luck but anxious to keep up appearances.*) Yes, Hoke isn't it?

**Hoke.**   Yassuh. Hoke Coleburn.

**Boolie.**   Have a seat there. I've got to sign these letters. I don't want Miss McClatchey fussing at me.

**Hoke.**   Keep right on with it. I got all the time in the worl'.

**Boolie.**   I see. How long you been out of work?

**Hoke.**   Since back befo' las' November.

**Boolie.**   Long time.

**Hoke.**   Well, Mist' Werthan, you try bein' me and looking for work. They hirin' young if they hirin' colored, an' they ain' even hirin' much young, seems like. (**Boolie** *is involved with his paperwork.*) Mist' Werthan? Y'all people Jewish, ain' you?

**Boolie.**   Yes we are. Why do you ask?

**Hoke.**   I'd druther drive for Jews. People always talkin' 'bout they stingy and they cheap, but don' say none of that 'roun' me.

**Boolie.**   Good to know you feel that way. Now, tell me where you worked before.

**Hoke.**   Yassuh. That's what I'm gettin' at. One time I workin' for this woman over near Little Five Points. What was that woman's name? I forget. Anyway, she president of the Ladies Auxiliary over yonder to the Ponce De Leon Baptist Church and seem like she always bringing up God and Jesus and do unto others. You know what I'm talkin' bout?

**Hoke.**   I'm not sure. Go on.

**Hoke.**   Well, one day, Mist' Werthan, one day that woman say to me, she say "Hoke, come on back in the back wid me. I got something for you." And we go on back yonder and, Lawd have mercy, she have all these old shirts and collars be on the bed, yellow, you know, and nasty like they been stuck off in a chiffarobe and forgot about. Thass' right. And she say "Ain' they nice? They b'long to my daddy befo' he pass and we fixin' to sell 'em to you for twenty five cent apiece."

**Boolie.**   What was her name?

**Hoke.**   Thass' what I'm thinkin'. What WAS that woman's name? Anyway, as I was goin' on to say, any fool see the whole bunch of them collars and shirts together ain' worth a nickel! Them's the people das callin' Jews cheap! So I say "Yassum, I think about it" and I get me another job fas' as I can.

**Boolie.**   Where was that?

**Hoke.**   Mist' Harold Stone, Jewish gentleman jes' like you. Judge, live over yonder on Lullwater Road.

**Boolie.**   I knew Judge Stone.

**Hoke.**   You doan' say! He done give me this suit when he finish wid it. An' this necktie too.

**Boolie.**    You drove for Judge Stone?

**Hoke.**    Seven years to the day nearabout. An' I be there still
    if he din' die, and Miz Stone decide to close up the house
    and move to her people in Savannah. And she say "Come
    on down to Savannah wid' me, Hoke." Cause my wife
    dead by then and I say "No thank you." I didn' want to
    leave my grandbabies and I don' get along with that
    Geechee trash they got down there.

**Boolie.**    Judge Stone was a friend of my father's.

**Hoke.**    You doan' mean! Oscar say you need a driver for yo'
    family. What I be doin'? Runnin' yo' children to school
    and yo' wife to the beauty parlor and like dat?

**Boolie.**    I don't have any children. But tell me—

**Hoke.**    Thass' a shame! My daughter bes' thing ever happen
    to me. But you young yet. I wouldn't worry none.

**Boolie.**    I won't. Thank you. Did you have a job after Judge
    Stone?

**Hoke.**    I drove a milk truck for the Avondale Dairy thru the
    whole war—the one jes' was.

**Boolie.**    Hoke, what I'm looking for is somebody to drive my
    mother around.

**Hoke.**    Excuse me for askin', but how come she ain' hire fo'
    herseff?

**Boolie.**    Well, it's a delicate situation.

**Hoke.**    Mmmm Hmm. She done gone 'roun' the bend a little?
    That'll happen when they get on.

**Boolie.**    Oh no. Nothing like that. She's all there. Too much
    there is the problem. It just isn't safe for her to drive any
    more. She knows it, but she won't admit it. I'll be frank
    with you. I'm a little desperate.

**Hoke.**    I know what you mean 'bout dat. Once I was outta
    work my wife said to me "Oooooh, Hoke, you ain' gon get
    noun nother job." And I say "What you talkin' bout,
    woman?" And the very next week I go to work for that

woman in Little Five Points. Cahill! Ms. Frances Cahill. And then I go to Judge Stone and they the reason I happy to hear you Jews.

**Boolie.** Hoke, I want you to understand, my mother is a little high-strung. She doesn't want anybody driving her. But the fact is you'd be working for me. She can say anything she likes but she can't fire you. You understand?

**Hoke.** Sho' I do. Don't worry none about it. I hold on no matter what way she run me. When I nothin' but a little boy down there on the farm above Macon, I use to wrastle hogs to the ground at killin' time, and ain' no hog get away from me yet.

**Boolie.** How does twenty dollars a week sound?

**Hoke.** Soun' like you got yo' Mama a chauffeur. (*Lights fade on them and come up on* **Daisy** *who enters her living room with the morning paper. She reads with interest.* **Hoke** *enters the living room. He carries a chauffeur's cap instead of his hat.* **Daisy**'s *concentration on the paper becomes fierce when she senses* **Hoke**'s *presence.*) Mornin', Miz Daisy.

**Daisy.** Good morning.

**Hoke.** Right cool in the night, wadn't it?

**Daisy.** I wouldn't know. I was asleep.

**Hoke.** Yassum. What yo plans today?

**Daisy.** That's my business.

**Hoke.** You right about dat. Idella say we runnin' outa coffee and Dutch Cleanser.

**Daisy.** We?

**Hoke.** She say we low on silver polish too.

**Daisy.** Thank you. I will go to the Piggly Wiggly on the trolley this afternoon.

**Hoke.** Now, Miz Daisy, how come you doan' let me carry you?

**Daisy.** No thank you.

**Hoke.**    Aint that what Mist' Werthan hire me for?

**Daisy.**    That's his problem.

**Hoke.**    All right den. I find something to do. I tend yo zinnias.

**Daisy.**    Leave my flower bed alone.

**Hoke.**    Yassum. You got a nice place back beyond the garage ain' doin' nothin' but sittin' there. I could put you in some butterbeans and some tomatoes and even some Irish potatoes could we get some ones with good eyes.

**Daisy.**    If I want a vegetable garden, I'll plant it for myself.

**Hoke.**    Well, I go out and set in the kitchen, then, like I been doin' all week.

**Daisy.**    Don't talk to Idella. She has work to do.

**Hoke.**    Nome. I jes sit there till five o'clock.

**Daisy.**    That's your affair.

**Hoke.**    Seem a shame, do. That fine Oldsmobile settin out there in the garage. Ain't move a inch from when Mist' Werthan rode it over here from Mitchell Motors. Only got nineteen miles on it. Seem like that insurance company give you a whole new car for nothin'.

**Daisy.**    That's your opinion.

**Hoke.**    Yassum. And my other opinion is a fine rich Jewish lady like you doan b'long draggin' up the steps of no bus, luggin' no grocery store bags. I come along and carry them fo' you.

**Daisy.**    I don't need you. I don't want you. And I don't like you saying I'm rich.

**Hoke.**    I won' say it, then.

**Daisy.**    Is that what you and Idella talk about in the kitchen? Oh, I hate this! I hate being discussed behind my back in my own house! I was born on Forsyth Street and, believe you me, I knew the value of a penny. My brother Manny brought home a white cat one day and Papa said we couldn't keep it because we couldn't afford to feed it. My sisters saved up money so I could go to school and be a teacher. We didn't have anything!

**Hoke.** Yassum, but look like you doin' all right now.

**Daisy.** And I've ridden the trolley with groceries plenty of times!

**Hoke.** Yassum, but I feel bad takin' Mist' Werthan's money for doin' nothin'. You understand? (*She cut him off in the speech.*)

**Daisy.** How much does he pay you?

**Hoke.** That between me and him, Miz Daisy.

**Daisy.** Anything over seven dollars a week is robbery. Highway robbery!

**Hoke.** Specially when I doan do nothin' but set on a stool in the kitchen all day long. Tell you what, while you goin on the trolley to the Piggly Wiggly, I hose down yo' front steps. (**Daisy** *is putting on her hat.*)

**Daisy.** All right.

**Hoke.** All right I hose yo' steps?

**Daisy.** All right the Piggly Wiggly. And then home. Nowhere else.

**Hoke.** Yassum.

**Daisy.** Wait. You don't know how to run the Oldsmobile!

**Hoke.** Miz Daisy, a gear shift like a third arm to me. Anyway, thissun automatic. Any fool can run it.

**Daisy.** Any fool but me, apparently.

**Hoke.** Ain' no need to be so hard on yoseff now. You cain' drive but you probably do alota things I cain' do. It all work out.

**Daisy.** (*calling offstage*) I'm gone to the market, Idella.

**Hoke.** (*also calling*) And I right behind her! (**Hoke** *puts on his cap and helps* **Daisy** *into the car. He sits at the wheel and backs the car down the driveway.* **Daisy**, *in the rear, is in full bristle.*) I love a new car smell. Doan' you? (**Daisy** *slides over to the other side of the seat.*)

**Daisy.** I'm nobody's fool, Hoke.

**Hoke.** Nome.

**Daisy.** I can see the speedometer as well as you can.

**Hoke.** I see dat.

**Daisy.** My husband taught me how to run a car.

**Hoke.** Yassum.

**Daisy.** I still remember everything he said. So don't you even think for a second that you can—Wait! You're speeding! I see it!

**Hoke.** We ain' goin' but nineteen miles an hour.

**Daisy.** I like to go under the speed limit.

**Hoke.** Speed limit thirty five here.

**Daisy.** The slower you go, the more you save on gas. My husband told me that.

**Hoke.** We barely movin'. Might as well walk to the Piggly Wiggly.

**Daisy.** Is this your car?

**Hoke.** Nome.

**Daisy.** Do you pay for the gas?

**Hoke.** Nome.

**Daisy.** All right then. My fine son may think I'm losing my abilities, but I am still in control of what goes on in my car. Where are you going?

**Hoke.** To the grocery store.

**Daisy.** Then why didn't you turn on Highland Avenue?

**Hoke.** Piggly Wiggly ain' on Highland Avenue. It on Euclid, down there near—

**Daisy.** I know where it is and I want to go to it the way I always go. On Highland Avenue.

**Hoke.** That three blocks out of the way, Miz Daisy.

**Daisy.** Go back! Go back this minute!

**Hoke.** We in the wrong lane! I cain' jes—

**Daisy.** Go back I said! If you don't, I'll get out of this car and walk!

**Hoke.** We movin'! You cain' open the do'!

**Daisy.** This is wrong! Where are you taking me?

**Hoke.** The sto'.

**Daisy.** This is wrong. You have to go back to Highland Avenue!

**Hoke.** Mmmm Hmmmm.

**Daisy.** I've been driving to the Piggly Wiggly since the day they put it up and opened it for business. This isn't the way! Go back! Go back this minute!

**Hoke.** Yonder the Piggly Wiggly.

**Daisy.** Get ready to turn now.

**Hoke.** Yassum.

**Daisy.** Look out! There's a little boy behind that shopping cart!

**Hoke.** I see dat.

**Daisy.** Pull in next to the blue car.

**Hoke.** We closer to the do' right here.

**Daisy.** Next to the blue car! I don't park in the sun! It fades the upholstery.

**Hoke.** Yassum. (*He pulls in, and gets out as Daisy springs out of the back seat.*)

**Daisy.** Wait a minute. Give me the car keys.

**Hoke.** Yassum.

**Daisy.** Stay right here by the car. And you don't have to tell everybody my business.

**Hoke.** Nome. Don' forget the Dutch Cleanser now. (*She fixes him with a look meant to kill and exits. **Hoke** waits by the car for a minute, then hurries to the phone booth at the corner.*) Hello? Miz McClatchey? Hoke Coleburn here. Can I speak to him? (*pause*) Mornin sir, Mist' Werthan. Guess where I'm at? I'm at dishere phone booth on Euclid Avenue right next to the Piggly Wiggly. I jes drove yo' Mama to the market. *(pause)* She flap a little on the way. But she all right. She in the store. Uh oh. Miz Daisy look out the store window and doan' see me, she liable to throw a fit right there by the checkout. *(pause)* Yassuh, only took six days. Same time it take the Lawd to make the worl'. *(Lights out on him. We hear a choir singing.)*

**CHOIR.**

May the words of my mouth
And the meditations of my heart
Be acceptable in Thy sight, O Lord
My strength and my redeemer. Amen.

*(Light up on **Hoke** waiting by the car, looking at a newspaper. Daisy enters in a different hat and a fur piece.)*

**Hoke.**   How yo' Temple this mornin', Miz Daisy?

**Daisy.**   Why are you here?

**Hoke.**   I bring you to de Temple like you tell me. *(He is helping her into the car.)*

**Daisy.**   I can get myself in. Just go. *(She makes a tight little social smile and a wave out the window.)* Hurry up out of here! (**Hoke** starts up the car.)

**Hoke.**   Yassum.

**Daisy.**   I didn't say speed. I said get me away from here.

**Hoke.**   Somethin' wrong back yonder?

**Daisy.**   No.

**Hoke.**   Somethin' I done?

**Daisy.**   No. *(a beat)* Yes.

**Hoke.**   I ain' done nothin'!

**Daisy.**   You had the car right in front of the front door of the Temple! Like I was Queen of Romania! Everybody saw you! Didn't I tell you to wait for me in the back?

**Hoke.**   I jes tryin' to be nice. They two other chauffeurs right behind me.

**Daisy.**   You made me look like a fool. A g.d. fool!

**Hoke.**   Lawd knows you ain' no fool, Miz Daisy.

**Daisy.**   Slow down. Miriam and Beulah and them, I could see what they were thinking when we came out of services.

**Hoke.**   What that?

**Daisy.**   That I'm trying to pretend I'm rich.

**Hoke.**   You is rich, Miz Daisy!

**Daisy.**   No I'm not! And nobody can ever say I put on airs. On Forsyth Street we only had meat once a week. We made a meal off of grits and gravy. I taught the fifth grade at the Crew Street School! I did without plenty of times, I can tell you.

**Hoke.**   And now you doin' with. What so terrible in that?

**Daisy.**   You! Why do I talk to you? You don't understand me.

**Hoke.**   Nome, I don't. I truly don't. Cause if I ever was to get ahold of what you got I be shakin' it around for everybody in the world to see.

**Daisy.**   That's vulgar.[3] Don't talk to me! (**Hoke** *mutters something under his breath.*) What? What did you say? I heard that!

**Hoke.**   Miz Daisy, you needs a chauffeur and Lawd know, I needs a job. Let's jes leave it at dat. (*Light out on them and up on* **Boolie**, *in his shirtsleeves. He has a phone to his ear.* )

**Boolie.**   Good morning, Mama. What's the matter? (*pause*) What? Mama, you're talking so fast I . . . What? All right. All right. I'll come by on my way to work. I'll be there as soon as I can. (*Light out on him and up on* **Daisy**, *pacing around her house in a winter bathrobe.* **Boolie** *enters in a topcoat and scarf.*) I didn't expect to find you in one piece.

**Daisy.**   I wanted you to be here when he comes. I wanted you to hear it for yourself.

**Boolie.**   Hear what? What is going on?

**Daisy.**   He's stealing from me!

---

[3]crude or coarse

**Boolie.** Hoke? Are you sure?

**Daisy.** I don't make empty accusations. I have proof!

**Boolie.** What proof?

**Daisy.** This! (*She triumphantly pulls an empty can of salmon out of her robe pocket.*) I caught him red handed! I found this hidden in the garbage pail under some coffee grounds.

**Boolie.** You mean he stole a can of salmon?

**Daisy.** Here it is! Oh I knew. I knew something was funny. They all take things, you know. So I counted.

**Boolie.** You counted?

**Daisy.** The silverware first and the linen dinner napkins and then I went into the pantry. I turned on the light and the first thing that caught my eye was a hole behind the corned beef. And I knew right away. There were only eight cans of salmon. I had nine. Three for a dollar on sale.

**Boolie.** Very clever, Mama. You made me miss my breakfast and be late for a meeting at the bank for a thirty-three cent can of salmon. (*He jams his hand in his pocket and pulls out some bills.*) Here! You want thirty-three cents? Here's a dollar! Here's ten dollars! Buy a pantry full of salmon!

**Daisy.** Why, Boolie! The idea! Waving money at me like I don't know what! I don't want the money. I want my things!

**Boolie.** One can of salmon?

**Daisy.** It was mine. I bought it and I put it there and he went into my pantry and took it and he never said a word. I leave him plenty of food every day and I always tell him exactly what it is. They are like having little children in the house. They want something so they just take it. Not a smidgin of manners. No conscience. He'll never admit this. "Nome," he'll say. "I doan know nothin' bout that." And I don't like it! I don't like living this way! I have no privacy.

**Boolie.** Mama!

**Daisy.** Go ahead. Defend him. You always do.

**Boolie.** All right. I give up. You want to drive yourself again, you just go ahead and arrange it with the insurance company. Take your blessed trolley. Buy yourself a taxicab. Anything you want. Just leave me out of it.

**Daisy.** Boolie . . . (**Hoke** *enters in an overcoat.*)

**Hoke.** Mornin, Miz Daisy. I b'leve it fixin' to clear up. S'cuse me, I didn't know you was here Mist' Werthan.

**Boolie.** Hoke, I think we have to have a talk.

**Hoke.** Jes' a minute. Lemme put my coat away. I be right back. (*He pulls a brown paper bag out of his overcoat.*) Oh, Miz Daisy. Yestiddy when you out with yo' sister I ate a can o' your salmon. I know you say eat the leff over pork chops, but they stiff. Here, I done buy you another can. You want me to put it in the pantry fo you?

**Daisy.** Yes. Thank you, Hoke.

**Hoke.** I'll be right wit you Mist' Werthan. (**Hoke** *exits.* **Daisy** *looks at the empty can in her hand.*)

**Daisy.** (*trying for dignity*) I've got to get dressed now. Goodbye, son. (*She pecks his cheek and exits. Lights out on him. We hear sounds of birds twittering. Lights come up brightly—hot sun.* **Daisy,** *in light dress, is kneeling, a trowel in her hand, working by a gravestone.* **Hoke,** *jacket in hand, sleeves rolled up, stands nearby.*)

**Hoke.** I jess thinkin', Miz Daisy. We bin out heah to the cemetery three times dis mont already and ain' even the twentieth yet.

**Daisy.** It's good to come in nice weather.

**Hoke.** Yassum. Mist' Sig's grave mighty well tended. I b'leve you the best widow in the state of Georgia.

**Daisy.** Boolie's always pestering me to let the staff out here tend to this plot. Perpetual care they call it.

**Hoke.** Doan' you do it. It right to have somebody from the family lookin' after you.

**Daisy.** I'll certainly never have that. Boolie will have me in perpetual care before I'm cold.

**Hoke.**    Come on now, Miz Daisy.

**Daisy.**    Hoke, run back to the car and get that pot of azaleas for me and set it on Leo Bauer's grave.

**Hoke.**    Miz Rose Bauer's husband?

**Daisy.**    That's right. She asked me to bring it out here for her. She's not very good about coming. And I believe today would've been Leo's birthday.

**Hoke.**    Yassum. Where the grave at?

**Daisy.**    I'm not exactly sure. But I know it's over that way on the other side of the weeping cherry. You'll see the head-stone. Bauer.

**Hoke.**    Yassum.

**Daisy.**    What's the matter?

**Hoke.**    Nothin' the matter. (*He exits. She works with her trowel. In a moment* **Hoke** *returns with flowers.*) Miz Daisy . . .

**Daisy.**    I told you it's over on the other side of the weeping cherry. It says Bauer on the headstone.

**Hoke.**    How'd that look?

**Daisy.**    What are you talking about?

**Hoke.**    (*deeply embarrassed*) I'm talkin' bout I cain' read.

**Daisy.**    What?

**Hoke.**    I cain' read.

**Daisy.**    That's ridiculous. Anybody can read.

**Hoke.**    Nome. Not me.

**Daisy.**    Then how come I see you looking at the paper all the time?

**Hoke.**    That's it. Jes' lookin'. I dope out what's happening from the pictures.

**Daisy.**    You know your letters, don't you?

**Hoke.**    My ABC's? Yassum, pretty good. I jes' cain' read.

**Daisy.**    Stop saying that. It's making me mad. If you know your letters then you can read. You just don't know you can read. I taught some of the stupidest children God ever put on the face of this earth and all of them could read enough to find a name on a tombstone. The name is Bauer. Buh buh buh buh Bauer. What does that buh letter sound like?

**Hoke.**  Sound like a B.

**Daisy.**  Of course. Buh Bauer. Er er er er er. BauER. That's the last part. What letter sounds like er?

**Hoke.**  R?

**Daisy.**  So the first letter is a—

**Hoke.**  B.

**Daisy.**  And the last letter is an—

**Hoke.**  R.

**Daisy.**  B-R. B-R. B-R. Brr. Brr. Brr. It even sounds like Bauer, doesn't it?

**Hoke.**  Sho' do Miz Daisy. Thass it?

**Daisy.**  That's it. Now go over there like I told you in the first place and look for a headstone with a B at the beginning and an R at the end and that will be Bauer.

**Hoke.**  We ain' gon' worry 'bout what come 'n the middle?

**Daisy.**  Not right now. This will be enough for you to find it. Go on now.

**Hoke.**  Yassum.

**Daisy.**  And don't come back here telling me you can't do it. You can.

**Hoke.**  Miz Daisy . . .

**Daisy.**  What now?

**Hoke**  I 'preciate this, Miz Daisy.

**Daisy.**  Don't be ridiculous! I didn't do anything. Now would you please hurry up? I'm burning up out here.

# REVIEWING AND INTERPRETING

Record your answers to these questions in your personal
literature notebook. Follow the directions for each part.

**REVIEWING**

*Recalling Facts*

*Identifying Sequence*

*Identifying Cause
and Effect*

*Understanding
Main Ideas*

Try to complete each of these sentences without looking back
at the play.

1. At the beginning of the play, Boolie is trying to persuade his
   mother to
   a. buy a new car.
   b. come live with him and his wife.
   c. move into a retirement home.
   d. hire a chauffeur to drive her around.

2. Hoke telephones Boolie from the phone booth
   a. after he drives Daisy to the grocery store.
   b. just before he meets Daisy for the first time.
   c. after Daisy and he visit the cemetery.
   d. before Boolie interviews him for the job.

3. Because Daisy grew up in a poor neighborhood, she
   a. gives a great deal of money to charity.
   b. is especially proud of the possessions she and her
      husband bought.
   c. is embarrassed to show off the money she has now.
   d. feels that she deserves special attention and sympathy.

4. Hoke is patient with Daisy mostly because
   a. she pays him so well.
   b. he needs the job.
   c. he doesn't notice that she is being rude.
   d. he likes Jewish people.

*Recognizing the Elements of a Play (Characters)*

**5.** This excerpt of *Driving Miss Daisy* must be performed by
    a. two actors.
    b. three actors.
    c. four actors.
    d. five actors.

**INTERPRETING**

To complete these sentences, you may look back at the play if you'd like.

*Making Inferences*

**6.** The fact that Daisy notices when a can of salmon is missing from her pantry indicates that she
    a. is confined to her house and never gets out to enjoy herself.
    b. always makes sure there are a certain number of salmon cans available.
    c. checks the pantry regularly to make sure no one is stealing from her.
    d. likes salmon and eats it every day.

*Predicting Outcomes*

**7.** The fact that Hoke immediately replaces the can of salmon will probably make Daisy
    a. trust him more.
    b. continue to check for thefts in her house.
    c. install a lock on her pantry.
    d. never distrust anyone again.

*Analyzing*

**8.** Daisy and Hoke are alike in many ways, but one thing they don't have in common is their
    a. hometown.
    b. racial prejudice.
    c. concern for their families.
    d. religion.

*Making
Generalizations*

**9.** The following saying comes closest to expressing the lesson that both Daisy and Hoke learn through their relationship:
  a. Oil and water don't mix.
  b. Birds of a feather flock together.
  c. You can't judge a book by its cover.
  d. God helps those who help themselves.

*Understanding the
Elements of a Play
(Stage Directions)*

**10.** The playwright shows that time has passed by
  a. changing the scenery and props.
  b. using new background music.
  c. dimming the lights and then raising them.
  d. displaying a calendar showing a new month or year.

Now check your answers with your teacher. Study the questions you answered incorrectly. What types of questions were they? Talk with your teacher about ways to work on those skills.

# Characters

As stated previously, one of the biggest challenges for an author is creating believable characters. Some authors say that before they begin to write, they have a clear picture of each character in their mind. They know how each character looks, sounds, and acts before they write a single word. Writing about these characters, then, is simply a matter of revealing them to the audience or reader.

Other authors, however, do not have such a clear picture of their characters before they begin to write. These authors' characters almost seem to create themselves as the story progresses.

No matter how an author goes about his or her job, the outcome should be the creation of characters who feel, speak, and act the way real, living human beings do. In order to make these characters "come to life," authors use a process called *characterization*. In plays, most characterization is accomplished through dialogue and action. You learn about characters through what they say and do, since you can't read about what they are thinking, as you can in a short story or novel. Every word a character says and every move he or she makes work together to create a complete person. Slowly, as the play progresses, you begin to know each of the characters as well as the playwright knows them, and you see how they grow and change over time.

In the lessons that follow, you will look at ways in which playwright Alfred Uhry reveals the characters in *Driving Miss Daisy:*

1. He reveals the characters by describing them in stage directions.

2. He reveals the characters through their dialogue and actions.

3. He makes the characters seem real by showing how they change and grow.

# LESSON ① WHAT IS SAID ABOUT THE CHARACTERS

Suppose you want to hire someone to take care of your cat while you are on vacation. Obviously, you will choose someone who is trustworthy and who likes cats. But how do you know that the person you have chosen will do the job well?

You might try to find out about the person by checking with his or her friends. How would they describe the person? Has he or she been dependable in other situations? You also might interview the potential cat-sitter. Does this person like cats and know how to take care of them? Can he or she point to proof of responsibility and trustworthiness in other jobs? Only after you gather this information can you say that you know the person well enough to hire him or her.

When you read a story or play, you learn about the characters in much the same way. You learn about each of the characters from other characters who know them, and from the characters' own descriptions of themselves.

In a play, the first source for information about a character is the stage directions. What do you learn about Daisy from these stage directions at the beginning of the play?

> **Daisy**, age 72, is wearing a summer dress and high heeled shoes. Her hair, her clothes, her walk, everything about her suggests bristle and feist and high energy. She appears to be in excellent health. Her son, **Boolie Werthan**, 40, is a businessman, Junior Chamber of Commerce style. He has a strong, capable air. The Werthans are Jewish, but they have strong Atlanta accents.

Although she is 72 years old, you learn that Daisy is energetic and spirited. You also learn that she is Jewish, she is healthy, and she has a 40-year-old son. To learn more about Daisy, you can read descriptions of her by others who know her well. How does Daisy's son Boolie describe her in his first conversation with Hoke?

**Boolie.**  Well, it's a delicate situation.

**Hoke.**  Mmmm Hmm. She done gone 'roun' the bend a little? That'll happen when they get on.

**Boolie.**  Oh no. Nothing like that. She's all there. Too much there is the problem. . . .

**Hoke.**  I know what you mean 'bout dat. . . .

**Boolie.**  Hoke, I want you to understand, my mother is a little high-strung. . . .

The readers and the audience have not seen much of Daisy at this point in the play, but based on what they *have* seen and heard, Boolie's description rings true. Daisy is bristling with energy.

EXERCISE ①

Read the following conversation between Daisy and Hoke. Then use what you have learned in this lesson to answer the questions that follow it.

**Daisy.**  I don't need you. I don't want you. And I don't like you saying I'm rich.

**Hoke.**  I won' say it, then.

**Daisy.**  Is that what you and Idella talk about in the kitchen? Oh, I hate this! I hate being discussed behind my back in my own house! I was born on Forsyth Street and, believe you me, I knew the value of a penny. My brother Manny brought home a white cat one day and Papa said we couldn't keep it because we couldn't afford to feed it. My sisters saved up money so I could go to school and be a teacher. We didn't have anything!

**Hoke.**  Yassum, but look like you doin' all right now.

**Daisy.**  And I've ridden the trolley with groceries plenty of times!

**1.** How does Daisy describe the economic conditions in which she grew up? How do they affect her image of herself at age 72?

**2.** Tell how Daisy's upbringing helps explain her attitude toward Hoke and the idea of having a chauffeur.

Now check your answers with your teacher. Review this part of the lesson if you don't understand why an answer was incorrect.

### WRITING ON YOUR OWN ①

Earlier in this unit, you listed descriptions of several elderly family members or friends. Now you will create a web about two of them, using details that you have observed. Follow these steps:

- Choose the two people you know best from the list you made earlier.
- Take out two sheets of paper. Write one person's name in the center of one sheet of paper and another person's name in the center of the other sheet.
- Around each name, arrange the following words: *sight, sound, smell, touch, taste*. Around each of these words, jot down words or ideas related to each sense that you associate with the person. For example, a web for your grandfather might look like this:

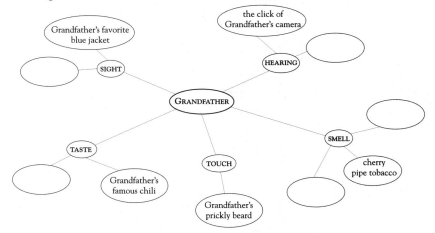

- Compare your two webs and then choose one person to write about. Write a paragraph about that person that includes most or all of the details that you listed in your web.

## LESSON ②   CHARACTERS, DIALOGUE, AND ACTION

You can only learn so much about characters through what others say about them and what they say about themselves. After all, people understand the world through their own point of view. Anything they claim to know has been filtered through their private way of thinking. Since people also can fool themselves about themselves, they are not always reliable sources either. For example, Daisy sees herself as poor, no matter how much money she has.

One of the most reliable ways to learn about people, then, is to observe what they say and do. They reveal much about their personalities, habits, and feelings through their words and actions. Read the following passage to learn more about Hoke. Daisy has just asked him to place a pot of azaleas on a friend's grave, and Hoke becomes confused and uncomfortable.

**Daisy.**   What's the matter?

**Hoke.**   Nothin' the matter. (*He exits. She works with her trowel. In a moment* **Hoke** *returns with flowers.*) Miz Daisy . . .

**Daisy.**   I told you it's over on the other side of the weeping cherry. It says Bauer on the headstone.

**Hoke.**   How'd that look?

**Daisy.**   What are you talking about?

**Hoke.**   (*deeply embarrassed*) I'm talkin' bout I cain' read.

**Daisy.**   What?

**Hoke.**   I cain' read.

**Daisy.**   That's ridiculous. Anybody can read.

**Hoke.**   Nome. Not me.

**Daisy.**    Then how come I see you looking at the paper all
the time?

**Hoke.**    That's it. Jes' lookin'. I dope out what's happening
from the pictures.

**Daisy.**    You know your letters, don't you?

**Hoke.**    My ABC's? Yassum, pretty good. I jes cain' read.

**Daisy.**    Stop saying that. It's making me mad. If you know
your letters then you can read. You just don't know you
can read. . . .

Hoke has been keeping a secret for his entire life—he
can't read. Naturally a quiet and dignified person, he has
never talked about his problem with Daisy, even though he
has known her for quite a while by this time. Hoke has been
covering up his secret for years, pretending to read the newspaper when he was only looking at the pictures. He would
have continued to keep his secret, but his desire to help Daisy
at the cemetery forces him to reveal it, no matter what the
cost is to him. Hoke's words and actions show him to be kind,
dignified, self-sufficient, and hardworking, even though he
hasn't had many advantages in life.

Daisy's reaction is typical of her approach to life. She is
positive, direct, and somewhat tactless. She has no time for
defeatist thinking. She believes that if you try hard enough,
you can do or overcome anything.

EXERCISE (2)

Read the following passage in which Daisy and Hoke discuss
Daisy's wealth. Then use what you have learned in this lesson
to answer the questions that follow the passage.

**Hoke.**    You is rich, Miz Daisy!

**Daisy.**    No I'm not! And nobody can ever say I put on
airs. On Forsyth Street we only had meat once a week.

We made a meal off of grits and gravy. I taught the fifth grade at the Crew Street School! I did without plenty of times, I can tell you.

**Hoke.** And now you doin' with. What so terrible in that?

**Daisy.** You! Why do I talk to you? You don't understand me.

**Hoke.** Nome, I don't. I truly don't. Cause if I ever was to get ahold of what you got I be shakin' it around for everybody in the world to see.

**Daisy.** That's vulgar. Don't talk to me! (**Hoke** *mutters something under his breath.*) What? What did you say? I heard that!

**Hoke.** Miz Daisy, you need a chauffeur and Lawd know, I needs a job. Let's jes leave it at dat.

1. Why is it so important to Daisy that she not be seen as "putting on airs"? Why does she think that Hoke has said something vulgar and unacceptable?

2. So far in the play, Hoke has usually given in to Daisy's fits of temper and her rudeness. How does he show that she has finally pushed him too far?

Now check your answers with your teacher. Review this part of the lesson if you don't understand why an answer was incorrect.

 WRITING ON YOUR OWN ②

You have written a paragraph recording observable details about an elderly relative or friend. Now you will write about a time when you learned about his or her inner personality. Follow these steps:

- You may have known your chosen person for a long time, or you may have come to know him or her just recently. Either way, your opinion of the person has been formed by shared experiences. Think about a time when the person's personality was revealed to you. For example, you may remember a time when your grandfather took you to the amusement park and had just as much fun as you did.
- Try to think of at least three different times when you saw a different side of your elderly friend or relative. Then choose one of those times to describe in a few paragraphs. Write from a first-person point of view, using the pronouns *I, me,* and *we.*
- Reread your description, looking for ways to improve it. Make any necessary changes.

## LESSON 3    CHARACTERS AND CHANGE

In some stories or plays, the characters stay the same from the beginning to the end. For example, if they were stingy at the beginning, they are stingy at the end no matter what happens to them in the course of the plot. Characters who don't change are called *static* characters.

In other stories or plays, the characters change in response to plot events. These characters are referred to as *dynamic* characters. Dynamic characters are quite realistic, since hardly anyone can experience life and remain unchanged.

In *Driving Miss Daisy*, Alfred Uhry has created dynamic characters. They not only grow older throughout the play, they also develop and grow in their attitudes and relationships toward each other. Compare this curt exchange between Hoke and Daisy at the beginning of the play to the one that follows it.

**Hoke.**   Mornin', Miz Daisy.
**Daisy.**   Good morning.

**Hoke.** Right cool in the night, wadn't it?

**Daisy.** I wouldn't know. I was asleep.

**Hoke.** Yassum. What yo plans today?

**Daisy.** That's my business.

Later in the play, Daisy and Hoke have this friendly conversation:

**Hoke.** I jess thinkin', Miz Daisy. We bin out heah to the cemetery three times dis mont already and ain' even the twentieth yet.

**Daisy.** It's good to come in nice weather.

**Hoke.** Yassum. Mist' Sig's grave mighty well tended. I b'leve you the best widow in the state of Georgia.

**Daisy.** Boolie's always pestering me to let the staff out here tend to this plot. Perpetual care they call it.

**Hoke.** Doan' you do it. It right to have somebody from the family lookin' after you.

**Daisy.** I'll certainly never have that. Boolie will have me in perpetual care before I'm cold.

**Hoke.** Come on now, Miz Daisy.

In the first passage, Daisy has closed herself off from Hoke. She makes it clear that he is not part of her life and that's the way she wants things to stay. She refuses even to comment on the weather and certainly does not want to share her plans for the day with this unwelcome stranger. In the second passage, however, you can see that Daisy confides her opinions and even her fears to Hoke and accepts his concern for her. In return, Hoke is now comfortable sharing his thoughts with Daisy, seemingly certain that his words will be considered and respected.

## EXERCISE ③

Read the following passage in which Daisy has called Boolie over to demand that he fire Hoke for stealing a can of salmon from her pantry. Then use what you have learned in this lesson to answer the questions that follow it.

**Daisy.**  It was mine. I bought it and I put it there and he went into my pantry and took it and he never said a word. I leave him plenty of food every day and I always tell him exactly what it is. They are like having little children in the house. They want something so they just take it. Not a smidgin of manners. No conscience. He'll never admit this. . . . (**Hoke** *enters in an overcoat.*)

**Hoke.**  Mornin, Miz Daisy. I b'leve it fixin' to clear up. S'cuse me, I didn't know you was here Mist' Werthan.

**Boolie.**  Hoke, I think we have to have a talk.

**Hoke.**  Jes' a minute. Lemme put my coat away. I be right back. (*He pulls a brown paper bag out of his overcoat.*) Oh, Miz Daisy. Yestiddy when you out with yo' sister I ate a can o' your salmon. I know you say eat the leff over pork chops, but they stiff. Here, I done buy you another can. You want me to put it in the pantry for you?

**Daisy.**  Yes. Thank you, Hoke.

**Hoke.**  I'll be right wit you Mist' Werthan. (**Hoke** *exits.* **Daisy** *looks at the empty can in her hand.*)

**Daisy.**  (*trying for dignity*) I've got to get dressed now. Goodbye, son. (*She pecks his cheek and exits.*)

1. What does Daisy say about Hoke's honesty before he enters?

2. How does her attitude change by the time Hoke exits? How does she feel about her own ability to judge others accurately now?

Now check your answers with your teacher. Review this part of the lesson if you don't understand why an answer was incorrect.

## WRITING ON YOUR OWN ③

In this exercise, you will write about how your relationship with your elderly friend or relative changed over time. Follow these steps:

- Divide a paper into two columns. At the top of the first column, write "When I was younger." At the top of the second column, write "Now."
- Think about what you thought, felt, or did with your friend or relative when you were much younger. Add these ideas in the column labeled "When I was younger." Under the column labeled "Now," record how your thoughts, ideas, and actions have changed. For example, you might write in the first column, "When I was little I cried and ran to my grandfather when I fell down." In the second column, you might write, "Now I go to my grandfather for advice when I need help."

## DISCUSSION GUIDES

1. Are Daisy and Hoke realistic characters? Use the following questions to help you decide: Have you ever known anyone like Daisy or Hoke? In what ways was this person similar to either character? Did the person have a strong personality or like to do things without help from anyone else? Did the person begin to have trouble driving, shopping, or meeting new people? Did he or she prejudge people based on their race, religion, style of dressing, or occupation? Discuss these questions with a small group of classmates and then decide if Hoke and Daisy are realistic characters.

2. When Boolie is interviewing Hoke, Hoke says, "My daughter bes' thing ever happen to me." What would you say is the best thing that ever happened to you? Write down at least three possible answers to that question. Then get together with a small group and share your answers. How many of the "best things" on your lists involve people you care about? How many of you share similar "best things"?

3. One of the most enjoyable elements in *Driving Miss Daisy* is the naturalness of the dialogue. The playwright uses familiar patterns of speech ("Anything over seven dollars is robbery. Highway robbery!") and references to real-life places (the Piggly Wiggly grocery store). Reading or hearing this dialogue makes the situation seem authentic and believable. With a partner, develop a two- or three-minute conversation that you might hear in the cafeteria or on a bus. Make the conversation seem real and believable. Then present the dialogue to the rest of the class.

# WRITE A CHARACTER SKETCH

You have seen how authors develop characters for stories and plays, and you have experimented with some of these techniques yourself. Now you will write a character sketch about an elderly person you know. Follow these steps to complete your character sketch.

If you have questions about the writing process, refer to Using the Writing Process on page 300.

- Assemble all the writing assignments you completed in this unit. You should have four pieces of writing: *1)* a list of elderly friends and relatives and short descriptions of each one, *2)* webs about two of these people and a paragraph about one of them, *3)* a description of a particular incident involving that person and you, *4)* a comparison of the relationship between that person and yourself when you were young and now. Refer to these assignments to complete this exercise.
- Using the first-person point of view, introduce your character. You may want to use details from the description you wrote earlier.
- Next, tell about your most memorable experience with your elderly friend or relative. Describe what the person said and did to reveal his or her personality.
- In the last paragraph, describe how your relationship has changed over the years. Include details about yourself, the other person, and your feelings toward him or her.
- Reread your character sketch. Does it make your character come alive? Did you include enough details about your character? Did you choose the best details to describe him or her? Make any necessary changes now.
- Proofread your character sketch for spelling, grammar, punctuation, and capitalization errors. Make a final copy and save it in your writing portfolio.

# Setting, Staging, and Dialogue

# The Devil and Daniel Webster

by Stephen Vincent Benét

## INTRODUCTION

*ABOUT THE SELECTION*

According to an old German legend, a scholar named Faust made a bargain with the devil. The devil would give Faust knowledge and magical powers that would enable him to satisfy his every desire. In return, at the end of a certain time, Faust would give the devil his soul. The legend ends disastrously for Faust when the devil calls for payment. This legend inspired many writers, composers, and artists to use the tale in creating plays, operas, paintings, and many other works of art. One of these works is the one-act play *The Devil and Daniel Webster* by Stephen Vincent Benét.

*The Devil and Daniel Webster* is an Americanized version of the German legend. The play is set in a New Hampshire town and, instead of a scholar, it is a Yankee farmer named Jabez Stone who sells his soul to the devil. Reflecting the optimism and self-confidence found in American tall tales, this play explores the possibility of outwitting the devil. It gives the soul-seller a thoroughly American champion, a character based on historical hero Daniel Webster (1782–1852). The real Webster was a New Hampshire lawyer who served in both the Senate and the House of Representatives and who also ran for President twice. He was such a persuasive speaker that many New Englanders said, "Daniel Webster could out-argue the devil himself." In this play, the fictional Webster takes on that job as he appoints himself Stone's defense lawyer and challenges Stone's agreement with the devil.

## ABOUT THE AUTHOR

Stephen Vincent Benét (1898–1943) was an American poet, short-story writer, novelist, dramatist, historian, critic, and editor. He was born in Bethlehem, Pennsylvania, into a military family. When he was young, he read extensively about American history, especially military history. He wrote a lengthy narrative poem about the Civil War, "John Brown's Body," which was awarded the Pulitzer Prize in 1929. In 1944, after his death, he was awarded the Pulitzer Prize for poetry for the epic poem "Western Star," which told of the settling of the first English colonies in America.

Benét also wrote five novels and numerous collections of short stories. "The Devil and Daniel Webster" was originally written as a short story in 1937. Benét later rewrote the story as the one-act play that you will read. The story also has been turned into an opera and a movie. All of Benét's short stories and poems display a great feeling for American folklore and legend. They celebrate America, the democratic form of government, American ideals, and most importantly, the value of the individual. *The Devil and Daniel Webster*, which is considered an American classic, conveys all of these qualities.

## ABOUT THE LESSONS

The lessons that follow *The Devil and Daniel Webster* focus on what happens on stage during a play performance. How the scenery is arranged, how it changes from scene to scene, how the stage is lit, what costumes and props are used, how the actors are positioned on stage, and how they speak their dialogue can all be grouped under the term *stagecraft*. The decisions on these issues for any one play depend on the director of that production. But the writer of the play can help the director through the stage directions and, often, the dialogue in his or her play.

Why is the playwright concerned with these details? How does lighting, for example, affect the actors' words? How does the way actors enter, exit, or move on the stage support or interfere with what they are saying? These are some of the issues that will be explored in this unit.

## WRITING: DESCRIBING A RISKY EVENT

Throughout history, there have been countless moments when people were on the verge of important discoveries and achievements. They hoped for good results from their actions but feared failure, and their moods changed back and forth between hope and fear. In this unit you will see how a playwright uses stagecraft to affect the mood of an audience. You also will use what you learn to write a short scene about a moment in history when people change moods as they struggle toward their goals. The following activities will help you begin:

- Consider advances in science and technology that required risky research. For example, new medicines had to be tested on human volunteers. Inventions such as planes and submarines had to be tested. Scientists of the Middle Ages who challenged old ideas had to hide or defend their work. Make a list of at least three areas of science or technology that interest you. Then do some reading to find out about risks that people took in these areas. Write a brief description of each risky situation.
- Consider changes in laws and governments that required risk-taking. For example, colonists in America who signed the Declaration of Independence risked being hanged as traitors.

Abolitionists were attacked for trying to change customs and laws. During World War II, civilians in countries under Nazi rule took great chances by hiding Jews. Do people who take risks on behalf of human rights interest you? Learn more about an individual or individuals who took a dangerous stand. Jot down some notes to describe the situation.

- Investigate a time in history that interests you. Choose an event that happened at least thirty years ago, anywhere on Earth, with these characteristics: *1)* its outcome was unknown to the people involved, and *2)* there was a physical, social, or financial risk. Learn about the event and the people who made it happen. Write a few sentences to describe what happened.

*AS YOU READ*

The questions below will point out some of the methods that Stephen Vincent Benét uses in *The Devil and Daniel Webster* to create specific effects on the stage. As you read the play, think about the answers to these questions:

- How do the scenery, props, and costumes set the time and place of the play? How do they help to establish a tone and mood?
- How does the author use lighting and sound effects to alter the mood?
- In what situations other than conversations do characters speak? How do these situations contribute to the plot or other elements of the play?

# The Devil and Daniel Webster

◉

by Stephen Vincent Benét

**SETTING**

*Place:* **Jabez Stone**'s *Farmhouse*
*Time: 1841*

*The scene is the main room of **Jabez Stone**'s New Hampshire farmhouse in 1841, a big, comfortable room that hasn't yet developed the stuffiness of a front parlor. A door leads to the kitchen, another door to the outside. Windows, in center, show a glimpse of summer landscape. Most of the furniture has been cleared away for a dance which follows the wedding of **Jabez** and **Mary Stone**, but there is a settle or* *bench by the fireplace, a table with some wedding presents upon it, at least three chairs by the table, and a cider barrel on which the* **Fiddler** *sits, in front of the table. Near the table there is a cupboard where there are glasses and a jug. There is a clock.*

*A country wedding has been in progress—the wedding of* **Jabez** *and* **Mary Stone**. *He is a husky young farmer, around twenty-eight or thirty. The bride is in her early twenties. He is dressed in stiff store clothes but not ridiculously—they are of good quality and he looks important. The bride is in a simple white or cream wedding dress and may carry a small, stiff bouquet of country flowers.*

*Now the wedding is over and the guests are dancing. The* **Fiddler** *is perched on the cider barrel. He plays and calls square-dance figures. The guests include the recognizable types of a small New England town—doctor, lawyer, store-keeper, old maid, schoolteacher, farmer, etc. There is an air of prosperity and hearty country mirth about the whole affair.*

*At rise,* **Jabez** *and* **Mary** *are left center, receiving the congratulations of a few last guests who talk to them and pass on to the dance. The others are dancing. There is a buzz of conversation that follows the tune of the dance music.*

---

**First Woman.**   Right nice wedding.

**First Man.**   Handsome couple.

**Second Woman.**   (*passing through crowd with dish of oyster stew*) Oysters for supper!

**Second Man.**   (*passing cake*) And layer cake—layer cake—

**An Old Man.**   (*hobbling toward cider barrel*) Makes me feel young again! Oh, by jingo!

**An Old Woman.** *(pursuing him)* Henry, Henry, you've been drinking cider!

**Fiddler.** Set to your partners! Dosy-do!

**Women.** Mary and Jabez

**Men.** Jabez and Mary.

**A Woman.** Where's the State Senator?

**A Man.** Where's the lucky bride?

*(With cries of "Mary—Jabez—strike it up, fiddler—make room for the bride and groom," the* **Crowd** *drags* **Mary** *and* **Jabez**, *pleased but embarrassed, into the center of the room, and* **Mary** *and* **Jabez** *do a little solo dance, while the* **Crowd** *claps, applauds, and makes various remarks.)*

**A Man.** Handsome steppers!

**A Woman.** She's pretty as a picture.

**A Second Man.** Cut your pigeon wing, Jabez!

**The Old Man.** Young again, young again, that's the way I feel! *(He tries to cut a pigeon wing himself.)*

**The Old Woman.** Henry, Henry, careful of your rheumatiz!

**A Third Woman.** Makes me feel all teary, seeing them so happy.

*(The solo dance ends, the music stops for a moment.)*

**The Old Man.** *(gossiping to a neighbor)* Wonder where he got it all. Stones was always poor.

**His Neighbor.** Ain't poor now. Makes you wonder just a mite.

**A Third Man.** Don't begrudge it to him—but I wonder where he got it.

**The Old Man.** *(starting to whisper)* Let me tell you something—

**The Old Woman.** *(quickly)* Henry, Henry, don't you start to gossip. *(She drags him away.)*

**Fiddler.**   *(cutting in)* Set to your partners! Scratch for corn!

*(The dance resumes, but as it does so, the* **Crowd** *chants back and forth.)*

**Women.**   Gossip's got a sharp tooth.

**Men.**   Gossip's got a mean tooth.

**Women.**   She's a lucky woman. They're a lucky pair.

**Men.**   That's true as gospel. But I wonder where he got it.

**Women.**   Money, land, and riches.

**Men.**   Just came out of nowhere.

**Women and Men.**   *(together)* Wonder where he got it all. But that's his business.

**Fiddler.**   Left and right—grand chain!

*(The dance rises to a pitch of ecstasy with the final figure. The fiddle squeaks and stops. The dancers mop their brows.)*

**First Man.**   Whew! Ain't danced like that since I was knee-high to a grasshopper!

**Second Man.**   Play us "The Portland Fancy," fiddler!

**Third Man.**   No, wait a minute, neighbor. Let's hear from the happy pair! Hey, Jabez!

**Fourth Man.**   Let's hear from the State Senator!

*(They crowd around* **Jabez** *and push him up on the settle.)*

**Old Man.**   Might as well. It's the last time he'll have the last word!

**Old Woman.**   Now, Henry Banks, you ought to be ashamed of yourself!

**Old Man.**   Told you so, Jabez!

**The Crowd.**   Speech!

**Jabez.**   *(embarrassed)* Neighbors, friends—I'm not much of a speaker, spite of your 'lecting me to State Senate—

**The Crowd.**   That's the ticket, Jabez. Smart man, Jabez. I voted for ye. Go ahead, Senator, you're doing fine.

**Jabez.**   But we're certainly glad to have you here—me and Mary. And we want to thank you for coming and—

**A Voice.**   Vote the Whig ticket!

**Another Voice.**   Hurray for Daniel Webster!

**Jabez.**   And I'm glad Hi Foster said that, for those are my sentiments, too. Mr. Webster has promised to honor us with his presence here tonight.

**The Crowd.**   Hurray for Dan'l! Hurray for the greatest man in the U.S.!

**Jabez.**   And when he comes, I know we'll give him a real New Hampshire welcome.

**The Crowd.**   Sure we will—Webster forever—and to hell with Henry Clay!

**Jabez.**   And meanwhile—well, there's Mary and me (*takes her hand*) and, if you folks don't have a good time, well, we won't feel right about getting married at all. Because I know I've been lucky—and I hope she feels that way, too. And, well, we're going to be happy or bust a trace! (*He wipes his brow to terrific applause. He and **Mary** look at each other.*)

**A Woman.**   (*in kitchen doorway*) Come and get the cider, folks!

(*The **Crowd** begins to drift away—a few to the kitchen, a few toward the door that leads to the outside. They furnish a shifting background to the next little scene, where **Mary** and **Jabez** are left alone by the fireplace.*)

**Jabez.**   Mary.

**Mary.**   Mr. Stone.

**Jabez.**   Mary.

**Mary.**   My husband.

**Jabez.**   That's a big word, husband.

**Mary.**   It's a good word.

**Jabez.**   Are you happy, Mary?

**Mary.**   Yes. So happy I'm afraid.

**Jabez.**   Afraid?

**Mary.**   I suppose it happens to every girl—just for a minute. It's like spring turning into summer. You want it to be summer. But the spring was sweet. (*dismissing the mood*) I'm sorry. Forgive me. It just came and went, like something cold. As if we'd been too lucky.

**Jabez.**   We can't be too lucky, Mary. Not you and me.

**Mary.**   (*rather mischievously*) If you say so, Mr. Stone. But you don't even know what sort of housekeeper I am. And Aunt Hepsy says—

**Jabez.**   Bother your Aunt Hepsy! There's just you and me and that's all that matters in the world.

**Mary.**   And you don't know something else—

**Jabez.**   What's that?

**Mary.**   How proud I am of you. Ever since I was a little girl. Ever since you carried my books. Oh, I'm sorry for women who can't be proud of their men. It must be a lonely feeling.

**Jabez.**   (*uncomfortably*) A man can't always be proud of everything, Mary. There's some things a man does, or might do, when he has to make his way.

**Mary.**   (*laughing*) I know—terrible things—like being the best farmer in the county and the best State Senator—

**Jabez.**   (*quietly*) And a few things besides. But you remember one thing, Mary, whatever happens. It was all for you. And nothing's going to happen. Because he hasn't come yet—and he would have come if it was wrong.

**Mary.**   But it's wonderful to have Mr. Webster come to us.

**Jabez.**   I wasn't thinking about Mr. Webster. (*He takes both her hands.*) Mary, I've got something to tell you. I should have told you before, but I couldn't seem to bear it. Only, now that it's all right, I can. Ten years ago—

**A Voice.**   (*from off stage*) Dan'l! Dan Webster!

(**Jabez** *drops* **Mary**'s *hands and looks around. The* **Crowd** *begins to mill and gather toward the door. Others rush in from the kitchen.*)

**Another Voice.**   Black Dan'l! He's come!

**Another Voice.**   Three cheers for the greatest man in the U.S.!

**Another Voice.**   Three cheers for Daniel Webster!

(*And, to the cheering and applause of the* **Crowd**, **Daniel Webster** *enters and stands for a moment upstage, in the familiar pose, his head thrown back, his attitude leonine.*[1] *He stops the cheering of the* **Crowd** *with a gesture.*)

**Webster.**   Neighbors, old friends—it does me good to hear you. But don't cheer me—I'm not running for President this summer. (*a laugh from the* **Crowd**) I'm here on a better errand—to pay my humble respects to a most charming lady and her very fortunate spouse.

(*There is a twang of a fiddle string breaking.*)

**Fiddler.**   'Tarnation! Busted a string!

**A Voice.**   He's always bustin' strings.

(**Webster** *blinks at the interruption but goes on.*)

**Webster.**   We're proud of State Senator Stone in these parts— we know what he's done. Ten years ago he started out with a patch of land that was mostly rocks and mortgages and now—well, you've only to look around you. I don't know that I've ever seen a likelier farm, not even at Marshfield,

---

[1]like a lion

and I hope, before I die, I'll have the privilege of shaking his hand as Governor of this state. I don't know how he's done it—I couldn't have done it myself. But I know this—Jabez Stone wears no man's collar. (*At this statement there is a discordant squeak from the fiddle and* **Jabez** *looks embarrassed.* **Webster** *knits his brows.*) And what's more, if I know Jabez, he never will. But I didn't come here to talk politics—I came to kiss the bride. (*He does so amid great applause. He shakes hands with* **Jabez**.) Congratulations, Stone—you're a lucky man. And now, if our friend in the corner will give us a tune on his fiddle—

(*The* **Crowd** *presses forward to meet the great man. He shakes hands with several.*)

**A Man.**　Remember me, Mr. Webster? Saw ye up at the State House at Concord.

**Another Man.**　Glad to see ye, Mr. Webster. I voted for ye ten times.

(**Webster** *receives their homage politely, but his mind is still on music.*)

**Webster.**　(*a trifle irritated*) I said, if our friend in the corner would give us a tune on his fiddle—

**Fiddler.**　(*passionately, flinging the fiddle down*) Hell's delight—excuse me, Mr. Webster. But the very devil's got into that fiddle of mine. She was doing all right up to just a minute ago. But now I've tuned her and tuned her and she won't play a note I want.

(*And, at this point,* **Mr. Scratch** *makes his appearance. He has entered, unobserved, and mixed with the* **Crowd** *while all eyes were upon* **Daniel Webster**. *He is, of course, the devil—a New England devil, dressed like a rather shabby attorney but with something just a little wrong in clothes and appearance. For one thing, he wears black gloves on his hands. He carries a large* *black tin box, like a botanist's collecting box, under one arm. Now he slips through the* **Crowd** *and taps the* **Fiddler** *on the shoulder.)*

**Scratch.** *(insinuatingly[2])* Maybe you need some rosin[3] on your bow, fiddler?

**Fiddler.** Maybe I do and maybe I don't. *(turns and confronts the stranger)* But who are you? I don't remember seeing you before.

**Scratch.** Oh, I'm just a friend—a humble friend of the bridegroom's. *(He walks toward* **Jabez.** *Apologetically.)* I'm afraid I came in the wrong way, Mr. Stone. You've improved the place so much since I last saw it that I hardly knew the front door. But, I assure you, I came as fast as I could.

**Jabez.** *(obviously shocked)* It—it doesn't matter. *(with a great effort)* Mary—Mr. Webster—this is a—a friend of mine from Boston—a legal friend. I didn't expect him today but—

**Scratch.** Oh, my dear Mr. Stone—an occasion like this—I wouldn't miss it for the world. *(He bows.)* Charmed, Mrs. Stone. Delighted, Mr. Webster. But—don't let me break up the merriment of the meeting. *(He turns back toward the table and the* **Fiddler.***)*

**Fiddler.** *(with a grudge, to* **Scratch***)* Boston lawyer, eh?

**Scratch.** You might call me that.

**Fiddler.** *(tapping the tin box with his bow)* And what have you got in that big box of yours? Law papers?

**Scratch.** Oh, curiosities for the most part. I'm a collector, too.

**Fiddler.** Don't hold much with Boston curiosities, myself.

---

[2]in such a way as to gain another's favor

[3]hard, yellowish substance used on violin bows to keep them from slipping

And you know about fiddling, too, do you? Know all about it?

**Scratch.**  Oh— (*a deprecatory[4] shrug*)

**Fiddler.**  Don't shrug your shoulders at me—I ain't no Frenchman. Telling me I needed more rosin!

**Mary.**  (*trying to stop the quarrel*) Isaac, please—

**Fiddler.**  Sorry, Mary—Mrs. Stone. But I been playing the fiddle at Cross Corners weddings for twenty-five years. And now here comes a stranger from Boston and tells me I need more rosin!

**Scratch.**  But, my good friend—

**Fiddler.**  Rosin, indeed! Here—play it yourself then and see what you can make of it! (*He thrusts the fiddle at* **Scratch.** *The latter stiffens, slowly lays his black collecting box on the table, and takes the fiddle.*)

**Scratch.**  (*with feigned[5] embarrassment*) But really, I— (*He bows toward* **Jabez.***) Shall I, Mr. Senator?

(**Jabez** *makes a helpless gesture of assent.[6]*)

**Mary.**  (*to* **Jabez**) Mr. Stone, Mr. Stone—are you ill?

**Jabez.**  No—no—but I feel—it's hot—

**Webster.**  (*chuckling*) Don't you fret, Mrs. Stone. I've got the right medicine for him. (*He pulls a flask from his pocket.*) Ten-year-old Medford, Stone. I buy it by the keg down at Marshfield. Here— (*He tries to give some of the rum to* **Jabez.***)

**Jabez.**  No— (*He turns.*) Mary—Mr. Webster— (*But he can-

---

[4] apologetic or belittling

[5] false; pretended

[6] agreement

*not explain. With a burst.)* Oh, let him play—let him play! Don't you see he's bound to? Don't you see there's nothing we can do?

*(A rustle of discomfort among the guests.* **Scratch** *draws the bow across the fiddle in a horrible discord.)*

**Fiddler.** *(triumphantly)* I told you so, stranger. The devil's in that fiddle!

**Scratch.** I'm afraid it needs special tuning. *(draws the bow in a second discord)* There, that's better. *(grinning)* And now for this happy—this very happy occasion—in tribute to the bride and groom—I'll play something appropriate—a song of young love—

**Mary.** Oh, Jabez, Mr. Webster—stop him! Do you see his hands? He's playing with gloves on his hands.

*(***Webster*** *starts forward, but, even as he does so,* **Scratch** *begins to play and all freeze as* **Scratch** *goes on with the extremely inappropriate song that follows. At first his manner is oily and mocking. It is not till he reaches the line "The devil took the words away" that he really becomes terrifying and the* **Crowd** *starts to be afraid.)*

**Scratch.** *(accompanying himself fantastically)*

Young William was a thriving boy.
(Listen to my doleful tale.)
Young Mary Clark was all his joy.
(Listen to my doleful tale.)

He swore he'd love her all his life.
She swore she'd be his loving wife.

But William found a gambler's den
And drank with livery-stable men.
He played the cards, he played the dice.
He would not listen to advice.

And when in church he tried to pray,
The devil took the words away.

(**Scratch**, *still playing, starts to march across the stage.*)

The devil got him by the toe,
And so, alas, he had to go.


"Young Mary Clark, young Mary Clark,
I now must go into the dark."

(*These last two verses have been directed at* **Jabez. Scratch**
*continues, now turning to* **Mary.**)

Young Mary lay upon her bed.
"Alas, my Will-i-am is dead."

He came to her a bleeding ghost—

(*He rushes at* **Mary** *but* **Webster** *stands between them.*)

**Webster.**   Stop! Stop! You miserable wretch, can't you see that
you're frightening Mrs. Stone? (*He wrenches the fiddle out of*
**Scratch**'s *hands and tosses it aside.*) And now, sir—out of this
house!

**Scratch.**   (*facing him*) You're a bold man, Mr. Webster.
Too bold for your own good, perhaps. And anyhow,
it wasn't my fiddle. It belonged to— (*He wheels and sees the*
**Fiddler** *tampering with the collecting box that has been left on
the table.*) Idiot! What are you doing with my collecting
box? (*He rushes for the* **Fiddler** *and chases him around the
table, but the* **Fiddler** *is just one jump ahead.*)

**Fiddler.**   Boston lawyer, eh? Well, I don't think so. I think
you've got something in that box of yours you're afraid to
show. And, by jingo— (*He throws open the lid of the box.*

*The lights wink and there is a clap of thunder. All eyes stare upward. Something has flown out of the box. But what?* **Fiddler**, *with relief.*) Why, 'tain't nothing but a moth.

**Mary.**   A white moth—a flying thing.

**Webster.**   A common moth—*Telea polyphemus*—

**The Crowd.**   A moth—just a moth—a moth—

**Fiddler.**   *(terrified)* But it ain't. It ain't no common moth! I seen it! And it's got a death's head on it! (*He strikes at the invisible object with his bow to drive it away.*)

**Voice of the Moth.**   Help me, neighbors! Help me!

**Webster.**   What's that? It wails like a lost soul.

**Mary.**   A lost soul.

**The Crowd.**   A lost soul—lost—in darkness—in the darkness.

**Voice of the Moth.**   Help me, neighbors!

**Fiddler.**   It sounds like Miser Stevens.

**Jabez.**   Miser Stevens!

**The Crowd.**   The miser—Miser Stevens—a lost soul—lost.

**Fiddler.**   *(frantically)* It sounds like Miser Stevens—and you had him in your box. But it can't be. He ain't dead.

**Jabez.**   He ain't dead—I tell you he ain't dead! He was just as spry and mean as a woodchuck Tuesday.

**The Crowd.**   Miser Stevens—soul of Miser Stevens—but he ain't dead.

**Scratch.**   *(dominating them)* Listen!

(*A bell off stage begins to toll a knell, slowly, solemnly.*)

**Mary.**   The bell—the church bell—the bell that rang at my wedding.

**Webster.**   The church bell—the passing bell.

**Jabez.**   The funeral bell.

**The Crowd.**    The bell—the passing bell—Miser Stevens—dead.

**Voice of the Moth.**    Help me, neighbors, help me! I sold my soul to the devil. But I'm not the first or the last. Help me. Help Jabez Stone!

**Scratch.**    Ah, would you! (*He catches the moth in his red bandanna, stuffs it back into his collecting box, and shuts the lid with a snap.*)

**Voice of the Moth.**    (*fading*) Lost—lost forever, forever. Lost, like Jabez Stone.

(*The* **Crowd** *turns on* **Jabez**. *They read his secret in his face.*)

**The Crowd.**    Jabez Stone—Jabez Stone—answer us—answer us.

**Mary.**    Tell them, dear—answer them—you are good—you are brave—you are innocent.

(*But the* **Crowd** *is all pointing hands and horrified eyes.*)

**The Crowd.**    Jabez Stone—Jabez Stone. Who's your friend in black, Jabez Stone? (*They point to* **Scratch**.)

**Webster.**    Answer them, Mr. State Senator.

**The Crowd.**    Jabez Stone—Jabez Stone. Where did you get your money, Jabez Stone?

(**Scratch** *grins and taps his collecting box.* **Jabez** *cannot speak.*)

**Jabez.**    I—I— (*He stops.*)

**The Crowd.**    Jabez Stone—Jabez Stone. What was the price you paid for it, Jabez Stone?

**Jabez.**    (*looking around wildly*) Help me, neighbors! Help me!

(*This cracks the built-up tension and sends the* **Crowd** *over the edge into fanaticism.*)

**A Woman's Voice.**    (*high and hysterical*) He's sold his soul to the devil! (*She points to* **Jabez.**)

**Other Voices.**  To the devil!

**The Crowd.**  He's sold his soul to the devil! The devil himself! The devil's playing the fiddle! The devil's come for his own!

**Jabez.**  *(appealing)* But, neighbors—I didn't know—I didn't mean—oh, help me!

**The Crowd.**  *(inexorably[7])* He's sold his soul to the devil!

**Scratch.**  *(grinning)* To the devil!

**The Crowd.**  He's sold his soul to the devil! There's no help left for him, neighbors! Run, hide, hurry, before we're caught! He's a lost soul—Jabez Stone—he's the devil's own! Run, hide, hasten! *(They stream across the stage like a flurry of bats, the cannier[8] picking up the wedding presents they have given to take along with them.)*

*(**Mr. Scratch** drives them out into the night, fiddle in hand, and follows them. **Jabez** and **Mary** are left with **Webster**. **Jabez** has sunk into a chair, beaten, with his head in his hands. **Mary** is trying to comfort him. **Webster** looks at them for a moment and shakes his head sadly. As he crosses to exit to the porch, his hand drops for a moment on **Jabez**'s shoulder, but **Jabez** makes no sign. **Webster** exits. **Jabez** lifts his head.)*

**Mary.**  *(comforting him)* My dear—my dear—

**Jabez.**  I—it's all true, Mary. All true. You must hurry.

**Mary.**  Hurry?

**Jabez.**  Hurry after them—back to the village—back to your folks. Mr. Webster will take you—you'll be safe with Mr. Webster. You see, it's all true and he'll be back in a minute. *(with a shudder)* The other one. *(He groans.)* I've got until twelve o'clock. That's the contract. But there isn't much time.

---

[7] in a way that cannot be changed
[8] more clever

**Mary.**   Are you telling me to run away from you, Mr. Stone?

**Jabez.**   You don't understand, Mary. It's true.

**Mary.**   We made some promises to each other. Maybe you've forgotten them. But I haven't. I said, it's for better or worse. It's for beter or worse. I said, in sickness or in health. Well, that covers the ground, Mr. Stone.

**Jabez.**   But, Mary, you must. I command you.

**Mary.**   "For thy people shall be my people and thy God my God." (*quietly*) That was Ruth, in the Book. I always liked the name of Ruth—always liked the thought of her. I always thought—I'll call a child Ruth, sometime. I guess that was just a girl's notion. (*She breaks.*) But, oh, Jabez—why?

**Jabez.**   It started years ago, Mary. I guess I was a youngster then—guess I must have been. A youngster with a lot of ambitions and no way in the world to get there. I wanted city clothes and a big white house. I wanted to be State Senator and have people look up to me. But all I got on the farm was a crop of stones. You could work all day and all night but that was all you got.

**Mary.**   (*softly*) It was pretty, that hill farm, Jabez. You could look all the way across the valley.

**Jabez.**   Pretty? It was fever and ague—it was stones and blight. If I had a horse, he got colic. If I planted garden truck, the woodchucks ate it. I'd lie awake nights and try to figure out a way to get somewhere—but there wasn't any way. And all the time you were growing up, in the town. I couldn't ask you to marry me and take you to a place like that.

**Mary.**   Do you think it's the place makes the difference to a woman? I'd—I'd have kept your house. I'd have stroked the cat and fed the chickens and seen you wiped your shoes on the mat. I wouldn't have asked for more. Oh, Jabez—why didn't you tell me?

**Jabez.**   It happened before I could. Just an average day—you know—just an average day. But there was a mean east wind and a mean small rain. Well, I was plowing, and the share broke clean off on a rock where there hadn't been any rock the day before. I didn't have money for a new one—I didn't have money to get it mended. So I said it and I said loud, "I'll sell my soul for about two cents," I said. *(He stops,* **Mary** *stares at him.)* Well, that's all there is to it, I guess. He came along that afternoon—that fellow from Boston—and the dog looked at him and ran away. Well, I had to make it more than two cents, but he was agreeable to that. So I pricked my thumb with a pin and signed the paper. It felt hot when you touched it, that paper. I keep remembering that. *(He pauses.)* And it's all come true and he's kept his part of the bargain. I got the riches and I've married you. And, oh, God almighty, what shall I do?

**Mary.**   Let us run away! Let us creep and hide!

**Jabez.**   You can't run away from the devil—I've seen his horses. Miser Stevens tried to run away.

**Mary.**   Lest us pray—let us pray to the God of Mercy that He redeem us.

**Jabez.**   I can't pray, Mary. The words just burn in my heart.

**Mary.**   I won't let you go! I won't! There must be someone who could help us. I'll get the judge and the squire—

**Jabez.**   Who'll take a case against old Scratch? Who'll face the devil himself and do him brown? There isn't a lawyer in the world who'd dare do that.

*(***Webster*** appears in the doorway.)*

**Webster.**   Good evening, neighbors. Did you say something about lawyers—

**Mary.**   Mr. Webster!

**Jabez.**   Dan'l Webster! But I thought—

**Webster.**   You'll excuse me for leaving for a moment. I was just taking a stroll on the porch, in the cool of the evening. Fine summer evening, too.

**Jabez.**   Well, it might be, I guess, but that kind of depends on the circumstances.

**Webster.**   Hm. Yes. I happened to overhear a little of your conversation. I gather you're in trouble, neighbor Stone.

**Jabez.**   Sore trouble.

**Webster.**   *(delicately)* Sort of a law case, I understand.

**Jabez.**   You might call it that, Mr. Webster. Kind of a mortgage case, in a way.

**Mary.**   Oh, Jabez!

**Webster.**   Mortgage case. Well, I don't generally plead now, except before the Supreme Court, but this case of yours presents some very unusual features and I never deserted a neighbor in trouble yet. So, if I can be of any assistance—

**Mary.**   Oh, Mr. Webster, will you help him?

**Jabez.**   It's a terrible lot to ask you. But—well, you see, there's Mary. And, if you could see your way to it—

**Webster.**   I will.

**Mary.**   *(weeping with relief)* Oh, Mr. Webster!

**Webster.**   There, there, Mrs. Stone. After all, if two New Hampshire men aren't a match for the devil, we might as well give the country back to the Indians. When is he coming, Jabez?

**Jabez.**   Twelve o'clock. The time's getting late.

**Webster.**   Then I'd better refresh my memory. The—er—mortgage was for a definite term of years?

**Jabez.**   Ten years.

**Webster.**   And it falls due—?

**Jabez.**   Tonight. Oh, I can't see how I came to be such a fool!

**Webster.**   No use crying over spilt milk, Stone. We've got to get you out of it now. But tell me one thing. Did you sign this precious document of your own free will?

**Jabez.**   Yes, it was my own free will. I can't deny that.

**Webster.**   Hm, that's a trifle unfortunate. But we'll see.

**Mary.**   Oh, Mr. Webster, can you save him? Can you?

**Webster.**   I shall do my best, madam. That's all you can ever say till you see what the jury looks like.

**Mary.**   But even you, Mr. Webster— Oh, I know you're Secretary of State. I know you're a great man. I know you've done wonderful things. But it's different—fighting the devil!

**Webster.**   (*towering*) I've fought John C. Calhoun, madam. And I've fought Henry Clay. And, by the great shade of Andrew Jackson, I'd fight ten thousand devils to save a New Hampshire man!

**Jabez.**   You hear, Mary?

**Mary.**   Yes. And I trust Mr. Webster. But—oh, there must be some way that I can help!

**Webster.**   There is one, madam, and a hard one. As Mr. Stone's counsel, I must formally request your withdrawal.

**Mary.**   No.

**Webster.**   Madam, think for a moment. You cannot help Mr. Stone. Since you are his wife, your testimony would be prejudiced. And frankly, madam, in a very few moments this is going to be no place for a lady.

**Mary.**   But I can't—I can't leave him. I can't bear it!

**Jabez.**   You must go, Mary. You must.

**Webster.**   Pray, madam—you can help us with your prayers. Are the prayers of the innocent unavailing?[9]

---

[9]without effect

**Mary.**    Oh, I'll pray—I'll pray. But a woman's more than a praying machine, whatever men think. And how do I know?

**Webster.**    Trust me, Mrs. Stone.

**Mary.**    (*turns to go, and with one hand on* **Jabez**'s *shoulder, as she moves to the door, says the following prayer*)

Now may there be a blessing and a light betwixt thee and
  me forever.
For, as Ruth unto Naomi, so do I cleave unto thee.
Set me as a seal upon thy heart, as a seal upon thine arm,
  for love is strong as death.
Many waters cannot quench love, neither can the floods
  drown it.
As Ruth unto Naomi, so do I cleave unto thee.
The Lord watch between thee and me when we are absent,
  one from the other.
Amen. Amen. (*She goes out.*)

**Webster.**    Amen.

**Jabez.**    Thank you, Mr. Webster. She ought to go. But I couldn't have made her do it.

**Webster.**    Well, Stone, I know ladies—and I wouldn't be surprised if she's still got her ear to the keyhole. But she's best out of this night's business. How long have we got to wait?

**Jabez.**    (*beginning to be terrified again*) No long—not long.

**Webster.**    Then I'll just get out the jug, with your permission, Stone. Somehow or other, waiting's wonderfully shorter with a jug. (*He crosses to the cupboard, gets out jug and glasses, pours himself a drink.*) Ten-year-old Medford. There's nothing like it. I saw an inchworm take a drop of it once, and he stood right up on his hind legs and bit a bee. Come, try a nip.

**Jabez.**    There's no joy in it for me.

**Webster.**    Oh, come, man, come! Just because you've sold your soul to the devil, that needn't make you a teetotaler. (*He laughs and passes the jug to* **Jabez**, *who tries to pour from it. But at that moment the clock whirs and begins to strike the three-quarters, and* **Jabez** *spills the liquor.*)

**Jabez.** Oh, God!

**Webster.** Never mind. It's a nervous feeling, waiting for a trial to begin. I remember my first case—

**Jabez.** 'Tain't that. (*He turns to* **Webster**.) Mr. Webster—Mr. Webster—for God's sake harness your horses and get away from this place as fast as you can!

**Webster.** (*placidly*) You've brought me a long way, neighbor, to tell me you don't like my company.

**Jabez.** I've brought you the devil's own way. I can see it all now. He's after both of us—him and his damn collecting box! Well, he can have me if he likes. I don't say I relish it, but I made the bargain. But you're the whole United States! He can't get you, Mr. Webster—he mustn't get you!

**Webster.** I'm obliged to you, neighbor Stone. It's kindly thought of. But there's a jug on the table and a case in hand. And I never left a jug or a case half finished in my life. (*There is a knock at the door.* **Jabez** *gives a cry.*) Ah, I thought your clock was a trifle slow, neighbor Stone. Come in!

(**Scratch** *enters from the night.*)

**Scratch.** Mr. Webster! This *is* a pleasure!

**Webster.** Attorney of record for Jabez Stone. Might I ask your name?

**Scratch.** I've gone by a good many. Perhaps Scratch will do for the evening. I'm often called that in these regions. May I? (*He sits at the table and pours a drink from the jug. The liquor steams as it pours into the glass while* **Jabez** *watches, ter-*

*rified.* **Scratch** *grins, toasting* **Webster** *and* **Jabez** *silently in the liquor. Then he becomes businesslike. To* **Webster.***)* And now I call upon you, as a law-abiding citizen, to assist me in taking possession of my property.

**Webster.** Not so fast, Mr. Scratch. Produce your evidence, if you have it.

**Scratch.** *(takes out a black pocketbook and examines papers)* Slattery—Stanley—Stone. *(takes out a deed)* There, Mr. Webster. All open and aboveboard and in due and legal form. Our firm has its reputation to consider—we deal only in the one way.

**Webster.** *(taking deed and looking it over)* Hm. This appears—I say it appears—to be properly drawn. But, of course, we contest the signature. *(tosses it back, contemptuously)*

**Scratch.** *(suddenly turning on* **Jabez** *and shooting a finger at him)* Is that your signature?

**Jabez.** *(wearily)* You know damn well it is.

**Webster.** *(angrily)* Keep quiet, Stone. *(to* **Scratch***)* But that is a minor matter. This precious document isn't worth the paper it's written on. The law permits no traffic in human flesh.

**Scratch.** Oh, my dear Mr. Webster! Courts in every state in the Union have held that human flesh is property and recoverable. Read your Fugitive Slave Act. Or shall I cite Brander versus McRae?

**Webster.** But, in the case of the State of Maryland versus Four Barrels of Bourbon—

**Scratch.** That was overruled, as you know, sir. North Carolina versus Jenkins and Co.

**Webster.** *(unwillingly)* You seem to have an excellent acquaintance with the law, sir.

**Scratch.**   Sir, that is no fault of mine. Where I come from we have always gotten the pick of the bar.

**Webster.**   *(changing his note, heartily)* Well, come now, sir. There's no need to make hay and oats of a trifling matter when we're both sensible men. Surely we can settle this little difficulty out of court. My client is quite prepared to offer a compromise. **(Scratch** *smiles.)* A very substantial compromise. **(Scratch** *smiles more broadly, slowly shaking his head.)* Hang it, man, we offer ten thousand dollars! **(Scratch** *signs No.)* Twenty thousand—thirty—name your figure! I'll raise it if I have to mortgage Marshfield!

**Scratch.**   Quite useless, Mr. Webster. There is only one thing I want from you—the execution of my contract.

**Webster.**   But this is absurd. Mr. Stone is now a State Senator. The property has greatly increased in value!

**Scratch.**   The principle of *caveat emptor*[10] still holds, Mr. Webster. *(He yawns and looks at the clock.)* And now, if you have no further arguments to adduce,[11] I'm rather pressed for time— *(He rises briskly as if to take* **Jabez** *into custody.)*

**Webster.**   *(thundering)* Pressed or not, you shall not have this man. Mr. Stone is an American citizen and no American citizen may be forced into the service of a foreign prince. We fought England for that, in 'twelve, and we'll fight all hell for it again!

**Scratch.**   Foreign? And who calls me a foreigner?

**Webster.**   Well, I never yet heard of the dev—of your claiming American citizenship.

---

[10]Latin phrase meaning "let the buyer beware"

[11]give as proof, a reason, or an example

**Scratch.**    And who with better right? When the first wrong
was done to the first Indian, I was there. When the first
slaver put out for the Congo, I stood on her deck. Am I
not in your books and stories and beliefs, from the first settlement on? Am I not spoken of still in every church in
New England? 'Tis true the North claims me for a
Southerner and the South for a Northerner, but I am neither. I am merely an honest American like yourself—and
of the best descent—for, to tell the truth, Mr. Webster,
though I don't like to boast of it, my name is older in the
country than yours.

**Webster.**    Aha! Then I stand on the Constitution! I demand
a trial for my client!

**Scratch.**    The case is hardly one for an ordinary jury—and
indeed, the lateness of the hour—

**Webster.**    Let it be any court you choose, so it is an American
judge and an American jury. Let it be the quick or the
dead, I'll abide the issue.

**Scratch.**    The quick or the dead! You have said it. (*He points
his finger at the place where the* **Jury** *is to appear. There is a
clap of thunder and a flash of light. The stage blacks out completely. All that can be seen is the face of* **Scratch***, lit with a
ghastly green light, as he recites the invocation that summons
the* **Jury.** *As, one by one, the important* **Jurymen** *are mentioned,
they appear.*)

I summon the jury Mr. Webster demands.
From churchyard mold and gallows grave,
Brimstone pit and burning gulf,
I summon them!
Dastard, liar, scoundrel, knave,
I summon them! Appear!
There's Simon Girty, the renegade,[12]

---

[12]one who abandons one side and goes over to the other side

The haunter of the forest glade,
Who joined with Indian and wolf
To hunt the pioneer.
The stains upon his hunting shirt
Are not the blood of the deer.
There's Walter Butler, the loyalist,
Who carried a firebrand in his fist
Of massacre and shame.
King Philip's eye is wild and bright.
They slew him in the great Swamp Fight,
But still, with terror and affright,
The land recalls his name.
Blackbeard Teach, the pirate fell,
Smeet the strangler, hot from hell,
Dale, who broke men on the wheel,
Morton, of the tarnished steel—
I summon them, I summon them
From their tormented flame!
Quick or dead, quick or dead,
Broken heart and bitter head,
True Americans, each one,
Traitor and disloyal son,
Cankered earth and twisted tree,
Outcasts of eternity,
Twelve great sinners, tried and true,
For the work they are to do!
I summon them, I summon them!
Appear, appear, appear!

(*The* **Jury** *has now taken its place in the box,* **Walter Butler** *in the place of foreman. They are eerily lit and so made up as to suggest the unearthly. They sit stiffly in their box. At first, when one moves, all move, in stylized gestures. It is not till the end of* **Webster***'s speech that they begin to show any trace of humanity. They speak rhythmically, and, at first, in low, eerie voices.*)

**Jabez.** *(seeing them, horrified)* A jury of the dead!

**Jury.** Of the dead!

**Jabez.** A jury of the damned!

**Jury.** Of the damned!

**Scratch.** Are you content with the jury, Mr. Webster?

**Webster.** Quite content. Though I miss General Arnold from the company.

**Scratch.** Benedict Arnold is engaged upon other business. Ah, you asked for a justice, I believe. *(He points his finger and* **Justice Hathorne,** *a tall, lean, terrifying Puritan, appears, followed by his* **Clerk.***)* Justice Hathorne is a jurist of experience. He presided at the Salem witch trials. There were others who repented of the business later. But not he, not he!

**Hathorne.** Repent of such notable wonders and undertakings? Nay, hang them, hang them all! *(He takes his place on the bench.)*

*(The* **Clerk,** *an ominous[13] little man with clawlike hands, takes his place. The room has now been transformed into a courtroom.)*

**Clerk.** *(in a gabble of ritual)* Oyes, oyes, oyes.[14] All ye who have business with this honorable court of special session this night, step forward!

**Hathorne.** *(with gavel)* Call the first case.

**Clerk.** The World, the Flesh, and the Devil versus Jabez Stone.

**Hathorne.** Who appears for the plaintiff?

**Scratch.** I, Your Honor.

**Hathorne.** And for the defendant?

**Webster.** I.

---

[13]threatening

[14]old English term meaning "Hear ye!" or "Attention!" (pronounced "oh-yes")

**Jury.**   The case—the case—he'll have little luck with this case.

**Hathorne.**   The case will proceed.

**Webster.**   Your Honor, I move to dismiss this case on the grounds of improper jurisdiction.

**Hathorne.**   Motion denied.

**Webster.**   On the grounds of insufficient evidence.

**Hathorne.**   Motion denied.

**Jury.**   Motion denied—denied. Motion denied.

**Webster.**   I will take an exception.

**Hathorne.**   There are no exceptions in this court.

**Jury.**   No exceptions—no exceptions in this court. It's a bad case, Daniel Webster—a losing case.

**Webster.**   Your Honor—

**Hathorne.**   The prosecution will proceed—

**Scratch.**   Your Honor—gentlemen of the jury. This is a plain, straightforward case. It need not detain us long.

**Jury.**   Detain us long—it will not detain us long.

**Scratch.**   It concerns one thing alone—the transference, barter, and sale of a certain piece of property, to wit, his soul, by Jabez Stone, farmer, of Cross Corners, New Hampshire. That transference, barter, or sale is attested[15] by a deed. I offer that deed in evidence and mark it Exhibit A.

**Webster.**   I object.

**Hathorne.**   Objection denied. Mark it Exhibit A.

(**Scratch** *hands the deed—an ominous and impressive document—to the* **Clerk**, *who hands it to* **Hathorne**. **Hathorne** *hands it back to the* **Clerk**, *who stamps it. All very fast and with mechanical gestures.*)

---

[15]serve as proof of

**Jury.**  Exhibt A—mark it Exhibit A. (**Scratch** *takes the deed from the* **Clerk** *and offers it to the* **Jury**, *who pass it rapidly among them, hardly looking at it, and hand it back to* **Scratch**.) We know the deed—the deed—it burns in our fingers—we do not have to see the deed. It's a losing case.

**Scratch.**  It offers incontestable evidence of the truth of the prosecution's claim. I shall now call Jabez Stone to the witness stand.

**Jury.**  *(hungrily)* Jabez Stone to the witness stand—Jabez Stone. He's a fine, fat fellow, Jabez Stone. He'll fry like a batter cake, once we get him where we want him.

**Webster.**  Your Honor, I move that this jury be discharged for flagrant and open bias!

**Hathorne.**  Motion denied.

**Webster.**  Exception.

**Hathorne.**  Exception denied.

**Jury.**  His motion's always denied. He thinks himself smart and clever—lawyer Webster. But his motion's always denied.

**Webster.**  Your Honor! (*He chokes with anger.*)

**Clerk.**  (*advancing*) Jabez Stone to the witness stand!

**Jury.**  Jabez Stone—Jabez Stone.

(**Webster** *gives* **Jabez** *an encouraging pat on the back, and* **Jabez** *takes his place on the witness stand, very scared.*)

**Clerk.**  (*offering a black book*) Do you solemnly swear—testify—so help you—and it's no good, for we don't care what you testify?

**Jabez.**  I do.

**Scratch.**  What's your name?

**Jabez.**  Jabez Stone.

**Scratch.**  Occupation?

**Jabez.**   Farmer.

**Scratch.**   Residence?

**Jabez.**   Cross Corners, New Hampshire.

(*These three questions are very fast and mechanical on the part of* **Scratch**. *He is absolutely sure of victory and just going through a form.*)

**Jury.**   A farmer—he'll farm in hell—we'll see that he farms in hell.

**Scratch.**   Now, Jabez Stone, answer me. You'd better, you know. You haven't got a chance, and there'll be a cooler place by the fire for you.

**Webster.**   I protest! This is intimidation! This mocks all justice!

**Hathorne.**   The protest is irrelevant, incompetent, and immaterial. We have our own justice. The protest is denied.

**Jury.**   Irrelevant, incompetent, and immaterial—we have our own justice—oho, Daniel Webster! (*The* **Jury's** *eyes fix upon* **Webster** *for an instant, hungrily.*)

**Scratch.**   Did you or did you not sign this document?

**Jabez.**   Oh, I signed it! You know I signed it. And if I have to go to hell for it, I'll go!

(*A sigh sweeps over the* **Jury**.)

**Jury.**   One of us—one of us now—we'll save a place by the fire for you, Jabez Stone.

**Scratch.**   The prosecution rests.

**Hathorne.**   Remove the prisoner.

**Webster.**   But I wish to cross-examine—I wish to prove—

**Hathorne.**   There will be no cross-examination. We have our own justice. You may speak, if you like. But be brief.

**Jury.**   Brief—be very brief—we're weary of earth—incompetent, irrelevant, and immaterial—they say he's a smart man, Webster, but he's lost his case tonight—be very brief—we have our own justice here.

(**Webster** *stares around him like a baited bull. He can't find words.*)

**Mary's Voice.**   (*from off stage*) Set me as a seal upon they heart, as a seal upon thine arm, for love is strong as death—

**Jury.** (*loudly*)   A seal!—ha, ha—a burning seal!

**Mary's Voice.**   Love is strong—

**Jury.** (*drowning her out*) Death is stronger than love. Set the seal upon Daniel Webster—the burning seal of the lost. Make him one of us—one of the damned—one with Jabez Stone!

(*The* **Jury's** *eyes all fix upon* **Webster.** *The* **Clerk** *advances as if to take him into custody. But* **Webster** *silences them all with a great gesture.*)

**Webster.**   Be still!

I was going to thunder and roar. I shall not do that.

I was going to denounce and defy. I shall not do that.

You have judged this man already with your abominable justice. See that you defend it. For I shall not speak of this man.

You are demons now, but once you were men. I shall speak to every one of you.

Of common things I speak, of small things and common.

The freshness of morning to the young, the taste of food to the hungry, the day's toil, the rest by the fire, the quiet sleep.

These are good things.

But without freedom they sicken, without freedom they are nothing.

Freedom is the bread and the morning and the risen sun.

It was for freedom we came in the boats and the ships. It
   was for freedom we came.
It has been a long journey, a hard one, a bitter one.
But, out of the wrong and the right, the sufferings and the
   starvations, there is a new thing, a free thing.
The traitors in their treachery, the wise in their wisdom,
   the valiant in their courage—all, all have played a part.
It may not be denied in hell or shall hell prevail against it.
Have you forgotten this? (*He turns to the* **Jury**.) Have you
   forgotten the forest?

**Girty.**   (*as in a dream*) The forest, the rustle of the forest, the
   free forest.

**Webster.**   (*to King Philip*) Have you forgotten your lost nation?

**King Philip.**   My lost nation—my fires in the wood—my war-
   riors.

**Webster.**   (*to* **Teach**) Have you forgotten the sea and the way of
   ships?

**Teach.**   The sea—and the swift ships sailing—the blue sea.

**Jury.**   Forgotten—remembered—forgotten yet remembered.

**Webster.**   You were men once. Have you forgotten?

**Jury.**   We were men once. We have not thought of it nor
   remembered. But we were men.

**Webster.**   Now here is this man with good and evil in his heart.
   Do you know him? He is your brother. Will you take the
   law of the oppressor and bind him down?
   It is not for him that I speak. It is for all of you.
   There is sadness in being a man but it is a proud thing, too.
   There is failure and despair on the journey—the endless
      journey of mankind.
   We are tricked and trapped—we stumble into the pit—but,
      out of the pit, we rise again.
   No demon that was ever foaled can know the inwardness of
      that—only men—bewildered men.

They have broken freedom with their hands and cast her
     out from the nations—yet shall she live while man lives.
She shall live in the blood and the heart—she shall live in
     the earth of this country—she shall not be broken.
When the whips of the oppressors are broken and their
     names forgotten and destroyed,
I see you, mighty, shining, liberty, liberty! I see free men
     walking and talking under a free star.
God save the United States and the men who have made
     her free.
The defense rests.

**Jury.** *(exultantly)* We were men—we were free—we were
     men—we have not forgotten—our children—our children
     shall follow and be free.

**Hathorne.** *(rapping with gravel)* The jury will retire to consider
     its verdict.

**Butler.** *(rising)* There is no need. The jury has heard Mr.
     Webster. We find for the defendant, Jabez Stone!

**Jury.** Not guilty.

**Scratch.** *(in a screech, rushing forward)* But, Your Honor—

*(But even as he does so, there is a flash and a thunderclap, the
stage blacks out again, and when the lights come on,* **Judge** *and*
**Jury** *are gone. The yellow light of dawn lights the windows.)*

**Jabez.** They're gone and it's morning—Mary, Mary!

**Mary.** *(in doorway)* My love—my dear. *(She rushes to him.)*

*(Meanwhile* **Scratch** *has been collecting his papers and is trying
to sneak out. But* **Webster** *catches him.)*

**Webster.** Just a minute, Mr. Scratch. I'll have that paper first,
     if you please. *(He takes the deed and tears it.)* And now, sir,
     I'll have *you!*

**Scratch.** Come, come, Mr. Webster. This sort of thing is

ridic—ouch—is ridiculous. If you're worried about the costs of the case, naturally I'd be glad to pay.

**Webster.**   And so you shall! First of all, you'll promise and covenant never to bother Jabez Stone or any other New Hampshire man from now till doomsday. For any hell we want to raise in this state we can raise ourselves, without any help from you.

**Scratch.**   Ouch! Well, they never did run very big to the barrel but—ouch—I agree!

**Webster.**   See you keep to the bargain! And then—well, I've got a ram named Goliath. He can butt through an iron door. I'd like to turn you loose in his field and see what he could do to you. (**Scratch** *trembles.*) But that would be hard on the ram. So we'll just call in the neighbors and give you a shivaree.

**Scratch.**   Mr. Webster, please—oh—

**Webster.**   Neighbors! Neighbors! Come in and see what a long-barreled, slab-sided, lantern-jawed, fortunetelling note-shaver I've got by the scruff of the neck! Bring on your kettles and your pans! (*a noise and murmur outside*) Bring on your muskets and your flails!

**Jabez.**   We'll drive him out of New Hampshire!

**Mary.**   We'll drive old Scratch away!

(*The **Crowd** rushes in, with muskets, flails, brooms, etc. They pursue **Scratch** around the stage, chanting.*)

**The Crowd.**   We'll drive him out of New Hampshire!
        We'll drive old Scratch away!
        Forever and a day, boys,
        Forever and a day!

(*They finally catch **Scratch** between two of them and fling him out of the door bodily.*)

**A Man.**   Three cheers for Dan'l Webster!

**Another Man.**   Three cheers for Daniel Webster! He's licked the devil!

**Webster.**   (*moving to center stage, and joining* **Jabez**'s *hands and* **Mary**'s) And whom God hath joined let no man put asunder. (*He kisses* **Mary** *and turns, dusting his hands.*) Well, that job's done. I hope there's a pie for breakfast, neighbor Stone.

(*Some of the women, dancing, bring in pies from the kitchen.*)

# REVIEWING AND INTERPRETING THE PLAY

Record your answers to these questions in your personal
literature notebook. Follow the directions for each part.

**REVIEWING**    Try to complete each of these sentences without looking back
at the play.

*Understanding*
*Main Ideas*

**1.** As the men and women at the party dance, they say
   "Money, land, and riches. Just came out of nowhere.
   Wonder where he got it all." They suspect that Jabez Stone
   a. is about to retire.
   b. has lied about how much money he has.
   c. achieved success through illegal or shameful methods.
   d. discovered gold.

*Recalling Facts*

**2.** Miser Stevens is being carried off by Mr. Scratch in the form of a
   a. botanist's collecting box.
   b. common moth.
   c. clap of thunder.
   d. fiddle.

*Identifying Sequence*

**3.** As soon as Webster hears Scratch claim American
   citizenship, he
   a. compliments Scratch on his knowledge of the law.
   b. raises an objection to Scratch's evidence.
   c. offers a cash settlement to break Jabez's contract.
   d. demands a jury trial for his client.

*Recognizing Literary*
*Elements (Theme)*

**4.** By telling Webster, "I am merely an honest American like
   yourself—and of the best descent—for . . . my name is older
   in the country than yours," Scratch is implying that
   a. evil has always existed.
   b. America has always been evil.
   c. the devil is not always evil.
   d. he is not really the devil.

*Identifying
Cause and Effect*

**5.** Webster changes his approach from thundering and denouncing to reminding the jurors of their humanity and freedom because
   a. Mary interrupts him and makes him forget what he was going to say.
   b. the Jury interrupts and asks him to be brief.
   c. he sees that his anger is giving Scratch power over him.
   d. he realizes he has lost the case and might as well save his energy.

**INTERPRETING**

To complete these sentences, you may look back at the play if you'd like.

*Making Inferences*

**6.** Jabez sold his soul to the devil for all these reasons *except* that he
   a. was a very ambitious person.
   b. wanted a nice home to bring Mary to.
   c. had lost hope that he would ever be anything but poor.
   d. was a very evil person.

*Making
Generalizations*

**7.** The motto that best describes the behavior of Jabez Stone's neighbors is
   a. "Love conquers all."
   b. "Look on the bright side."
   c. "Look out for Number One."
   d. "Fortune favors the brave."

*Analyzing*

**8.** After Webster appeals to the Jury to remember life and freedom, individual jurors, including Girty, King Philip, and Teach, speak out. This indicates all of the following *except* that
   a. the jurors are beginning to listen to him.
   b. he is beginning to get through to the jurors.
   c. the jurors are not getting along any more.
   d. the memory of freedom is making the jurors act more independently.

*Understanding*
*Literary Elements*
*(Plot)*

**9.** At a certain moment Webster recognizes that Scratch and the Jury think they have him and Jabez, and he therefore changes his approach. This moment in the plot is
   a. part of the introduction.
   b. the turning point.
   c. part of the falling action.
   d. the resolution.

*Predicting Outcomes*

**10.** If any of Mr. Scratch's victims ever asks for a jury trial in the future, Mr. Scratch probably will
   a. call on a different set of jurors.
   b. let that person out of the contract.
   c. refuse the request without hesitation.
   d. see that the judge is better at enforcing the rules.

Now check your answers with your teacher. Study the questions you answered incorrectly. What types of questions were they? Talk with your teacher about ways to work on those skills.

# Setting, Staging, and Dialogue

As you know, plays are not written just to be read. The script is only the frame around which a complete production is fashioned. Playwrights know that the objects and actions on a stage all help to support the dialogue and convey meaning to the audience. Therefore, most playwrights use stage directions to guide the directors, actors, and crew who bring the dialogue to life.

In *The Devil and Daniel Webster*, Benét presents a tale of the supernatural, and he chooses to tell his story with a certain attitude, or tone, that supports the message he has in mind. Unlike horror-story author Edgar Allan Poe, Benét has no desire to start with a scary situation and build steadily to terror. He wants to change the mood, or feeling, from scene to scene. The dialogue mixes humor with fear, and the staging of the play must reflect a back-and-forth motion between despair and hope. In his stage directions, Benét calls for specific sights, sounds, and special effects that will further the plot as well as stress the alternating moods and the theme of the play.

In these lessons, you will look at some of the ways in which Benét uses stagecraft to support his dialogue:

1. He specifies scenery, props, and costumes that establish the setting, indicate the mood, and give hints about other elements of the play.

2. He suggests lighting and sound effects to influence the mood of each scene and, occasionally, to carry the plot forward.

3. He uses stylized movements and dialogue to help develop the plot.

## LESSON 1  SCENERY, PROPS, AND COSTUMES

If a stage's curtain were to rise on a shadowy scene draped with cobwebs, how would you react? Before a single word was spoken, you probably would suspect that something eerie was going to happen on stage. You might even feel a slight shudder of fear. However, you probably would not know from the scenery alone where or when the action of the play takes place. You would have to see how the actors are dressed or how they speak before you would be sure of the specific setting.

On the other hand, if the scenery were to show a brightly-lit living room with familiar furnishings, you would recognize the setting but you probably wouldn't be sure what the mood of the play would be. That setting might be right for a comedy, a murder mystery, or a serious family drama. In this case, you would have to see and hear the actors before you decide on the mood.

In each of these examples, the playwright chose where to put the emphasis—either on the mood or setting. Read this passage from Benét's stage directions for the set design of *The Devil and Daniel Webster*. Picture what the audience would see as the curtain goes up. How does Benét manage both to establish time and place and to suggest a mood?

*The scene is the main room of **Jabez Stone**'s New Hampshire farmhouse in 1841, a big, comfortable room that hasn't yet developed the stuffiness of a front parlor. A door leads to the kitchen, another door to the outside. Windows, in center, show a glimpse of summer landscape. Most of the furniture has been cleared away for the dance which follows the wedding of **Jabez** and **Mary Stone**, but there is a settle or bench by the fireplace, a table with some wedding presents upon it, at least three chairs by the table, and a cider barrel on which the **Fiddler** sits, in front of the table. Near the table there is a cupboard where there are glasses and a jug. There is a clock.*

*A country wedding has been in progress—the wedding of **Jabez** and **Mary Stone**. He is a husky young farmer, around twenty-eight or thirty. The bride is in her early twenties. He is dressed in stiff store clothes but not ridiculously—they are of good quality and he looks important. The bride is in a simple white or cream wedding dress and may carry a small, stiff bouquet of country flowers.*

*Now the wedding is over and the guests are dancing. The **Fiddler** is perched on the cider barrel. He plays and calls square-dance figures. . . . There is an air of prosperity and hearty country mirth about the whole affair.*

Unless theater-goers are given a program that lists the setting of each scene, they will not know the exact year of this scene. However, parts of the scenery—the fireplace, the settle, the style of the table and chairs, and the cider barrel—will suggest that the time is well over a hundred years ago. An additional hint is given by the costumes of the actors on stage as the curtain rises. These clues help the audience make an intelligent estimate of the decade.

From the scenery alone, the audience cannot guess the mood any more than you could with the scene of the modern family-room discussed earlier. However, Benét doesn't make the audience wait for dialogue. The curtain goes up on guests dancing to merry music. A happy, cheerful mood is unmistakable.

Although it is not immediately obvious, this setting also suggests the tone, or attitude, that the writer takes toward the plot. This home is down-to-earth, practical, and friendly. The view of the summer landscape seen through the center windows links the people in the house to the land. As the play progresses, we will become aware of an attitude of cheerful optimism, a confidence in anyone native to this land.

## EXERCISE ①

Read the following stage direction. Then use what you have learned in this lesson to answer the questions.

*(And, at this point, **Mr. Scratch** makes his appearance. He has entered, unobserved, and mixed with the **Crowd** while all eyes were upon **Daniel Webster**. He is, of course, the devil— a New England devil, dressed like a rather shabby attorney but with something just a little wrong in clothes and appear-*

*ance. For one thing, he wears black gloves on his hands. He carries a large black tin box, like a botanist's collecting box, under one arm. Now he slips through the* **Crowd** *and taps the* **Fiddler** *on the shoulder.)*

**1.** How does Mr. Scratch's costume alert the audience to the idea that there is something wrong about him?

**2.** What do you learn about the author's tone from the fact that he portrays the devil as a "shabby attorney"? Does this portrayal suggest an attitude of respect or disrespect toward the character?

Now check your answers with your teacher. Review this part of the lesson if you don't understand why an answer was incorrect.

## WRITING ON YOUR OWN ①

In this exercise you will use what you have learned in the lesson about scenery and props to describe a stage setting. Follow these steps.

- Review your notes from the first writing exercise. Decide which event in history you will write about. Focus on what happened to build up to the event. Choose a specific place where some of this action occurred or where you imagine it occurred.
- Determine what must be on the stage at the beginning of your scene to indicate the time and place of the action. Do whatever research is needed to discover the type of furniture, machinery, or household objects that were in use at the time. Describe the set completely enough to guide a production crew in preparing the scenery and props.

## LESSON ② LIGHTING AND SOUND DIRECTIONS

Lighting is a very important element of play production. Besides the concrete objects the audience sees on the stage—

the backdrop, the props, and the actors—they also see light. The director and lighting crew in a theater work hard to control that light. When the play's action is spread across the stage, the entire stage is lit with an even, smooth illumination. When attention must be focused on a single speaker, a spotlight shines on that person and the rest of the stage is hidden in darkness. The color of the light, too, is managed skillfully. A warm yellow light can stress the comfort of a calm scene; a harsh red light can impose tension; a cool blue light can suggest a feeling of detachment, as in a dream sequence. In addition to setting or supporting the mood of a scene, light can advance the action. Flashes of light, for example, can represent lightning that starts a fire. A gradual darkening of the stage can suggest the coming of evening, movement into a dark cave, or a similar plot development.

Sound, too, is a vital element in stagecraft. The actors' voices, background music, all sorts of sound effects, and even silence are parts of the playwright's and director's tool kit. Like lighting, sound can be used over a span of time to suggest or support a mood, or in a short burst to signify an event in the plot.

Note how Benét uses light and sound in *The Devil and Daniel Webster*. In the first part of the play, he leaves most of the lighting decisions up to the director. However, he suggests where the focus on the stage should be. Read this stage direction. If you were directing a production of the play, where would you put the strongest light in this scene?

> (*The* **Crowd** *begins to drift away—a few to the kitchen, a few toward the door that leads to the outside. They furnish a shifting background to the next little scene, where* **Mary** *and* **Jabez** *are left alone by the fireplace.*)

When all the dancers needed to be seen, the whole stage required fairly even lighting. But now the people in the background need relatively little light, and the strong lighting should be only on Jabez and Mary.

Review, also, the stage directions quoted in Exercise 1 that describe Mr. Scratch's entrance. To make sure the audience sees this actor and notes his costume and collecting box, a director would naturally make sure he is in strong light.

In the following passage, Benét specifically calls for lighting to present a major plot development. Scratch has upset the entire wedding party by his threatening song, and Webster has pulled the fiddle out of his hands.

**Scratch.** *(facing him)* You're a bold man, Mr. Webster. Too bold for your own good, perhaps. And anyhow, it wasn't my fiddle. It belonged to— *(He wheels and sees the* **Fiddler** *tampering with the collecting box that has been left on the table.)* Idiot! What are you doing with my collecting box? *(He rushes for the* **Fiddler** *and chases him around the table, but the* **Fiddler** *is just one jump ahead.)*

**Fiddler.** Boston lawyer, eh? Well, I don't think so. I think you've got something in that box of yours you're afraid to show. And, by jingo— *(He throws open the lid of the box. The lights wink and there is a clap of thunder. All eyes stare upward. Something has flown out of the box. But what?* **Fiddler**, *with relief.)* Why, 'tain't nothing but a moth. . . . *(terrified)* But it ain't. It ain't no common moth! I seen it! And it's got a death's head on it! *(He strikes at the invisible object with his bow to drive it away.)*

Without the wink of the lights and the clap of thunder, the opening of the box could go unnoticed. The change in lighting, in particular, alerts the audience to the presence of something fast-moving and barely seen.

The clap of thunder that accompanies that flash of light is not the first use of sound effects in *The Devil and Daniel Webster*. From the rising of the curtain, fiddle music has supported the mood and notable events in the plot. What is the significance of the fiddle sounds in the following passage?

**Webster.**    Neighbors, old friends—it does me good to hear you. But don't cheer me—I'm not running for President this summer. (*a laugh from the* **Crowd**) I'm here on a better errand—to pay my humble respects to a most charming lady and her very fortunate spouse.
(*There is a twang of a fiddle string breaking.*)

**Fiddler.**    'Tarnation! Busted a string!

**A Voice.**    He's always bustin' strings.

(**Webster** *blinks at the interruption but goes on.*)

**Webster.**    We're proud of State Senator Stone in these parts—we know what he's done. . . . I know this—Jabez Stone wears no man's collar. (*At this statement there is a discordant squeak from the fiddle and* **Jabez** *looks embarrassed.* **Webster** *knits his brows.*)

The first time the fiddle makes an unpleasant sound, the wedding guests assume it's an accident. But when a second annoying sound interrupts Webster's speech, both Jabez and Webster begin to take the noises personally. The audience soon realizes that these noises are more than accidents. They are Mr. Scratch's first reactions to Mr. Webster's remarks about Jabez Stone. A few moments later, the Fiddler unknowingly identifies the problem when he uses what he thinks is a figure of speech:

**Fiddler.**    (*passionately, flinging the fiddle down*) Hell's delight—excuse me, Mr. Webster. But the very devil's got into that fiddle of mine.

EXERCISE ②

Read this passage, which ends the wedding party. Use what you have learned to answer the questions that follow the passage.

**The Crowd.**    He's sold his soul to the devil! There's no help left for him, neighbors! Run, hide, hurry, before we're caught! He's a lost soul—Jabez Stone—he's the devil's own! Run, hide, hasten! (*They stream across the stage like a flurry of bats, the cannier picking up the wedding presents they have given to take along with them.*)

(**Mr. Scratch** *drives them out into the night, fiddle in hand, and follows them.* **Jabez** *and* **Mary** *are left with* **Webster**. **Jabez** *has sunk into a chair, beaten, with his head in his hands.* **Mary** *is trying to comfort him.* **Webster** *looks at them for a moment and shakes his head sadly. As he crosses to exit to the porch, his hand drops for a moment on* **Jabez**'s *shoulder, but Jabez makes no sign.* **Webster** *exits.* **Jabez** *lifts his head.*)

1. What hints about lighting effects do you find in the phrases *like a flurry of bats* and *drives them out into the night?* If you were the director, how would you light the scene to match Benét's description? What changes would be needed during these few minutes?

2. What sounds does Benét want on the stage at the beginning of this passage? What sounds does he want at the end? How does the change in sound indicate a change in mood?

Now check your answers with your teacher. Review this part of the lesson if you don't understand why an answer was incorrect.

### WRITING ON YOUR OWN ②

In this exercise you will use what you have learned to describe lighting and sound effects that contribute to the mood and plot of the scene you are developing. Follow these steps:

Think about the problem with which the people in your scene are struggling and the actions that they will take or react to in this scene. The scene may begin at a low point, when the characters are discouraged, frightened, or confused. Or it may begin at a high point, when the characters are hopeful, enthusiastic, or cheered by whatever happened in the previous scene. What can the characters do or say, or what news can they receive, that will change that mood?

- On your paper, make a chart with three columns. Label the columns *Actions, Lighting,* and *Sounds.*
- In the first column, list the characters on stage at the beginning of this scene and summarize their initial positions. Then list three or four events in the scene and describe important movements of the actors. For example, several characters might be sitting anxiously when a new character enters with news, and then everyone might jump up in delight, slump in despair, or run in terror.
- In the second column, describe the lighting effects you want on the stage. For example, do the lights get brighter or dimmer? Is there a spotlight on the messenger or on the leader of the group waiting for news? Write the direction for each lighting change next to the note describing what's happening on stage.
- Determine what sound effects will support the action on the stage. Is there a battle raging? Is an angry crowd milling outside? Does soft music play in the background? How is the sound affected by the change in mood? In the third column, list sound effects that will help to establish the first mood, show the change in mood, and support the new mood. (Don't forget that silence is also considered a sound effect.)

## LESSON ③　 USES OF DIALOGUE

Whatever a character says that is not part of a back-and-forth conversation, or dialogue, is called a *monologue.* A *speech* is one kind of monologue. In a speech, one character talks for several minutes without interruption, knowing that others are listening to him or her. A second type of monologue is a *soliloquy.* In a soliloquy, a character talks to himself or herself; the speaker is not conscious of anyone else listening. In the past, playwrights often gave characters *asides*. In an aside, the character is aware of the audience and speaks directly to it, without other characters hearing.

In *The Devil and Daniel Webster*, Benét makes use of several types of monologue. Both Scratch and Webster deliver long speeches. The following passage leads into Scratch's invocation of the jury from hell and includes its ending. What is special about the staging of Scratch's speech? What is the effect of this speech being in the form of a poem? How does the speech advance the plot?

**Scratch.**    The quick or the dead! You have said it. (*He points his finger at the place where the* **Jury** *is to appear. There is a clap of thunder and a flash of light. The stage blacks out completely. All that can be seen is the face of* **Scratch**, *lit with a ghastly green light, as he recites the invocation that summons the* **Jury**. *As, one by one, the important* **Jurymen** *are mentioned, they appear.*)
I summon the jury Mr. Webster demands.
From churchyard mold and gallows grave,
Brimstone pit and burning gulf,
I summon them!
Dastard, liar, scoundrel, knave,
I summon them! Appear! . . .
I summon them, I summon them
From their tormented flame!
Quick or dead, quick or dead,
Broken heart and bitter head,
True Americans, each one,
Traitor and disloyal son,
Cankered earth and twisted tree,
Outcasts of eternity,
Twelve great sinners, tried and true,
For the work they are to do!
I summon them, I summon them!
Appear, appear, appear!

*(The **Jury** has now taken its place in the box . . . They are eerily lit and so made up as to suggest the unearthly. . . .)*

The stage directions call for special lighting. The stage goes dark except for a green light on Scratch's face, and the light increases only enough to make the entrances of the jurors detectable. Limiting the light and sound only to Scratch gives him a power over the stage and sets up an eerie mood that would be lost if anyone were to interrupt him. The poem format, with irregular rhythm and rhyme, makes the speech sound like a magic incantation. Although Scratch's arrival at the wedding party was somewhat strange, the action was still in Jabez's comfortable, realistic home. Now Scratch's words move the action to an unearthly courtroom where Scratch—not law or logic—rules.

A second kind of monologue appears in the words of the ghostly jury. Up to Webster's speech, the jury members speak as one. What they say is directed to no one in particular. Instead, it is a comment on what others say and do, as if someone were musing to himself or herself in a soliloquy. As you read this passage, notice how the Jury intensifies Jabez's fears by repeating them.

**Jabez.**    *(seeing them, horrified)* A jury of the dead!
**Jury.**    Of the dead!
**Jabez.**    A jury of the damned!
**Jury.**    Of the damned!

Read the passage below, in which the Jury again comments almost to itself. The passage ends in a speech by Webster. What additional kind of monologue does Benét use here?

**Webster.**    But I wish to cross-examine—I wish to prove—
**Hathorne.**    There will be no cross-examination. We have our own justice. You may speak, if you like. But be brief.

**Jury.**  Brief—be very brief—we're weary of earth—incompetent, irrelevant, and immaterial—they say he's a smart man, Webster, but he's lost his case tonight—be very brief—we have our own justice here.

(**Webster** *stares around him like a baited bull. He can't find words.*)

**Mary's Voice.**  (*from off stage*) Set me as a seal upon they heart, as a seal upon thine arm, for love is strong as death—

**Jury.**  (*loudly*) A seal!—ha, ha—a burning seal!

**Mary's Voice.**  Love is strong—

**Jury.**  (*drowning her out*) Death is stronger than love. Set the seal upon Daniel Webster—the burning seal of the lost. Make him one of us—one of the damned—one with Jabez Stone!

(*The **Jury's** eyes all fix upon **Webster**. The **Clerk** advances as if to take him into custody. But **Webster** silences them all with a great gesture.*)

**Webster.**  Be still!

I was going to thunder and roar. I shall not do that.

I was going to denounce and defy. I shall not do that.

In addition to the Jury's rambling and threatening soliloquies and Webster's speech, Mary's lines in this passage are a third kind of monologue. Her voice comes from another room—almost another world—and is not directed to anyone in this scene. Yet what she says arouses the Jury and makes its members put into words what they have been thinking all along: Daniel Webster is their target as much as Jabez Stone. This series of monologues has carried the conflict to its climax.

## EXERCISE ③

Read the following passage. The action in it occurs shortly before the passage above. Use the two passages and what you have learned to answer the questions that follow.

**Scratch.**    . . . I shall now call Jabez Stone to the witness stand.

**Jury.**    *(hungrily)* Jabez Stone to the witness stand—Jabez Stone. He's a fine, fat fellow, Jabez Stone. He'll fry like a batter cake, once we get him where we want him.

**Webster.**    Your Honor, I move that this jury be discharged for flagrant and open bias!

**Hathorne.**    Motion denied.

**Webster.**    Exception.

**Hathorne.**    Exception denied.

**Jury.**    His motion's always denied. He thinks himself smart and clever—lawyer Webster. But his motion's always denied.

**Webster.**    Your Honor! *(He chokes with anger.)*

1.  In this excerpt, which characters are involved in dialogue, that is, conversation?

2.  Is the Jury speaking to Scratch, Jabez, Hathorne, Webster, or itself? How can you tell? Do the other characters hear the Jury? Again, how can you tell?

3.  Note the stage direction concerning Webster that ends this excerpt. Compare it to the Jury's demands and stage directions in the lesson above. How does this stage direction relate to the later developments?

Now check your answers with your teacher. Review this part of the lesson if you don't understand why an answer was incorrect.

### WRITING ON YOUR OWN ③

In this exercise you will examine a real-life situation involving movement by a group, and you will transfer it to the stage. Follow these steps:

- List all the situations you can think of that involve a large number of people moving together in a similar way. These situations could include fans doing the wave at a sports event or jumping up to cheer a home run, touchdown, or goal. They could include a stream of commuters entering a train station, hundreds of students switching classrooms between periods, or many runners starting a marathon.
- Choose a situation with which you link strong feelings. For example, if you are part of a crowd going in one direction, you might feel forceful or helplessly swept along; if you are meeting that crowd as you go the opposite direction, you might feel overpowered or adventurous. Circle that situation on your list. Below the list, describe your feelings.
- How could you represent that situation on a stage and express one of the feelings you described? Suppose you have about a dozen actors. What props would you give them, if any? How would they move on the stage? Would they need lines? Would you need lighting or sound effects to emphasize the mood? Write stage directions and any necessary dialogue that let a director and actors know what effect you want on the stage.

## DISCUSSION GUIDES

**1.** Despite modern skepticism about the devil, the concept of selling your soul to the devil is still often used in movies, television programs, and other entertainment. Does the lasting fascination with this legend tell us anything about ourselves? Discuss these questions with a small group. Report your conclusions and discuss them with your class.

**2.** What do you think the message of this play is? Choose one or two speeches that you think are significant. When you state what you think the theme is, read the lines that support your opinion.

**3.** In *The Devil and Daniel Webster,* Mr. Scratch is presented as a fiddler. This portrayal of the devil appears in other literature and music, from classical to country. Work with a small group to investigate other works of art that use either the idea of the devil as a fiddler or the legend of Faust. Make a chart or poster to display what you find. For each work, list this information: *a)* the name of the work; *b)* its creator, if known; *c)* the country and century in which its creator lived; *d)* the type of literature, music, or art it belongs to; and *e)* a brief description of the work. Explain your chart to the class and, if possible, play some of the music you discovered that is inspired by either of these themes.

**4.** Working independently or with a partner, research one of the people or events in American history mentioned in this play— for example: any of the named jurors, the War of 1812, or the introduction of slavery. Write a few paragraphs about what you discover. Then work with the rest of the class to put together a poster or bulletin board showing a time line from 1600 to 1850. Attach cards containing the paragraphs at the appropriate years.

# WRITE A SCENE FOR THE STAGE

In this unit you have looked at ways in which playwrights can use objects, people, lighting, sound effects, and dialogue to express or support elements of a play. In the writing exercises, you have practiced using some of these methods. Now you will apply what you have learned to write a scene based on a historical theme, using stagecraft to develop the mood and other dramatic elements.

If you have questions about the writing process, refer to Using the Writing Process on page 300.

- Assemble and review the writing assignments you did for this unit: *1)* a description of a stage setting presenting a specific era in history, *2)* a chart listing certain elements of a single scene, *3)* directions for a scene involving a group in movement which expresses a mood.
- Using your stage description and chart to guide you, write a part of your scene about a risky moment in a historical event. For this short scene, don't worry about developing characters or conflict fully. Your main concern is to develop a setting and a mood and then to change that mood through dialogue, action, lighting, and sound effects. Set off your stage directions with underlining. Make sure the speakers are clearly identified.
- Ask a classmate to read your scene and identify the different moods at the beginning and end of the passage. If your classmate cannot see the different moods, rework the scene to make it stronger. Use your classmate's comments to clarify your stage directions.
- Proofread your scene for spelling, grammar, punctuation, capitalization, and formatting errors. Then make a final copy and save it in your portfolio.

# Theme

# A Marriage Proposal

by Anton Chekov,
*translated by Joachim Neugroschel*

## INTRODUCTION

**ABOUT THE SELECTION**

Lómov, a Russian landowner who habitually and needlessly worries about his health, visits his neighbor, Choobookóv, to ask for his daughter Natália's hand in marriage. As soon as the complaining Lómov and the impatient and headstrong Natália begin their conversation, however, hilarious conflicts develop. Read this classic play to see how a situation that should be romantic deteriorates rapidly into foolishness.

*A Marriage Proposal* is a comedy. As do all of Chekhov's plays, it depicts a real-life situation typical of the Russian middle class at the end of the 19th century. Despite their settings, Chekhov's plays have been described as having a timeless quality because they depict the problems of everyday people.

**ABOUT THE AUTHOR**

Anton Chekhov was born in 1860. He was the grandson of a serf—a peasant who was bound to the land he lived on and who could not leave without the landowner's permission. Chekhov studied medicine at the University of Moscow and became a doctor in 1884. While he was a student, Chekhov wrote articles for a variety of comic papers. His first book, *Motley Stories*, was published in 1886. It was so successful that Chekhov was able to devote most of his time to writing, although he always considered himself a doctor rather than a writer.

Although Chekhov's short stories became popular quickly, his plays did not meet with immediate success. When his play *The Sea Gull* failed in 1896, Chekhov vowed to stop writing plays forever. "Never will I write these plays or try to produce them," he wrote, "not if I live to be 700 years old." Fortunately, the Moscow Art Theatre persuaded him to change his mind. Their revival of *The Sea Gull* was a triumph. Chekhov then wrote *The Three Sisters* and his last play, *The Cherry Orchard*, for the Art Theatre. Chekhov died in 1904 from tuberculosis, which he had contracted while studying at the University of Moscow.

## ABOUT THE LESSONS

The lessons that follow *A Marriage Proposal* focus on theme. *Theme* refers to the lesson or message that a writer wants to share with his or her readers. Through the theme, the author shares insights about human nature and suggests ways to live or behave. In most modern stories and plays, the theme is not stated directly but is implied instead. To understand the theme of a play, you need to analyze what the characters say and do.

## WRITING: DEVELOPING A THEME

At the end of this unit, you will write a scene about a quarrel that develops a theme. Follow these steps to help you get started:

First, think about the qualities you admire in people, such as generosity or kindness. List these qualities in one column on a sheet of paper.

- Next, think about the qualities that frustrate or anger you in people, such as laziness, selfishness, or greed. List them in another column.
- Save your lists. You will refer to them for ideas when you write your quarrel at the end of the unit.

**AS YOU READ**

As you read this selection, think about the answers to these questions:

- What is the author's purpose for writing this play?
- What theme, or message, is the author trying to convey?
- How do you feel about the characters in this play?
- How does the author use the characters to help him express the theme?

# A Marriage Proposal

by Anton Chekov,
*translated by Joachim Neugroschel*

**CAST**

**Stepán Stepánovich Choobookóv,** *a landowner*

**Natália Stepánovna,** *his twenty-five-year-old daughter*

**Iván Vassílievich Lómov,** *Choobookóv's neighbor, a healthy and well-fed, but terribly hypochondriac[1] landowner*

**SETTING**

*The action takes place in the drawing room of* **Choobookóv***'s country house.*

---

**SCENE 1** (**Choobookóv** *and* **Lómov.** *The latter enters, wearing tails and white gloves.*)

**Choobookóv.** *(going over to welcome his guest)* Why, of all people! My old friend, Iván Vassílievich! How nice to see you! *(shakes his hand)* This really is a surprise, old boy. . . . How *are* you?

**Lómov.** Very well, thank you. And may I ask how *you* are?

---

[1] overly concerned about one's health

**Choobookóv.** Not bad at all, old friend, with the help of your prayers and so on. . . . Please have a seat. . . . Now, really, it's not very nice of you to neglect your neighbors, my dear boy. And what are you all dressed up for? Morning coat, gloves, and so on! Are you off on a visit, old boy?

**Lómov.** No, I'm just calling on you, my esteemed neighbor.

**Choobookóv.** But why the morning coat, old friend? This isn't New Year's Day!

**Lómov.** Well, you see, the fact of the matter is . . . (*takes his arm*) I've burst in on you like this, Stepán Stepánovich, my esteemed neighbor, in order to ask a favor of you. I've already had the honor more than once of turning to you for help and you've always, so to speak, uh! . . . But forgive me, my nerves . . . I must have a sip of water, dear Stepán Stepánovich. (*drinks some water*)

**Choobookóv.** (*aside*) He's after money. Fat chance! (*to **Lómov***) What is it, my dear fellow?

**Lómov.** Well, you see, my Stepán dearovich, uh! I mean dear Stepánovich . . . uh! I mean, my nerves are in a terrible condition, which you yourself are so kind as to see. In short, you're the only one who can help me, although, of course, I've done nothing to deserve it and . . . and I don't even have the right to count on your help. . . .

**Choobookóv.** Now, now; don't beat about the bush, old friend. Out with it! . . . Well?

**Lómov.** All right, here you are. The fact of the matter is, I've come to ask for your daughter Natália's hand in marriage.

**Choobookóv.** (*overjoyed*) My *dearest* friend! Iván Vassílievich. Could you repeat that—I'm not sure I heard right!

**Lómov.** I have the honor of asking—

**Choobookóv.** (*breaking in*) My oldest and dearest friend . . . I'm *so* delighted and so on . . . Yes really, and all that sort of thing. (*hugging and kissing him*) I've been yearning for this for ages. It's been my constant desire. (*sheds a tear*) And

I've always loved you like a son, you wonderful person, you. May God grant you love and guidance and so on, it's been my most fervent wish. . . . But why am I standing here like a blockhead? I'm dumbstruck by the sheer joy of it, completely dumbstruck. Oh, with all my heart and soul . . . I'll go get Natália, and so on.

**Lómov.**    (*deeply moved*) Stepán Stepánovich, my esteemed friend, do you think I may count on her accepting me?

**Choobookóv.**    A handsome devil like you? How could she possibly resist? She's *madly* in love with you, don't worry, *madly*, and so on . . . I'll call her right away. (*exit*)


## SCENE 2

**Lómov.**    (*alone*) It's so cold . . . I'm shaking all over, like before a final exam. The important thing is to make up your mind. If you think about it too long, or waver, talk about it too much, and wait for the ideal woman or for true love, you'll never marry. . . . Brr! It's cold! Natália Stepánovna is an excellent housekeeper, she's not bad-looking, and she's got some education. . . . What more could I ask for? Oh, I'm so nervous, I can hear a buzzing in my ears. (*Drinks some water.*) It would be best for me to get married . . . First of all, I'm thirty-five years old already—and that, as they say, is a critical age. And then, I have to start leading a steady and regular life. . . . I've got a heart condition, with palpitations[2] all the time. . . . I've got an awful temper, and I'm always getting terribly wrought up. . . . Even now, my lips are trembling and my right eyelid is twitching. . . . But the worst thing is when I try to sleep. The instant I get to bed and start dropping off, something *stabs* me in my left side—ungh! And it cuts right through my shoulder straight into my head—ungh! I jump like a lunatic, walk about a little, and then I lie down again, but

---

[2]irregular, rapid beating of the heart

the moment I start to doze off, I feel it in my side again—ungh! And it keeps on and on for at least twenty times. . . .

### SCENE 3   (Natália Stepánovna *and* Lómov.)

**Natália.**   (*entering*) Ah, it's you. And Papa said a customer had come for the merchandise. How do you do Iván Vassílievich!

**Lómov.**   How do you do, my esteemed Natália Stepánovna!

**Natália.**   I'm sorry about my apron and not being dressed. . . . We're shelling peas for drying. Where've you been keeping yourself? Have a seat. . . . (*They sit down.*) Would you like a bite of lunch?

**Lómov.**   Thank you so much, but I've already eaten.

**Natália.**   Well, then have a cigarette. . . . The matches are over here. . . . The weather's magnificent today, but yesterday it rained so hard that the men couldn't do a thing all day long. How much hay did *you* get done? Can you imagine, I was so greedy that I had the whole meadow mown, and now I regret it, I'm scared that all my hay may rot. I should have waited. But what's this? I do believe you're wearing a morning coat! How original! Are you going to a ball or something? Incidentally, you're getting quite handsome. . . . But honestly, why are you all dolled up?

**Lómov.**   (*nervously*) You see, my esteemed Natália Stepánovna . . . the fact is I've made up my mind to ask you to listen to me. . . . Naturally you'll be surprised and even angry, but I . . . (*aside*) God, it's cold!

**Natália.**   What is it? (*pause*) Well?

**Lómov.**   I'll try to be brief. You are well aware, my esteemed Natália Stepánovna, that for a long time now, in fact since my childhood, I have had the honor of knowing your family. My late aunt and her husband, whose estate as you know I inherited, always held your father and your late mother in utmost esteem. The Lómov family and the

Choobookóv family have always maintained extremely friendly, one might even say, intimate relations. Furthermore, as you know, my property borders on yours. Perhaps you will be so kind as to recall that my Ox Meadows run along your birch forest.

**Natália.** Excuse me for interrupting you. You said "*my* Ox Meadows" . . . are they *yours?*

**Lómov.** Of course. . . .

**Natália.** Oh, come now! The Ox Meadows belong to us, not you!

**Lómov.** Oh no! They're mine, dear Natália Stepánovna.

**Natália.** That's news to me. How did they ever get to be yours?

**Lómov.** What do you mean? I'm talking about the Ox Meadows that are wedged in between your birch forest and the Burnt Marsh.

**Natália.** Exactly. . . . They're ours.

**Lómov.** No, you're mistaken, dear Natália Stepánovna— they're mine.

**Natália.** Do be reasonable, Iván Vassílievich! Since when have they been yours?

**Lómov.** Since when? They've always been ours, as far back as I can remember.

**Natália.** Excuse me, but this is too much!

**Lómov.** You can look at the documents, dear Natália Stepánovna. At one time, there *were* some quarrels about the Ox Meadows, you're quite right. But now, everyone knows they're mine. Why argue about it? If you will permit me to explain: my aunt's grandmother lent them to your paternal great-grandfather's peasants for an indefinite period and free of charge in return for their firing her bricks. Your great-grandfather's peasants used the Meadows free of charge for some forty years and began thinking of them as their own . . . and then after the Emancipation, when a statute[3] was passed—

**Natália.**    You've got it all wrong! Both my grandfather and great-grandfather regarded their property as reaching all the way to the Burnt Swamp—which means that the Ox Meadows were ours. What's there to argue about?—I don't understand. How annoying!

**Lómov.**    I'll show you the documents, Natália Stepánovna.

**Natália.**    No; you're joking or trying to tease me. . . . What a surprise! We've owned that land for practically three hundred years and now suddenly we're told it's not ours! I'm sorry, Iván Vassílievich, but I just can't believe my ears. Those Meadows don't mean a thing to me. The whole area probably doesn't come to more than forty acres, it's worth about three hundred rubles;[4] but I'm terribly upset by the injustice of it all. You can say what you like, but I simply can't stand injustice.

**Lómov.**    Please listen to me, I beseech you. Your paternal great-grandfather's peasants, as I have already had the honor of telling you, fired bricks for my aunt's grandmother. Now, my aunt's grandmother, wishing to do them a favor in return—

**Natália.**    Grandfather, grandmother, aunt . . . I don't know *what* you're talking about! The Meadows are *ours*, and that's that.

**Lómov.**    They're *mine!*

**Natália.**    They're ours! You can keep arguing for two days, you can put on fifteen morning coats if you like, but they're ours, ours, ours! . . . I don't desire *your* property, but I don't care to lose mine. . . . Do as you like!

**Lómov.**    I don't need the Meadows, Natália Stepánovna, but

[3]law

[4]Russian unit of money

it's the principle of the thing. If you want, I'll *give* them to you.

**Natália.**    It would be *my* privilege to give them to *you*, they're mine! . . . All this is rather odd—to put it mildly, Iván Vassílievich. Up till now we've always considered you a good neighbor and friend. Last year we let you borrow our threshing machine, and as a result we couldn't finish our own grain until November, and now you're treating us like Gypsies. You're *giving* me my own land. Excuse me, but that's not a neighborly thing to do! To *my* mind, it's impertinent,[5] if you care to—

**Lómov.**    Are you trying to tell me that I'm a land-grabber? Madam, I've never seized anyone else's property, and I won't allow anyone to *say* I have. . . . (*hurries over to the carafe and drinks some water*) The Ox Meadows are mine!

**Natália.**    That's not true, they're ours.

**Lómov.**    They're mine.

**Natália.**    That's not true. I'll prove it to you! I'll send my men over to mow them this afternoon.

**Lómov.**    What?!

**Natália.**    My men will be there this afternoon!

**Lómov.**    I'll kick them out!

**Natália.**    You wouldn't dare!

**Lómov.**    (*clutching at his heart*) The Ox Meadows are mine! Do you hear! Mine!

**Natália.**    Stop shouting! Please! You can shout your lungs out in your own place, but I must ask you to control yourself here.

**Lómov.**    Madam, if it weren't for these awful, excruciating palpitations and the veins throbbing in my temples, I'd speak to you in a totally different way! (*shouting*) The Ox Meadows are mine.

---

[5]rude; disrespectful

**Natália.**   Ours!

**Lómov.**   Mine!

**Natália.**   Ours!

**Lómov.**   Mine!


## SCENE 4   (*Enter* **Choobookóv.**)

**Choobookóv.**   What's going on? What's all the shouting about?

**Natália.**   Papa, please tell this gentleman whom the Ox Meadows belong to. Us or him.

**Choobookóv.**   (*to* **Lómov**) Why, the Meadows belong to us, old friend.

**Lómov.**   But for goodness' sake, Stepán Stepánovich, how can that be? Can't *you* be reasonable at least? My aunt's grandmother lent the Meadows to your grandfather's peasants for temporary use and free of charge. His peasants used the land for forty years and got in the habit of regarding it as their own, but after the Land Settlement—

**Choobookóv.**   Excuse me, old boy . . . You're forgetting that our peasants didn't pay your grandmother and so on precisely *because* the Meadows were disputed and what not . . . But now every child knows that they're ours. I guess you've never looked at the maps.

**Lómov.**   I'll *prove* they're mine.

**Choobookóv.**   You won't prove a thing, my boy.

**Lómov.**   I will *so* prove it!

**Choobookóv.**   My dear boy, why carry on like this? You won't prove a thing by shouting. I don't want anything of yours, but I don't intend to let go of what's mine. Why should I? If it comes to that, dear friend, if you mean to dispute my ownership of the Meadows, and so on, I'd sooner let my peasants have them than you. So there!

**Lómov.**   I don't understand. What right do you have to give away other people's property?

**Choobookóv.**   Allow me to decide whether or not I've got the right. Really, young man, I'm not accustomed to being spoken to in that tone of voice, and what not. I'm old enough to be your father, and I must ask you to calm down when you speak to me, and so forth.

**Lómov.**   No! You're treating me like an idiot, and laughing at me. You tell me that *my* property is yours, and then you expect me to remain calm and talk to you in a normal fashion. That's not a very neighborly thing to do, Stepán Stepánovich. You're no neighbor, you're a robber baron.

**Choobookóv.**   What?! What did you say, my good man?

**Natália.**   Papa, have the men mow the Ox Meadows right now!

**Choobookóv.**   (*to* **Lómov**) What did you say, sir?

**Natália.**   The Ox Meadows are our property, and I won't let anyone else have them. I won't, I won't, I won't!

**Lómov.**   We'll see about that! I'll prove to you in court that they're mine.

**Choobookóv.**   In court? My good man, you can take it to court and what not. Go right ahead! I know you, you've just been waiting for a chance to litigate, and so on. You're a quibbler from the word go. Your whole family's nothing but a bunch of pettifoggers.[6] All of them!

**Lómov.**   I must ask you not to insult my family. The Lómovs have always been law-abiding folk. None of them was ever hauled into court for embezzlement the way your uncle was.

**Choobookóv.**   Every last one of them was insane.

**Natália.**   Every last one of them, every last one!

**Choobookóv.**   Your grandfather drank like a fish, and the whole country knows that your youngest aunt, Nastasia, ran off with an architect, and what not—

---

[6]one who argues about insignificant matters

**Lómov.** And your mother was a hunchback! (*clutching at his heart*) There's a twitching in my side. . . . My head's throbbing. . . . Oh, God . . . Water!

**Choobookóv.** And your father was a gambler and he ate like a pig!

**Natália.** And no one could beat your aunt at scandalmongering.[7]

**Lómov.** My left leg's paralyzed. . . . And you're a schemer. . . . Oooh! My heart! . . . And it's no secret to anyone that just before the elections you—There are stars bursting before my eyes. . . . Where's my hat?

**Natália.** Vermin! Liar! Brute!

**Choobookóv.** You're a spiteful, double-dealing schemer! So there!

**Lómov.** Ah, my hat . . . My heart. Where am I? Where's the door? Oooh! . . . I think I'm dying . . . My foot's totally paralyzed. (*drags himself to the door*)

**Choobookóv.** (*calling after him*) And don't ever set your foot in my home again!

**Natália.** Go to court! Sue us! Just wait and see!

(**Lómov** *staggers out.*)


## SCENE 5   (**Choobookóv** *and* **Natália Stepánovna**.)

**Choobookóv.** He can go straight to hell, damn him! (*walks about, all wrought up*)

**Natália.** Isn't he the worst crook? Catch me trusting a good neighbor after this!

**Choobookóv.** The chiseler! The scarecrow!

**Natália.** The monster! He not only grabs other people's property, he calls them names, to boot.

[7]dealing with gossip or rumors

**Choobookóv.** And that clown, that . . . freak had the colossal nerve to ask me for your hand in marriage, and so on. Can you imagine? He wanted to propose.

**Natália.** Propose?

**Choobookóv.** Exactly? That's what he came for. To propose to you.

**Natália.** Propose? To me? Why didn't you *say* so?

**Choobookóv.** And he got all dolled up in a morning coat. That pipsqueak. That upstart.

**Natália.** Propose? To me? Ohhh! (*collapses into an armchair and wails*) Bring him back. Get him. Ohh! Get him!

**Choobookóv.** Get whom?

**Natália.** Hurry up, hurry! I feel sick. Bring him back. (*hysterical*)

**Choobookóv.** What is it? What's wrong? (*grabbing his head*) This is awful! I'll shoot myself. I'll hang myself. They've worn me out.

**Natália.** I'm dying! Bring him back!

**Choobookóv.** All right. Stop yelling! (*runs out*)

**Natália.** (*alone, wailing*) What've we done? Bring him back! Bring him back!

**Choobookóv.** (*running in*) He's coming and all that, damn him. Ughh! *You* talk to him, alone, I really don't feel like . . .

**Natália.** (*wailing*) Bring him back!

**Choobookóv.** (*shouting*) He's coming, I tell you. Oh God! What did I ever do to deserve a grown-up daughter? I'll cut my throat. I swear, I'll cut my throat. We insulted and abused him, and it's all your fault!

**Natália.** My fault? It was yours!

**Choobookóv.** Now *I'm* the culprit!

(**Lómov** *appears at the French doors.* **Choobookóv** *exits.*)

## SCENE 6 (Natalia *and* Lómov)

**Lómov.** *(entering, exhausted)* What horrible palpitations . . . my foot's gone numb . . . there's a jabbing in my side . . .

**Natália.** My apologies, Iván Vassílievich, we got so worked up. . . . I do recall now that the Ox Meadows are actually *your* property.

**Lómov.** My heart's palpitating. . . . The Meadows *are* mine. . . . There are stars bursting in both my eyes.

*(They sit down.)*

**Natália.** We were wrong.

**Lómov.** It's the principle of the thing. . . . I don't care about the land, it's the principle of the thing—

**Natália.** Exactly, the principle . . . Let's talk about something else.

**Lómov.** Particularly since I have proof. My aunt's grandmother let your paternal great-grandfather's peasants—

**Natália.** All right, all right . . . *(aside)* I don't know how to go about it. . . . *(to* **Lómov***)* Will you start hunting soon?

**Lómov.** Yes, for grouse,[8] Natália Stepánovna. I think I shall begin after the harvest. Oh, have you heard what bad luck I had? My hound Guess—you know the one—he's gone lame.

**Natália.** What a pity! How did it happen?

**Lómov.** I don't know. He must have twisted his leg, or else some other dog bit him. . . . *(sighs)* My very best hound, not to mention the money! Why, I paid Mirónov a hundred and twenty-four rubles for him.

**Natália.** You overpaid him, Iván Vassílievich.

**Lómov.** I don't think so. It was very little for a wonderful dog.

**Natália.** Papa bought his dog Leap for eighty-five rubles, and Leap is vastly superior to your Guess.

---

[8] type of bird

**Lómov.** Leap superior to Guess? Oh, come now. *(laughs)* Leap superior to Guess!

**Natália.** Of course he is! I know that Leap is still young, he's not a full-grown hound yet. But for points and action, not even Volchanietsky has a better dog.

**Lómov.** Excuse me, Natália Stepánovna, but you're forgetting that he's pug-jawed, which makes him a poor hunting dog.

**Natália.** Pug-jawed? That's news to me.

**Lómov.** I can assure you, his lower jaw is shorter than his upper jaw.

**Natália.** Have you measured it?

**Lómov.** Indeed, I have. He'll do for pointing, of course, but when it comes to retrieving, he can hardly hold a cand—

**Natália.** First of all, our Leap is a pedigreed grey-hound—he's the son of Harness and Chisel, whereas your Guess is so pie-bald[9] that not even Solomon could figure out his breed.. . . Furthermore, he's as old and ugly as a broken-down nag—

**Lómov.** He may be old, but I wouldn't trade him for five of your Leaps. . . . The very idea! Guess is a real hound, but Leap . . . Why argue? It's ridiculous. . . . Every huntsman's assistant has a dog like your Leap. At twenty-five rubles he'd be overpriced.

**Natália.** You seem to be possessed by some demon of contradiction, Iván Vassílievich. First you fancy that the Ox Meadows are yours, then you pretend that Guess is a better hound than Leap. If there's one thing I don't like it's a person who says the opposite of what he thinks. You know perfectly well that Leap is a hundred times better than . . . than that stupid Guess of yours. Why do you insist on denying it?

**Lómov.** You obviously must think, Natália Stepánovna, that I'm either blind or mentally retarded. Can't you see that your Leap has a pug jaw?

---

[9]spotted or patched in two colors, usually black and white

**Natália.**   That's not true.

**Lómov.**   A pug jaw.

**Natália.**   (*screaming*) That's not true.

**Lómov.**   Why are you screaming, Madam?

**Natália.**   Why are you talking such rubbish? It's exasperating! Your Guess is just about ready to be put out of his misery, and you compare him to Leap.

**Lómov.**   Excuse me, but I can't keep on arguing like this. My heart's palpitating.

**Natália.**   I've noticed that the sportsmen who argue most don't understand the first thing about hunting.

**Lómov.**   Madam, pleeeease, keep quiet . . . My heart's bursting. . . . (*shouts*) Keep quiet!

**Natália.**   I won't keep quiet until you admit that Leap is a hundred times superior to your Guess.

**Lómov.**   He's a hundred times *inferior*. Someone ought to shoot him. My temples . . . my eyes . . . my shoulder . . .

**Natália.**   No one has to wish that idiotic mutt of yours dead, because he's just skin and bones anyway.

**Lómov.**   Keep quiet! I'm having heart failure!

**Natália.**   I will *not* keep quiet!


## SCENE 7

**Choobookóv.**   (*entering*) What's going on now?

**Natália.**   Papa, tell me, honestly and sincerely: which is the better dog—our Leap, or his Guess?

**Lómov.**   Stepán Stepánovich, I beseech you, just tell me one thing: is your Leap pug-jawed or isn't he? Yes or no?

**Choobookóv.**   So what! Who cares? He's still the best hound in the country, and what not.

**Lómov.**   And my Guess isn't better? Tell the truth.

**Choobookóv.**   Don't get all worked up, old boy. . . . Let me explain. . . . Your Guess *does* have a few good qualities. . . . He's pure-bred, he's got solid legs, he's well put together, and what not. But if you must know, my good man, your dog's got two basic faults: he's old, and his muzzle's too short.

**Lómov.**   Excuse me, my heart's racing madly. . . . Let's examine the facts. . . . Please don't forget that when we were hunting in the Mapooskin Fields, my Guess ran neck and neck with the count's dog Waggy, while your Leap lagged behind by half a mile.

**Choobookóv.**   That was because the count's assistant struck him with his riding crop.

**Lómov.**   Naturally. All the other dogs were chasing the fox, but yours started running after sheep.

**Choobookóv.**   That's a lie! My dear boy, I fly off the handle easily, so please let's stop arguing. The man whipped him because people are always envious of everyone else's dogs. Yes, they're all filled with spite! And you, sir, are no exception. Why, the minute you notice that anyone else's dog is better than your Guess, you instantly start up something or other . . . and what not. I've got the memory of an elephant!

**Lómov.**   And so do I.

**Choobookóv.**   (*mimicking him*) "And so do I." . . . And what does your memory tell you?

**Lómov.**   My heart's palpitating. . . . My foot's paralyzed. . . . I can't anymore . . .

**Natália.**   (*mimicking*) "My heart's palpitating . . ." What kind of hunter are you anyway? You ought to be home in bed catching cockroaches instead of out hunting foxes. Palpitations! . . .

**Choobookóv.**   That's right, what kind of hunter are you? If you've got palpitations, stay home; don't go wobbling around the countryside on horseback. It wouldn't be so bad if you really hunted, but you only tag along in order to start arguments or meddle with other people's dogs, and what not. We'd better stop, I fly off the handle easily. You, sir, are not a hunter, and that's that.

**Lómov.**   And you *are*, I suppose. The only reason *you* go hunting is to flatter the count and carry on your backstabbing little intrigues. . . . Oh, my heart! . . . You schemer!

**Choobookóv.**   Me, a schemer. (*shouting*) Shut up!

**Lómov.**   Schemer!

**Choobookóv.**   Upstart! Pipsqueak!

**Lómov.**   You old fogy! You hypocrite!

**Choobookóv.**   Shut up, or I'll blast you with a shotgun like a partridge.

**Lómov.**   The whole county knows that—Oh, my heart!—your late wife used to beat you. . . . My leg . . . my temples . . . I see stars . . . I'm falling, falling . . .

**Choobookóv.**   And your housekeeper henpecks you all over the place!

**Lómov.**   There, you see . . . my heart's burst! My shoulder's torn off. . . . Where's my shoulder? . . . I'm dying! (*collapses into armchair*) Get a doctor! (*faints*)

**Choobookóv.**   Pipsqueak. Weakling. Windbag. I feel sick. (*drinks some water*) I feel sick.

**Natália.**   What kind of hunter are you anyway? You don't even know how to sit in a saddle! (*to her father*) Papa! What's the matter with him? Papa! Look, Papa! (*screams*) Iván Vassílievich! He's dead!

**Choobookóv.**   I feel sick! . . . I can't breathe! . . . Air!

**Natália.**   He's dead! (*tugs at* **Lómov**'s *sleeve*) Iván Vassílievich!

Iván Vassílievich! What've we done? He's dead. (*collapses into easy chair*) Get a doctor. (*She becomes hysterical.*)

**Choobookóv.** Oh! . . . What is it? What's wrong?

**Natália.** (*moaning*) He's dead . . . he's dead!

**Choobookóv.** Who's dead? (*glancing at* **Lómov**) He really is dead! Oh, my God! Get some water! Get a doctor! (*holds a glass to* **Lómov**'s *mouth*) Go ahead and drink! . . . He won't drink. . . . I guess he's dead and so on. . . . Why does everything have to happen to me? Why didn't I put a bullet through my head long ago? Why didn't I cut my throat? What am I waiting for? Give me a knife! Give me a gun! (**Lómov** *stirs.*) He's reviving, I think. . . . Drink some water! . . . That's right.

**Lómov.** Stars . . . fog . . . where am I?

**Choobookóv.** You two'd better hurry up and get married . . . Dammit! She accepts. . . . (*joins* **Lómov's** *hand with* **Natalia**'s) She accepts. . . . My blessings and so forth. . . . Just do me a favor and leave me in peace.

**Lómov.** What? (*getting up*) Who?

**Choobookóv.** She accepts. Well? Kiss her.

**Natália.** (*moaning*) He's alive. . . . I accept, I accept. . . .

**Choobookóv.** Kiss and make up.

**Lómov.** What? Who? (*kisses* **Natalia**) Enchanté . . . Excuse me, but what's going on? Oh yes, I remember. . . . My heart . . . stars . . . I'm very happy, Natália Stepánovna. (*kisses her hands*) My leg's paralyzed. . . .

**Natália.** I . . . I'm very happy, too. . . .

**Choobookóv.** That's a load off my back. . . . Whew!

**Natália.** But . . . all the same, why don't you finally admit that Guess isn't as good as Leap?

**Lómov.** He's much better.

**Natália.**   He's worse.

**Choobookóv.**   The launching of marital bliss! Champagne!

**Lómov.**   He's better.

**Natália.**   Worse! Worse! Worse!

**Choobookóv.**   (*trying to outshout them*) Champagne! Champagne!

## REVIEWING AND INTERPRETING

Record your answers to these questions in your personal
literature notebook. Follow the directions for each part.

REVIEWING

Try to complete each of these sentences without looking back
at the play.

*Recalling Facts*

**1.** Lómov visits Choobookóv in order to
   a. get help for his medical problems.
   b. ask for a loan.
   c. ask to marry his daughter.
   d. start a quarrel.

*Identifying Cause
and Effect*

**2.** Lómov and Natália first begin to quarrel because
   a. their ancestors were enemies.
   b. Natália can't stand Lómov's complaining.
   c. they keep interrupting each other.
   d. they both claim the Ox Meadows for their own.

*Indentifying Sequence*

**3.** Natália orders her father to bring Lómov back to her
   a. after she finds out he wants to marry her.
   b. after they begin to quarrel about their hounds.
   c. before Lómov complains of palpitations.
   d. after Lómov is revived from his faint.

*Understanding
Main Ideas*

**4.** Lómov wants to marry Natália because
   a. he is deeply in love with her.
   b. he wants her land.
   c. he is getting older and thinks it's time to settle down.
   d. his family and her family have always been friendly.

*Recognizing the Elements of a Play (Stage Directions)*

**5.** All of these props and costumes are mentioned in the stage directions *except*
   a. a glass of water.
   b. champagne.
   c. white gloves.
   d. an armchair.

**INTERPRETING**

To complete these sentences, you may look back at the play if you'd like.

*Making Inferences*

**6.** When Lómov hurries to get a drink of water, it usually means that he
   a. has forgotten what he was going to say next.
   b. especially enjoys the water at Choobookóv's house.
   c. needs to take a pill.
   d. is nervous or upset.

*Analyzing*

**7.** The word that best describes the conversation between Lómov and his neighbors is
   a. childish.
   b. friendly.
   c. intelligent.
   d. boring.

*Predicting Outcomes*

**8.** The marriage of Lómov and Natália probably will be
   a. called off immediately.
   b. full of arguments.
   c. peaceful.
   d. full of laughter.

*Making Generalizations*

**9.** When Lómov looks for a wife, he follows this rule:
   a. Find a woman who is easy to get along with.
   b. Be sure you enjoy the woman's family.
   c. Marry a woman who can take care of you in your old age.
   d. Make sure you love the woman before you marry her.

*Understanding*
*Literary Elements*
*(Conflict)*

**10.** Most of the conflict in this play occurs
   a. between a character and a force of nature.
   b. between characters.
   c. within a character's own mind.
   d. between a character and society in general.

Now check your answers with your teacher. Study the questions you answered incorrectly. What types of questions were they? Talk with your teacher about ways to work on those skills.

# *Theme*

Have you ever heard the saying, "With age comes wisdom"? Most people believe that you need to live through a number of interesting or difficult situations before you can begin to understand yourself, other people, and the world in general. One of the reasons that writers write is to share the insights they have gained in their lives. Sometimes the theme, or message, they share is simple and straightforward, and they actually state it somewhere in the work. For example, a character may say, "There's no place like home," as Dorothy does in *The Wizard of Oz*. At other times, however, readers must study the characters, the dialogue, the action, and their own reaction to all of these elements to understand the message that the author wants to communicate.

In any work of literature, there may be more than one theme. The major, or most important, theme is often easy to spot. It may come up over and over again throughout the story, novel, or play. Minor themes are not quite as important as the major theme. They usually work together to support the major theme.

As you read *A Marriage Proposal*, you may first be struck by the silliness of the plot and the humor of the dialogue. But if you reflect on what the author is trying to say with this glimpse into the childish behavior of adults, you will understand the serious message he is trying to communicate.

In these lessons, you will look at the ways in which playwright Anton Chekhov develops his themes:

1. He creates characters whose words and behavior communicate the theme.

2. He manipulates his readers' or audience's feelings to convey the theme.

3. He stresses the theme to influence readers' and audience's behavior.

## LESSON ① THEMES AND CHARACTERS

The characters in *A Marriage Proposal* are not realistic. The author has exaggerated their qualities to get across his theme about the childish behavior of so-called adults. In Lómov, Choobookóv, and Natália, Chekhov has created characters who are fickle, insincere, selfish, and ridiculous. For example, read this passage from the beginning of the play, when Choobookóv finds out that Lómov is not interested in borrowing money from him after all but wants to marry his daughter instead. Choobookóv's relief at not having to loan money and the possibility of marrying off his daughter make him appear to be filled with love and praise.

> **Choobookóv.** *(breaking in)* My oldest and dearest friend . . . I'm *so* delighted and so on . . . Yes really, and all that sort of thing. *(hugging and kissing him)* I've been yearning for this for ages. It's been my constant desire. *(sheds a tear)* And I've always loved you like a son, you wonderful person, you. May God grant you love and guidance and so on, it's been my most fervent wish. . . . But why am I standing here like a blockhead? I'm dumbstruck by the sheer joy of it, completely dumbstruck. Oh, with all my heart and soul . . . I'll go get Natália, and so on.

Now compare the previous passage with Choobookóv's later speech. Lómov has just claimed the Ox Meadows and is threatening legal action against Choobookóv. Remember that only a few minutes have passed.

> **Choobookóv.** In court? My good man, you can take it to court and what not. Go right ahead! I know you, you've just been waiting for a chance to litigate, and so on. You're a quibbler from the word go. Your whole family's nothing but a bunch of pettifoggers. All of them!

Clearly, Choobookóv was not sincere when he said earlier that he loved Lómov "like a son." Lómov could not have changed from a "wonderful person" to a "quibbler from the word go" in five minutes. It is difficult to believe anything that Choobookóv says because he blurts out the first thing that enters his mind without thinking, as a child would.

## EXERCISE ①

Read this passage from the play, in which Natália and Lómov quarrel about their hunting dogs. Then use what you have learned in this lesson to answer the questions that follow the passage.

> **Lómov.** Madam, pleeeease, keep quiet . . . My heart's bursting. . . . (*shouts*) Keep quiet!
>
> **Natália.** I won't keep quiet until you admit that Leap is a hundred times superior to your Guess.
>
> **Lómov.** He's a hundred times *inferior*. Someone ought to shoot him. My temples . . . my eyes . . . my shoulder . . .
>
> **Natália.** No one has to wish that idiotic mutt of yours dead, because he's just skin and bones anyway.
>
> **Lómov.** Keep quiet! I'm having heart failure!
>
> **Natália.** I will *not* keep quiet!

1. Lómov complains that he is having heart failure because he is so upset by the conversation. What is Natália's reaction to his problem? What does her reaction show about her maturity and her concern for Lómov?

2. Lómov knows that he is upsetting Natália, the woman he says he wants to marry, but he doesn't seem to care. How does his behavior differ from the way you would expect a suitor to act?

3. How do the words and actions of these two characters help the author express his theme?

Now check your answers with your teacher. Review this part of the lesson if you don't understand why an answer was incorrect.

### WRITING ON YOUR OWN ①

Use what you have learned in this lesson to complete the following writing activity:

- Review the lists of positive and negative human qualities that you created earlier.
- Choose one or two qualities from each list. Can you think of real people—personal acquaintances or people in the news—who show these qualities? Write the people's names next to the qualities they represent.
- Now choose one quality or trait to write about. Try to picture an imaginary person who exemplifies your chosen quality. Jot down notes about the person. For example, a proud person would brag a great deal. He or she might fail to recognize the good qualities in others, concentrating only on himself or herself. Write a short paragraph about the person and title it with the quality you feel he or she represents.
- Last, state a theme that helps explain your chosen human trait. For example, for the trait of pride, you might use the theme "Pride can make it difficult to admit when you are wrong."

## LESSON ② THEMES AND FEELINGS

When you read stories, novels, and plays, you often will feel a connection to the characters you read about. You put yourself in their situations and share their emotions. As the characters grow and develop in positive ways, you may find that you admire their perseverance or creativity. Your regard for the characters helps you understand the theme of the story—which might be the importance of personal courage or the power of love, for example.

On the other hand, you may grow to dislike some of the characters. You might become frustrated by their selfishness or foolishness. Sometimes, if you put yourself in the story, you might fear or strongly dislike the characters. Again, the author has influenced the way you feel about the characters in order to make you understand themes such as intolerance or cruelty.

When you were first introduced to the characters in *A Marriage Proposal,* you probably had no opinions of them. They probably seemed like pleasant, well-adjusted people. Soon, however, you probably realized their rudeness and lack of maturity as you read passages such as this one:

**Lómov**.   . . . The Ox Meadows are mine!
**Natália**.   That's not true, they're ours.
**Lómov**.   They're mine.
**Natália**.   That's not true. I'll prove it to you! I'll send my men over to mow them this afternoon.
**Lómov**.   What?!
**Natália**.   My men will be there this afternoon!
**Lómov**.   I'll kick them out!
**Natália**.   You wouldn't dare!
**Lómov**.   *(clutching at his heart)* The Ox Meadows are mine! Do you hear! Mine! . . .
**Natália**.   Ours!
**Lómov**.   Mine!
**Natália**.   Ours!
**Lómov**.   Mine!

When these characters quarrel, you may be reminded of the way toddlers fight over a toy. You may think that Lómov and Natália are funny, or you may think that they are ridiculous. However, it is unlikely that you would want to have either one for a friend, and you probably don't want to resemble them in any way. The author has used your feelings about the characters to convey his theme that childish behavior is not limited to children.

## EXERCISE ②

Read the following passage. Then use what you have learned in this lesson to answer the questions.

> **Natália.** (*moaning*) He's dead . . . he's dead!
> **Choobookóv.** Who's dead? (*glancing at* **Lómov**) He really is dead! Oh, my God! Get some water! Get a doctor! (*holds a glass to* **Lómov**'s *mouth*) Go ahead and drink! . . . He won't drink. . . . I guess he's dead and so on. . . . Why does everything have to happen to me? . . .

1. How does Choobookóv react to what seems to be the death of Lómov? Do you like or dislike Choobookóv at this point in the play? Why?

2. Consider the way you feel about Choobookóv. Based on your feelings, identify a minor theme of this play.

Now check your answers with your teacher. Review this part of the lesson if you don't understand why an answer was incorrect.

 WRITING ON YOUR OWN ②

In this exercise you will use what you have learned to write a brief monologue expressing a theme. (Remember that a monologue is a speech by only one person.) Follow these steps:

- Review the character and the theme that you wrote about in Writing on Your Own 1. What might that character say to himself or herself to express the theme? Jot down some thoughts that might go through the character's mind.
- Write a short monologue similar to the one in Scene 2 of *A Marriage Proposal.* In that monologue, you learn about Lómov's self-centered reasons for wanting to find a wife. Be sure that your character's monologue reveals your chosen quality clearly. Try to reinforce the theme by making your readers like or dislike the character.
- Reread your monologue aloud to a classmate. How does he or she feel about the character? See if your classmate can guess the theme you are trying to express. If necessary, make changes to make the theme clearer.

## LESSON ③   THEMES AND AUTHOR'S PURPOSE

Every author has a reason for writing. He or she may want to entertain, teach, or persuade. Or, like Chekhov, the author may want to achieve all three purposes.

Have you ever had someone say to you, "Grow up! Act your age! Don't be such a baby!"? If so, you probably didn't exactly welcome the advice. You may have felt defensive and angry. The chances are good that you didn't say dutifully, "I suppose you're right. I'm acting childish and selfish. I'll try to do better from now on."

Anton Chekhov understood how people think and react. He knew that they resent being reminded of their weaknesses and failings. Even so, he felt that people need to understand that occasionally they slip and don't live up to their highest ambitions. So he presented an entertaining comedy with ridiculous characters and outrageous dialogue to reflect people's actions and behaviors in a nonthreatening way and to persuade them to act with more kindness and less selfishness. Because he does not directly accuse his readers and audiences of being like these silly characters, people are free to see themselves in the play and change their behavior voluntarily.

What type of behavior is the author ridiculing in the following passage?

> **Choobookóv.**    My dear boy, why carry on like this? You won't prove a thing by shouting. I don't want anything of yours, but I don't intend to let go of what's mine. Why should I? If it comes to that, dear friend, if you mean to dispute my ownership of the Meadows, and so on, I'd sooner let my peasants have them than you. So there!

Readers and audiences recognize the greed and pettiness in Choobookóv's character. As they laugh, they recall people they know who act like Choobookóv. Finally, they may secretly admit that they themselves act or have acted like him on occasion.

## EXERCISE ③

Read this passage from the play. Then use what you have learned in this lesson to answer the questions that follow the passage.

> **Natália.**    But . . . all the same, why don't you finally admit that Guess isn't as good as Leap?
> **Lómov.**    He's much better.
> **Natália.**    He's worse.
> **Choobookóv.**    The launching of marital bliss! Champagne!
> **Lómov.**    He's better.
> **Natália.**    Worse! Worse! Worse!
> **Choobookóv.**    (*trying to outshout them*) Champagne! Champagne!

1. Between the angry jibes of Lómov and Natália, Choobookóv calls for a toast to the "launching of marital bliss." Based on this scene, how would you describe the author's opinion of marriage?

2. The author paints an unflattering picture of the way some people treat each other in marriage. What type of behavior between marriage partners is he encouraging by showing its opposite?

Now check your answers with your teacher. Review this part of the lesson if you don't understand why an answer was incorrect.

## WRITING ON YOUR OWN ③

In this exercise you will write a paragraph explaining how you might try to help a person change a negative behavior. Follow these steps:

- Do you have a pet peeve about certain people's behaviors? For example, perhaps you don't like it when people are not tactful or careful of others' feelings. Maybe you don't like it when people criticize others but fail to recognize their own faults. Make a list of your pet peeves.
- Then write a paragraph explaining how you might try to change a person who is often guilty of one of these unwelcome behaviors. Would you try to persuade the person to change by pointing out the problem and discussing it, would you try to trick him or her into changing, or would you try a different approach?

## DISCUSSION GUIDES

1. Chekhov has written a play that calls for exaggerated over-acting. Since the characters are almost cartoon-like in their reactions and overreactions, the actors need not be extremely sensitive or careful in their portrayal. You might have fun presenting a scene from this play. Work with one or two classmates to choose a scene, practice it, and present it to the rest of the class.

2. Chekhov ridicules the behavior of some of the wealthiest members of Russian society in the 1880s. Work with a partner to research the living conditions of the Russian people at the end of the nineteenth century. How many Russians were landowners at that time and how many were peasants? What were the rights of peasants as opposed to landowners? Write a short report and present it to the class.

3. At the end of the play, it appears that Lómov and Natália will get married despite their uncontrollable tendencies to argue and upset each other. Do you think this marriage is a good idea? Why do you think they probably will go through with it? What would be the advantages of the marriage, from both partners' points of view? Would the advantages outweigh the disadvantages? Discuss these questions with a small group and then compare your opinions with those of other groups in the class.

# WRITE A QUARREL THAT EXPRESSES A THEME

In this unit you have seen how authors use characters and feelings to develop themes and accomplish their purpose or purposes for writing. You also have worked on developing ideas for a theme of your own. Now it is time to express a theme by writing a quarrel similar to the one in *A Marriage Proposal*.

Follow these steps to complete your dialogue. If you have questions about the writing process, refer to Using the Writing Process on page 300.

- Assemble all the writing you did for this unit: *1)* two lists of positive and negative human qualities, *2)* a paragraph describing someone who displays one of the qualities and a statement of the theme that explains or illustrates that quality, *3)* a short monologue by that character, and *4)* a paragraph explaining how you would try to change someone's negative behavior.
- After reviewing all of your writing assignments, choose one quality or habit that angers you. State a theme about that quality, such as "People who are always late are frustrating."
- Decide who the characters in your quarrel will be. Limit the argument to two or three characters. At least one of the characters should display the quality or habit at the heart of your theme.
- Keeping the quarrels from *A Marriage Proposal* in mind, make notes about how the quarrel might begin and what each person might say. Decide how the quarrel will end.
- Now write the quarrel in the form of a scene from a play. See the plays in this book for the proper format.
- Proofread your writing for spelling, grammar, punctuation, capitalization, and formatting errors and then make a final copy. If possible, ask one or two classmates to help you present your scene to the rest of the class. When you have finished, save your scene in your writing portfolio.

# The Radio Play

# Sorry, Wrong Number

by Lucille Fletcher

## INTRODUCTION

*ABOUT THE SELECTION*

By mistake, Mrs. Stevenson, a bedridden invalid, overhears two men on the telephone plotting a murder. Upset and frightened, she calls a number of places, trying to prevent the murder from happening, but she cannot get anyone to help her.

The radio play *Sorry, Wrong Number* was written for a popular radio program called *Suspense*. *Suspense* was an anthology series—a different suspense story was aired every week, and there were no regular characters or settings. The series began in 1942 and ran for about 20 years, featuring some of the best mystery writers and major film stars of the time. The series tried to "chill you a little, thrill you a little. . . ." When you read this radio play, use your imagination and see if it chills and thrills you.

*ABOUT THE AUTHOR*

Lucille Fletcher was born in 1912 in Brooklyn and later attended Vassar College. In 1949, she married John Douglas Wallop III, also a writer, but continued to write under the name Lucille Fletcher. Although she has written fiction, she is best known for her plays for radio and television. Fletcher wrote 20 radio plays and a number of television scripts for *Chrysler Theatre* and *Lights Out*. Her most famous radio play, *Sorry, Wrong Number,* was written in 1948. It was so popular that it was made into a movie for which Fletcher also wrote the screenplay. In addition to her plays, Lucille Fletcher wrote several mystery novels, including *And Presumed Dead* and *The Girl in Cabin B54*.

**ABOUT THE LESSONS**

The lessons that follow *Sorry, Wrong Number* focus on a special kind of play, the radio play. Unlike a play that is presented on the stage, in films, or on television, the radio play must rely on only words and sounds to tell the story. Audiences cannot see the action, so they must use their imaginations to fill in what is happening as they listen to the words, music, and sound effects. Sitting in their living rooms instead of in a theater audience, radio-play listeners connect with the actors and actresses in a way that is impossible in other forms of drama. After all, radio listeners don't simply listen; they also help create the characters, the setting, and the action in their minds.

**WRITING:** DEVELOPING A PHONE CONVERSATION

At the end of this unit, you will write the dialogue for a phone conversation involving someone in an emergency situation. Follow these steps to get started:

- Cellular phones allow you to make telephone calls from almost anyplace on earth. Some people feel that having such a phone will allow them to call for help in any emergency. Think of a few emergency situations in which a cell phone would come in handy. Jot down your ideas.

- Now think of situations in which a person in trouble would need to talk to another person for a period longer than the time it takes to report an address and a problem. An example of such a situation might be finding yourself trapped in an elevator or being lost in the woods. Make a list of emergency situations that would require one person to talk with another for an extended period of time.
- Save your list to use in later writing exercises.

**AS YOU READ**

As you read this play, keep the following questions in mind. They will help you understand some of the ways in which Lucille Fletcher has created an effective radio play.

- How does the author create believable characters?
- What does she do to build suspense?
- How does she use sound effects to help advance the plot?

# Sorry, Wrong Number

◉

## by Lucille Fletcher

◉

◉

(*Sound: Number being dialed on phone; busy signal.*)

**Mrs. Stevenson.** (*a querulous,[1] self-centered neurotic[2]*) Oh—dear! (*Slams down receiver. Dials* **Operator**.)

**Operator.** Your call, please?

**Mrs. Stevenson.** Operator? I've been dialing Murray Hill 4-0098 now for the last three-quarters of an hour, and the line is always busy. But I don't see how it *could* be busy that long. Will you try it for me, please?

---

[1]complaining

[2]one who is anxious and fearful

**Operator.**   Murray Hill 4-0098? One moment, please.

**Mrs. Stevenson.**   I don't see how it could be busy all this time. It's my husband's office. He's working late tonight, and I'm all alone here in the house. My health is very poor—and I've been feeling so nervous all day—

**Operator.**   Ringing Murray Hill 4-0098.

*(Sound: Phone buzz. It rings three times. Receiver is picked up at the other end.)*

**Man.**   Hello.

**Mrs. Stevenson.**   Hello? *(a little puzzled)* Hello. Is Mr. Stevenson there?

**Man.**   *(into phone, as though he had not heard)* Hello. *(louder)* Hello.

**Second Man.**   *(slow, heavy quality, faintly foreign accent)* Hello.

**First Man.**   Hello. George?

**George.**   Yes, sir.

**Mrs. Stevenson.**   *(louder and more imperious,[3] to phone)* Hello. Who's this? What number am I calling, please?

**First Man.**   We have heard from our client. He says the coast is clear for tonight.

**George.**   Yes, sir.

**First Man.**   Where are you now?

**George.**   In a phone booth.

**First Man.**   Okay. You know the address. At eleven o'clock the private patrolman goes around to the bar on Second Avenue for a beer. Be sure that all the lights downstairs are out. There should be only one light visible from the street. At eleven fifteen a subway train crosses the bridge. It makes a noise in case her window is open and she should scream.

**Mrs. Stevenson.**   *(shocked)* Oh—hello! What number is this, please?

---

[3]overbearing and demanding

**George.**    Okay, I understand.

**First Man.**    Make it quick. As little blood as possible. Our client does not wish to make her suffer long.

**George.**    A knife okay, sir?

**First Man.**    Yes, a knife will be okay. And remember—remove the rings and bracelets, and the jewelry in the bureau drawer. Our client wishes it to look like simple robbery.

**George.**    Okay, I get— (*sound: a bland[4] buzzing signal*)

**Mrs. Stevenson.**    (*clicking phone*) Oh! (*Bland buzzing signal continues. She hangs up.*) How awful! How unspeakably— (*sound of dialing; phone buzz*)

**Operator.**    Your call, please?

**Mrs. Stevenson.**    (*unnerved[5] and breathless, into phone*) Operator, I—I've just been cut off.

**Operator.**    I'm sorry, madam. What number were you calling?

**Mrs. Stevenson.**    Why—it was supposed to be Murray Hill 4-0098, but it wasn't. Some wires must have crossed—I was cut into a wrong number—and—I've just heard the most dreadful thing—a—a murder—and— (*imperiously*) Operator, you'll simply have to retrace that call at once.

**Operator.**    I beg you pardon, madam—I don't quite—

**Mrs. Stevenson.**    Oh—I know it was a wrong number, and I had no business listening—but these two men—they were cold-blooded fiends—and they were going to murder somebody—some poor innocent woman—who was all alone—in a house near a bridge. And we've got to stop them—we've got to—

**Operator.**    (*patiently*) What number were you calling, madam?

**Mrs. Stevenson.**    That doesn't matter. This was a *wrong* number. And *you* dialed it. And we've got to find out what it was—immediately!

---

[4]soothing; dull

[5]destroyed calmness or composure

**Operator.**    But—madam—

**Mrs. Stevenson.**    Oh, why are you so stupid? Look, it was obviously a case of some little slip of the finger. I told you to try Murray Hill 4-0098 for me—you dialed it—but your finger must have slipped—and I was connected with some other number—and I could hear them, but they couldn't hear me. Now, I simply fail to see why you couldn't make that same mistake again—on purpose—why you couldn't *try* to dial Murray Hill 4-0098 in the same careless sort of way—

**Operator.**    *(quickly)* Murray Hill 4-0098? I will try to get it for you, madam.

**Mrs. Stevenson.**    *(sarcastically) Thank* You.

*(sound of ringing; busy signal)*

**Operator.**    I am sorry. Murray Hill 4-0098 is busy.

**Mrs. Stevenson.**    *(frantically clicking receiver)* Operator. Operator.

**Operator.**    Yes, madam.

**Mrs. Stevenson.**    *(angrily)* You *didn't* try to get that wrong number at all. I asked explicitly.[6] And all you did was dial correctly.

**Operator.**    I am sorry. What number were you calling?

**Mrs. Stevenson.**    Can't you, for once, forget what number I was calling, and do something specific? Now I want to trace that call. It's my civic duty—it's *your* civic duty—to trace that call—and to apprehend those dangerous killers—and if *you* won't—

**Operator.**    I will connect you with the Chief Operator.

**Mrs. Stevenson.**    *Please!*

*(sound of ringing)*

**Chief Operator.**    *(coolly and professionally)* This is the Chief Operator.

**Mrs. Stevenson.**    Chief Operator? I want you to trace a call. A

---

[6]plainly; clearly

telephone call. Immediately. I don't know where it came from, or who was making it, but it's absolutely necessary that it be tracked down. Because it was about a murder. Yes, a terrible cold-blooded murder of a poor innocent woman—tonight—at eleven fifteen.

**Chief Operator.**    I see.

**Mrs. Stevenson.**    *(high-strung, demanding)* Can you trace it for me? Can you track down those men?

**Chief Operator.**    It depends, madam.

**Mrs. Stevenson.**    Depends on what?

**Chief Operator.**    It depends on whether the call is still going on. If it's a live call, we can trace it on the equipment. If it's been disconnected, we can't.

**Mrs. Stevenson.**    Disconnected?

**Chief Operator.**    If the parties have stopped talking to each other.

**Mrs. Stevenson.**    Oh—but—but of course they must have stopped talking to each other by *now*. That was at least five minutes ago—and they didn't sound like the type who would make a long call.

**Chief Operator.**    Well, I can try tracing it. Now—what is your name, madam?

**Mrs. Stevenson.**    Mrs. Stevenson. Mrs. Elbert Stevenson. But—listen—

**Chief Operator.**    *(writing it down)* And your telephone number?

**Mrs. Stevenson.**    *(more irritated)* Plaza 4-2295. But if you go on wasting all this time—

**Chief Operator.**    And what is your reason for wanting this call traced?

**Mrs. Stevenson.**    My reason? Well—for heaven's sake—isn't it obvious? I overheard two men—they're killers—they're planning to murder this woman—it's a matter for the police.

**Chief Operator.**    Have you told the police?

**Mrs. Stevenson.**    No. How could I?

**Chief Operator.**    You're making this check into a private call purely as a private individual?

**Mrs. Stevenson.**    Yes. But meanwhile—

**Chief Operator.**    Well, Mrs. Stevenson—I seriously doubt whether we could make this check for you at this time just on your say-so as a private individual. We'd have to have something more official.

**Mrs. Stevenson.**    Oh, for heaven's sake! You mean to tell me I can't report a murder without getting tied up in all this red tape? Why, it's perfectly idiotic. All right, then, I *will* call the police. (*She slams down receiver.*) Ridiculous!

(*sound of dialing*)

**Second Operator.**    Your call, please?

**Mrs. Stevenson.**    (*very annoyed*) The Police Department— please.

**Second Operator.**    Ringing the Police Department.

(*Rings twice. Phone is picked up.*)

**Sergeant Duffy.**    Police Department. Precinct 43. Duffy speaking.

**Mrs. Stevenson.**    Police Department? Oh. This is Mrs. Stevenson—Mrs. Elbert Smythe Stevenson of 53 North Sutton Place. I'm calling to report a murder.

**Sergeant Duffy.**    Eh?

**Mrs. Stevenson.**    I mean—the murder hasn't been committed yet. I just overheard plans for it over the telephone . . . over a wrong number that the operator gave me. I've been trying to trace down the call myself, but everybody is so stupid—and I guess in the end you're the only people who could *do* anything.

**Duffy.**    (*not too impressed*) Yes, ma'am.

**Mrs. Stevenson.**    (*trying to impress him*) It was a perfectly *definite* murder. I heard their plans distinctly. Two men were talking, and they were going to murder some woman at eleven fifteen tonight—she lived in a house near a bridge.

**Duffy.**    Yes, ma'am.

**Mrs. Stevenson.**    And there was a private patrolman on the street. He was going to go around for a beer on Second Avenue. And there was some third man—a client—who was paying to have this poor woman murdered— They were going to take her rings and bracelets—and use a knife— Well, it's unnerved me dreadfully—and I'm not well—

**Duffy.**    I see. When was all this, ma'am?

**Mrs. Stevenson.**    About eight minutes ago. Oh . . . (*relieved*) then you *can* do something? You *do* understand—

**Duffy.**    And what is your name, ma'am?

**Mrs. Stevenson.**    (*impatiently*) Mrs. Stevenson. Mrs. Elbert Stevenson.

**Duffy.**    And your address?

**Mrs. Stevenson.**    53 North Sutton Place. *That's* near a bridge, the Queensborough Bridge, you know—and *we* have a private patrolman on *our* street—and Second Avenue—

**Duffy.**    And what was that number you were calling?

**Mrs. Stevenson.**    Murray Hill 4-0098. But—that wasn't the number I overheard. I mean Murray Hill 4-0098 is my husband's office. He's working late tonight, and I was trying to reach him to ask him to come home. I'm an invalid, you know—and it's the maid's night off—and I *hate* to be alone—even though he says I'm perfectly safe as long as I have the telephone right beside my bed.

**Duffy.**    (*stolidly*) Well, we'll look into it, Mrs. Stevenson, and see if we can check it with the telephone company.

**Mrs. Stevenson.**    (*getting impatient*) But the telephone company said they couldn't check the call if the parties had stopped talking. I've already taken care of *that*.

**Duffy.**  Oh, yes?

**Mrs. Stevenson.**  (*highhanded[7]*) Personally I feel you ought to do something far more immediate and drastic than just check the call. What good does checking the call do, if they've stopped talking? By the time you track it down, they'll already have committed the murder.

**Duffy.**  Well, we'll take care of it, lady. Don't worry.

**Mrs. Stevenson.**  I'd say the whole thing calls for a search—a complete and thorough search of the whole city. I'm very near a bridge, and I'm not far from Second Avenue. And I know *I'd* feel a whole lot better if you sent a radio car to *this* neighborhood at once.

**Duffy.**  And what makes you think the murder's going to be committed in your neighborhood, ma'am?

**Mrs. Stevenson.**  Oh, I don't know. This coincidence is so horrible. Second Avenue—the patrolman—the bridge—

**Duffy.**  Second Avenue is a very long street ma'am. And do you happen to know how many bridges there are in the city of New York alone? Not to mention Brooklyn, Staten Island, Queens, and the Bronx? And how do you know there isn't some little house out on Staten Island—on some little Second Avenue you've never heard about? How do you know they were even talking about New York at all?

**Mrs. Stevenson.**  But I heard the call on the New York dialing system.

**Duffy.**  How do you know it wasn't a long-distance call you overheard? Telephones are funny things. Look, lady, why don't you look at it this way? Supposing you hadn't broken in on that telephone call? Supposing you'd got your husband the way you always do? Would this murder have made any difference to you then?

---

[7]proud and haughty

**Mrs. Stevenson.**    I suppose not. But it's so inhuman—so cold-blooded—

**Duffy.**    A lot of murders are committed in this city every day, ma'am. If we could do something to stop 'em, we would. But a clue of this kind that's so vague isn't much more use to us than no clue at all.

**Mrs. Stevenson.**    But surely—

**Duffy.**    Unless, of course, you have some reason for thinking this call is phony—and that someone may be planning to murder *you?*

**Mrs. Stevenson.**    *Me?* Oh, no, I hardly think so. I—I mean— why should anybody? I'm alone all day and night—I see nobody except my maid Eloise—she's a big two-hundred-pounder—she's too lazy to bring up my breakfast tray—and the only other person is my husband Elbert—he's crazy about me—adores me—waits on me hand and foot—he's scarcely left my side since I took sick twelve years ago—

**Duffy.**    Well, then, there's nothing for you to worry about, is there? And now, if you'll just leave the rest to us—

**Mrs. Stevenson.**    But what will you *do?* It's so late—it's nearly eleven o'clock.

**Duffy.**    (*firmly*) We'll take care of it, lady.

**Mrs. Stevenson.**    Will you broadcast it all over the city? And send out squads? And warn your radio cars to watch out— especially in suspicious neighborhoods like mine?

**Duffy.**    (*more firmly*) Lady, I *said* we'd take care of it. Just now I've got a couple of other matters here on my desk that require my immediate—

**Mrs. Stevenson.**    Oh! (*She slams down receiver hard.*) Idiot. (*looking at phone nervously*) Now, why did I do that? Now he'll think I *am* a fool. Oh, why doesn't Elbert come home? *Why* doesn't he?

(*sound of dialing operator*)

**Operator.**   Your call, please?

**Mrs. Stevenson.**   Operator, for heaven's sake, will you ring that Murray Hill 4-0098 number again? I can't think what's keeping him so long.

**Operator.**   Ringing Murray Hill 4-0098. (*Rings. Busy signal.*) The line is busy. Shall I—

**Mrs. Stevenson.**   (*nastily*) I can hear it. You don't have to tell me. I know it's busy. (*slams down receiver*) If I could only get out of this bed for a little while. If I could get a breath of fresh air—or just lean out the window—and see the street— (*The phone rings. She darts for it instantly.*) Hello. Elbert? Hello. Hello. Hello. Oh, what's the *matter* with this phone? *Hello? Hello?* (*slams down receiver*) (*The phone rings again, once. She picks it up.*) Hello? Hello— Oh, for heaven's sake, who *is* this? Hello. Hello. *Hello.* (*Slams down receiver. Dials operator.*)

**Third Operator.**   Your call, please?

**Mrs. Stevenson.**   (*very annoyed and imperious*) Hello, operator. I don't know what's the matter with this telephone tonight, but it's positively driving me crazy. I've never seen such inefficient, miserable service. Now, look. I'm an invalid, and I'm very nervous, and I'm *not* supposed to be annoyed. But if this keeps on much longer—

**Third Operator.**   (*a young, sweet type*) What seems to be the trouble, madam?

**Mrs. Stevenson.**   Well, everything's wrong. The whole world could be murdered, for all you people care. And now, my phone keeps ringing—

**Operator.**   Yes, madam?

**Mrs. Stevenson.**   Ringing and ringing and ringing every five seconds or so, and when I pick it up, there's no one there.

**Operator.**   I am sorry, madam. If you will hang up, I will test it for you.

**Mrs. Stevenson.**    I don't want you to test it for me. I want you to put through that call—whatever it is—at once.

**Operator.**    (*gently*) I am afraid that is not possible, madam.

**Mrs. Stevenson.**    (*storming*) Not possible? And why, may I ask?

**Operator.**    The system is automatic, madam. If someone is trying to dial your number, there is no way to check whether the call is coming through the system or not—unless the person who is trying to reach you complains to his particular operator—

**Mrs. Stevenson.**    Well, of all the stupid, complicated—! And meanwhile *I've* got to sit here in my bed, *suffering* every time that phone rings, imagining everything—

**Operator.**    I will try to check it for you, madam.

**Mrs. Stevenson.**    Check it! Check it! That's all anybody can do. Of all the stupid, idiotic . . . ! (*She hangs up.*) Oh—what's the use . . . (*Instantly* **Mrs. Stevenson**'s *phone rings again. She picks up the receiver. Wildly.*) Hello, HELLO. Stop ringing, do you hear me? Answer me? What do you want? Do you realize you're driving me crazy? Stark, staring—

**Man.**    (*dull, flat voice*) Hello. Is this Plaza 4-2295?

**Mrs. Stevenson.**    (*catching her breath*) Yes. Yes. This is Plaza 4-2295.

**Man.**    This is Western Union. I have a telegram here for Mrs. Elbert Stevenson. Is there anyone there to receive the message?

**Mrs. Stevenson.**    (*trying to calm herself*) I am Mrs. Stevenson.

**Western Union.**    (*reading flatly*) The telegram is as follows: "Mrs. Elbert Stevenson. 53 North Sutton Place, New York, New York. Darling. Terribly sorry. Tried to get you for last hour, but line busy. Leaving for Boston 11 P.M. tonight on urgent business. Back tomorrow afternoon. Keep happy. Love. Signed. Elbert."

**Mrs. Stevenson.**    (*breathing, aghast to herself*) Oh—no—

**Western Union.** That is all, madam. Do you wish us to deliver a copy of the message?

**Mrs. Stevenson.** No—no, thank you.

**Western Union.** Thank you, madam. Good night. (*He hangs up phone.*)

**Mrs. Stevenson.** (*mechanically, to phone*) Good night. (*She hangs up slowly, suddenly bursting into tears.*) No—no—it isn't true! He couldn't do it. Not when he knows I'll be all alone. It's some trick—some fiendish— (*She dials* operator.)

**Operator.** (*coolly*) Your call, please?

**Mrs. Stevenson.** Operator—try that Murray Hill 4-0098 number for me just once more, please.

**Operator.** Ringing Murray Hill 4-0098 (*Call goes through. We hear ringing at other end. Ring after ring.*)

**Mrs. Stevenson.** He's gone. Oh, Elbert, how could you? How could you—? (*She hangs up phone, sobbing pityingly to herself, turning restlessly.*) But I can't be alone tonight. I can't. If I'm alone one more second— I don't care what he says—or what the expense is—I'm a sick woman—I'm entitled— (*She dials* **Information**.)

**Information.** This is Information.

**Mrs. Stevenson.** I want the telephone number of Henchley Hospital.

**Information.** Henchley Hospital? Do you have the address, madam?

**Mrs. Stevenson.** No. It's somewhere in the seventies, though. It's a very small, private, and exclusive hospital where I had my appendix out two years ago. Henchley, H–E–N–C—

**Information.** One moment, please.

**Mrs. Stevenson.** Please—hurry. And please—what *is* the time?

**Information.** I do not know, madam. You may find out the time by dialing Meridian 7-1212.

**Mrs. Stevenson.** (*irritated*) Oh, for heaven's sake! Couldn't you—?

**Information.** The number of Henchley Hospital is Butterfield 7-0105, madam.

**Mrs. Stevenson.** Butterfield 7-0105. (*She hangs up before she finishes speaking, and immediately dials number as she repeats it.*) (*Phone rings.*)

**Woman.** (*middle-aged, solid, firm, practical*) Henchley Hospital, good evening.

**Mrs. Stevenson.** Nurses' Registry.

**Woman.** Who was it you wished to speak to, please?

**Mrs. Stevenson.** (*highhanded*) I want the Nurses' Registry at once. I want a trained nurse. I want to hire her immediately. For the night.

**Woman.** I see. And what is the nature of the case, madam?

**Mrs. Stevenson.** Nerves. I'm very nervous. I need soothing—and companionship. My husband is away—and I'm—

**Woman.** Have you been recommended to us by any doctor in particular, madam?

**Mrs. Stevenson.** No. But I really don't see why all this catechizing[8] is necessary. I want a trained nurse. I was a patient in your hospital two years ago. And after all, I *do* expect to *pay* this person—

**Woman.** We quite understand that, madam. But registered nurses are very scarce just now—and our superintendent has asked us to send people out only on cases where the physician in charge feels it is absolutely necessary.

**Mrs. Stevenson.** (*growing hysterical*) Well, it *is* absolutely necessary. I'm a sick woman. I—I'm very upset. Very. I'm alone in this house—and I'm an invalid—and tonight I overheard a telephone conversation that upset me dreadfully.

---

[8]careful questioning

About a murder—a poor woman who was going to be murdered at eleven fifteen tonight—in fact, if someone doesn't come at once—I'm afraid I'll go out of my mind— (*almost off handle by now*)

**Woman.** (*calmly*) I see. Well, I'll speak to Miss Phillips as soon as she comes in. And what is your name, madam?

**Mrs. Stevenson.** Miss Phillips. And when do you expect her in?

**Woman.** I really don't know, madam. She went out to supper at eleven o'clock.

**Mrs. Stevenson.** Eleven o'clock. But it's not eleven yet. (*She cries out.*) Oh, my clock *has* stopped. I thought it was running down. What time is it?

**Woman.** Just fourteen minutes past eleven.

(*Sound of phone receiver being lifted on same line as* **Mrs. Stevenson**'s. *A click.*)

**Mrs. Stevenson.** (*crying out*) What's that?

**Woman.** What was what, madam?

**Mrs. Stevenson.** That—that click just now—in my own telephone? As though someone had lifted the receiver off the hook of the extension phone downstairs—

**Woman.** I didn't hear it, madam. Now—about this—

**Mrs. Stevenson.** (*scared*) But I *did*. There's someone in this house. Someone downstairs in the kitchen. And they're listening to me now. They're— (*Hangs up phone. In a suffocated voice.*) I won't pick it up. I won't let them hear me. I'll be quiet—and they'll think— (*with growing terror*) But if I don't call someone now—while they're still down there—there'll be no time. (*She picks up receiver. Bland buzzing signal. She dials operator. Ring twice.*)

**Operator.** (*fat and lethargic*[9]) Your call, please?

---

[9]sluggish

**Mrs. Stevenson.** *(a desperate whisper)* Operator, I—I'm in desperate trouble—I—

**Operator.** I cannot hear you, madam. Please speak louder.

**Mrs. Stevenson.** *(still whispering)* I don't dare. I—there's someone listening. Can you hear me now?

**Operator.** Your call, please? What number are you calling, madam?

**Mrs. Stevenson.** *(desperately)* You've got to hear me. Oh, please. You've got to help me. There's someone in this house. Someone who's going to murder me. And you've got to get in touch with the— *(Click of receiver being put down in* **Mrs. Stevenson***'s line. Bursting out wildly.)* Oh, there it is—he's put it down—he's put down the extension—he's coming— *(She screams.)* He's coming up the stairs— *(hoarsely)* Give me the Police Department— *(screaming)* The police!

**Operator.** Ringing the Police Department.

*(Phone is rung. We hear sound of a train beginning to fade in. On second ring,* **Mrs. Stevenson** *screams again, but roaring of train drowns out her voice. For a few seconds we hear nothing but roaring of train, then dying away, phone at police headquarters ringing.)*

**Duffy.** Police Department. Precinct 43. Duffy speaking. *(pause)* Police Department. Duffy speaking.

**George.** Sorry. Wrong number. *(hangs up)*

# REVIEWING AND INTERPRETING

Record your answers to these questions in your personal literature notebook. Follow the directions for each part.

**REVIEWING**   Try to complete each of these sentences without looking back at the play.

*Recalling Facts*

1. Mrs. Stevenson needs the operator to help her dial her husband's office because
   a. she can't see the phone well enough to dial by herself.
   b. the line has been busy and she thinks there is something wrong with it.
   c. she is too nervous to dial.
   d. her phone isn't working correctly.

*Identifying Sequence*

2. Mrs. Stevenson calls the police the first time
   a. after the operator refuses to trace the frightening call.
   b. after someone picks up her phone.
   c. before the operator connects her to the frightening call.
   d. after she calls the hospital.

*Understanding Main Ideas*

3. The following are all reasons why Mrs. Stevenson is upset *except* that
   a. she is home alone and can't get out of bed.
   b. the men planning the crime sound so cold-blooded.
   c. the operator gives her the number of the hospital instead of connecting her immediately.
   d. her husband's phone line has been busy for a long time.

*Recognizing Literary Elements (Character)*

4. It may be that Mrs. Stevenson gets little sympathy from the people she speaks to because she is
   a. an invalid.
   b. fat and lethargic.
   c. difficult to understand.
   d. an unpleasant complainer.

*Identifying Cause and Effect*

**5.** Duffy, the police officer, refuses to do much about Mrs. Stevenson's request because
   a. he has no available officers at that time.
   b. some murders are not important enough to stop.
   c. he doesn't care about every murder that takes place in New York.
   d. the information Mrs. Stevenson has overheard is too vague to act upon.

**INTERPRETING**

To complete these sentences, you may look back at the play if you'd like.

*Making Inferences*

**6.** From the way Mrs. Stevenson speaks and treats people on the phone, you can tell that
   a. she is not used to talking to strangers.
   b. she probably complains to her husband a great deal.
   c. her illness is all in her mind.
   d. everyone she speaks to is incompetent.

*Prediciting Outcomes*

**7.** If Officer Duffy finds out about Mrs. Stevenson's murder, he probably will
   a. try to trace the murderers' phone call.
   b. not make any connection between her call and her death.
   c. know right away that her husband paid to have her killed.
   d. regret not having paid more attention to her call.

*Making Generalizations*

**8.** Mrs. Stevenson would probably agree that
   a. big cities are sometimes uncaring and dangerous.
   b. you are safe if you have strong locks on your doors.
   c. you can always trust your family.
   d. you can always get help in an emergency if you have a phone.

*Analyzing*      **9.** An implied motive for Mr. Stevenson to want his wife dead is
that he is
a. tired of caring for his invalid wife.
b. unaware that his wife is having any problems.
c. completely devoted to her.
d. involved with another woman.

*Understanding*      **10.** The climax of this play occurs when
*Literary Elements*      a. Mrs. Stevenson hears the men planning the murder.
*(Plot)*      b. George says, "Sorry. Wrong number."
c. Mrs. Stevenson shouts that someone's coming and then
screams.
d. Mrs. Stevenson hears someone pick up the extension.

Now check your answers with your teacher. Study the
questions you answered incorrectly. What types of questions
were they? Talk with your teacher about ways to work on
those skills.

# The Radio Play

For thousands of years, the only way to present a play was to have actors and actresses act out the story on a stage in front of an audience. However, in the 1920s a new way of presenting a play was born. By that time there were millions of radios in homes all across America. Advertisers realized that they could present entertainment over the radio and hold the attention of millions of listeners, while urging them to buy their products. For that reason, they sponsored all kinds of shows, from comedy and music to adventure and melodrama. For almost thirty years—until television took its place—the radio was the major source of entertainment for American families. Playwrights began writing specifically for the radio, taking into account the unique advantages and limitations of the format.

What made radio plays so popular? For one thing, they allowed listeners to use their imaginations to picture characters, settings, and events. In addition, listeners' favorite radio plays displayed the same qualities as any other good play—for example, believable characters, well-constructed plots, and intelligent themes. Radio plays also offered a new and exciting format for storytelling, using voices and sound effects as they had never been used before.

The Golden Age of Radio is remembered fondly by those who enjoyed it during the 1920s, 1930s, and 1940s. The radio gave families a chance to be entertained by skilled playwrights right in their own homes. In these lessons, you will look at what makes Lucille Fletcher's radio play effective:

1.  Fletcher creates well-drawn, believable characters by using effective dialogue and action.

2.  She builds suspense through the rapid pacing of plot events and dialogue.

3.  She adds to the plot and moves it along with important sound effects.

## LESSON 1    CHARACTERS IN A RADIO PLAY

Storytellers of long ago understood the power of the human voice. To tell their stories and hold the attention of their audiences, they used their voices like instruments, whispering softly when a secret was told and shouting when the characters were in danger. They varied their tone and pitch to communicate both the mood and the action of each story. Like those storytellers, the actors in a radio play must use their voices to tell the story clearly to audiences who can only hear but not see them.

Authors of radio plays help actors use their voices to create the characters in two ways. First, they create characters with strong personalities that can be communicated effectively using just the voice. See how Lucille Fletcher lets you know Mrs. Stevenson's personality in a few well-chosen words:

**Operator.**    (*patiently*) What number were you calling, madam?

**Mrs. Stevenson.**    That doesn't matter. This was a *wrong* number. And *you* dialed it. And we've got to find out what it was—immediately!

**Operator.**    But—madam—

**Mrs. Stevenson.**    Oh, why are you so stupid? Look, it was obviously a case of some little slip of the finger. I told you to try Murray Hill 4-0098 for me—you dialed it— but your finger must have slipped—and I was connected with some other number—and I could hear them, but they couldn't hear me. Now, I simply fail to see why you couldn't make that same mistake again—on purpose— why you couldn't *try* to dial Murray Hill 4-0098 in the same careless sort of way—

**Operator.**    (*quickly*) Murray Hill 4-0098? I will try to get it for you, madam.

**Mrs. Stevenson.**    (*sarcastically*) *Thank* you.

Mrs. Stevenson is rude, impatient, and sarcastic. She calls the operator stupid and accuses her of misdialing, instead of considering the possibility that what she heard happened because of a mechanical malfunction. She is also unreasonable. She expects the operator to remember how she misdialed the number and somehow repeat it. It is no wonder that the operator jumps at the chance to get away from her and simply dials the number she hears in Mrs. Stevenson's ranting conversation. An actress trying to portray Mrs. Stevenson would find it easy to imagine what her voice should sound like.

The second way in which authors help actors create characters is by writing clear stage directions. In *Sorry, Wrong Number*, Fletcher inserts plenty of instructions about how the lines are to be delivered. Usually these directions appear after the name of the character, as in this passage:

**Man.**    Hello.

**Mrs. Stevenson.**    Hello? (*a little puzzled*) Hello. Is Mr. Stevenson there?

**Man.**    (*into phone, as though he had not heard*) Hello. (*louder*) Hello.

**Second Man.**    (*slow, heavy quality, faintly foreign accent*) Hello.

**First Man.**    Hello. George?

**George.**    Yes, sir.

**Mrs. Stevenson.**    (*louder and more imperious, to phone*) Hello. Who's this? What number am I calling, please?

The stage directions specify that George's voice is slow and heavy and has a faint foreign accent. Such a voice could sound dangerous and frightening, even before it turns to a discussion of murder. Mrs. Stevenson's voice is described as "louder and more imperious." This demanding tone matches the bad temper and impatience she displays with the operator in the preceding passage.

EXERCISE (1)

Read this passage from the play. Then use what you have learned in this lesson to answer the questions that follow.

> **Duffy.**    Well, then, there's nothing for you to worry about, is there? And now, if you'll just leave the rest to us—
> **Mrs. Stevenson.**    But what will you *do*? It's so late—it's nearly eleven o'clock.
> **Duffy.**    (*firmly*) We'll take care of it, lady.
> **Mrs. Stevenson.**    Will you broadcast it all over the city? And send out squads? And warn your radio cars to watch out—especially in suspicious neighborhoods like mine?
> **Duffy.**    (*more firmly*) Lady, I *said* we'd take care of it. Just now I've got a couple of other matters here on my desk that require my immediate—
> **Mrs. Stevenson.**    Oh! (*She slams down receiver hard.*) Idiot!

1. What do you learn about Duffy's personality from this conversation? How has the playwright helped the actor know how to say Duffy's lines?

2. Suppose the playwright had Duffy say his lines timidly, kindly, or angrily? Using what you know about her personality, predict how Mrs. Stevenson might react to each of these ways of speaking.

Now check your answers with your teacher. Review this part of the lesson if you don't understand why an answer was incorrect.

WRITING ON YOUR OWN (1)

Review the emergency situations you listed in the first writing exercise. Now you will decide on two people who could be talking on the phone during an emergency. Follow these steps:

- In any emergency phone call, one person is relating a problem and the other person is trying to help. To decide who will be having the emergency, first make a list of possibilities. Include different kinds of people, from young children to senior citizens.
- Then decide who will be receiving the phone call. Will it be a police officer, a member of the armed forces, a parent, a private citizen? Jot down ideas for people who might become involved in helping someone through a troubling situation.
- Look over both lists. Decide on both participants in the conversation. Imagine how each person would look and act in normal daily life. Write at least three sentences describing each person.

## LESSON ②    SUSPENSE AND TEMPO

Most radio plays are fairly short. They usually fill a half-hour time slot, which includes commercials. For this reason, if a playwright wants to build a suspenseful story, he or she must plunge into the action quickly in order to have time to build to an exciting climax.

Look again at the beginning of *Sorry, Wrong Number*. About how many minutes of the play do you think have gone by before Mrs. Stevenson overhears the phone conversation detailing the murder? One? Maybe two? The action begins quickly and then picks up steam. The *tempo*, or speed, of this play is quite rapid. Mrs. Stevenson seems to be in an endless round of calling numbers and answering the telephone, one call after the other. For example, see how quickly one call ends and the other begins:

**Mrs. Stevenson.**     Oh, for heaven's sake! You mean to tell me I can't report a murder without getting tied up in all this red tape? Why, it's perfectly idiotic. All right, then, I *will* call the police. (*She slams down receiver.*) Ridiculous!

*(sound of dialing)*

**Second Operator.** Your call, please?

**Mrs. Stevenson.** *(very annoyed)* The Police Department—please.

**Second Operator.** Ringing the Police Department.

*(Rings twice. Phone is picked up.)*

**Sergeant Duffy.** Police Department. Precinct 43. Duffy speaking.

Not even a minute passes between the end of one call and the beginning of the next. This hurried pace is maintained throughout the play. Audiences become more and more on edge, both because of the frustration Mrs. Stevenson experiences and the rapidity with which events occur. The playwright builds tension until the final, climactic moment when Mrs. Stevenson screams to the uncaring operator that "he's coming."

## EXERCISE ②

Read this passage from the play. Then use what you have learned in the lesson to answer the questions that follow.

**Mrs. Stevenson.** *(nastily)* I can hear it. You don't have to tell me. I know it's busy. *(slams down receiver)* If I could only get out of this bed for a little while. If I could get a breath of fresh air—or just lean out the window—and see the street— *(The phone rings. She darts for it instantly.)* Hello. Elbert? Hello. Hello. Hello. Oh, what's the *matter* with this phone? *Hello? Hello?* *(slams down receiver)* *(The phone rings again, once. She picks it up.)* Hello? Hello— Oh, for heaven's sake, who *is* this? Hello. Hello. *Hello.* *(Slams down receiver. Dials operator.)*

1. How does the author create tension and build suspense in this passage? How does the pace of the action contribute to the nervous mood?

**2.** How does the rapidity with which Mrs. Stevenson speaks add to the tension and suspense? How might the mood of the play change if Mrs. Stevenson stopped repeating the word *hello* and spoke more calmly?

Now check your answers with your teacher. Review this part of the lesson if you don't understand why an answer was incorrect.

### WRITING ON YOUR OWN ②

So far, you have listed possible emergency situations in which two people could be having a phone conversation. You also have chosen the two people who will be involved in the call. Now do the following:

* In the middle of a sheet of paper, write the name of the person in trouble. Then review the list of possible emergencies. Some of those problems are more likely than others for the character you have chosen. For example, a teenager is more likely to experience an emergency while hiking than a toddler is. Describe the most logical emergencies in balloons around the name in the center of the page.
* Now choose the situation you wish to write about. Write a short paragraph explaining what happened to cause the emergency.
* Next, imagine the person's state of mind at the time of the phone call. Keeping in mind the way your character would speak, write the first few sentences that he or she would say to the person who answers the emergency call.

## LESSON ③   SOUND EFFECTS

*Sound effects* are the sounds that are called for in the script of a play. Listeners hearing the rain on the window, the whistle of a teakettle, or the chirping of crickets can paint a mental picture to match each sound.

Many stage plays, films, and television plays rely on sounds to help set the mood or tell part of the story. In a radio play, however, sound effects are absolutely essential. Without the ability to see what is happening, audiences need to hear clues about events. The creaking of a door can suggest a ghost entering the room. The clatter of assorted items falling can suggest the opening of the door to an overfilled, cluttered closet. Every sound that listeners hear is necessary for picturing the action. Without the sound effects in *Sorry, Wrong Number*, audiences would find it very difficult to follow the plot events.

In the following passage, Mrs. Stevenson is listening to the murderers making their final plans. Imagine trying to follow the action in the passage without the sound effects.

> **George.**   Okay, I get— (*Sound: A bland buzzing signal.*)
> **Mrs. Stevenson.**   (*clicking phone*) Oh! (*Bland buzzing signal continues. She hangs up.*) How awful! How unspeakably—
> (*Sound: Dialing. Phone buzz.*)
> **Operator.**   Your call, please?

Without sound effects, the passage would read this way:

> **George.**   Okay, I get—
> **Mrs. Stevenson.**   Oh! How awful! How unspeakably—
> **Operator.**   Your call, please?

The first buzzing signal explains why George's voice is cut off in mid-sentence. The sound of the clicking phone tells audiences that Mrs. Stevenson is frantically trying to renew the connection. The continued buzzing sound lets you know why Mrs. Stevenson is feeling frustrated. Sound effects tell you that she has hung up her phone and then immediately dialed it again. Without sound effects, this entire passage would be very confusing.

EXERCISE ③

Read this passage, paying particular attention to the sound effects. Then use what you have learned in this lesson to answer the questions that follow it.

> (*Sound of phone receiver being lifted on same line as* **Mrs. Stevenson**'s. *A click.*)
> **Mrs. Stevenson.**   (*crying out*) What's that?
> **Woman.**   What was what, madam?
> **Mrs. Stevenson.**   That—that click just now—in my own telephone? As though someone had lifted the receiver off the hook of the extension phone downstairs—
> **Woman.**   I didn't hear it, madam. Now—about this—

1. How does the sound effect in this passage move the plot forward?

2. At this point in the play, considering Mrs. Stevenson's frame of mind, would you believe that Mrs. Stevenson really hears the phone click if you didn't hear the sound effect yourself? Do you think the sound effect is necessary for audiences to believe that Mrs. Stevenson is really in danger? Why or why not?

Now check your answers with your teacher. Review this part of the lesson if you don't understand why an answer was incorrect.

 WRITING ON YOUR OWN ③

Work with a partner or a small group to complete this exercise. Follow these steps:

* At the scene of many emergencies, the air is full of sounds. Perhaps a child is crying or sirens are blaring. First make a list of as many emergency situations as you

can. You may want to refer to your original list for ideas. Then for each situation, think of at least one sound that accompanies it. Write the sound or sounds next to each emergency.

- Next, work with a partner or group to choose sounds that might be heard on the scene of the emergency you chose in earlier writing exercises. Then, working by yourself, write a short paragraph that explains why you chose those sounds and how they fit into your chosen emergency situation.

## DISCUSSION GUIDES

1.  Although Mrs. Stevenson asks several people for help, she can't persuade anyone to take action on her suspicions. In a small group, discuss why each of the people she contacts doesn't take her seriously. Are they justified in the way they act, or are they shirking their responsibilities as human beings to help another person in distress? In your opinion, what are the responsibilities of a telephone operator, a hospital nurse, and a police officer when they get calls like Mrs. Stevenson's? Let one member of the group record your responses, and then share them with the rest of the class.

2.  Mrs. Stevenson complains about the red tape she has to deal with in order to do something as important as report a murder. Discuss other situations in which you or someone you know has felt tied up in red tape—that is, frustrated by the necessity of going through annoying and sometimes useless procedures, forms, and rules to get something done. How did you feel? With a partner, make a list of situations in which you feel that normal operating procedures could or should be dispensed with, for the sake of a person in trouble.

3.  In a small group, select a scene from the play. Then take turns reading the dialogue aloud. While group members read, make notes about the best sound effects to use and the best way to read each line—the best voice pitch, the proper speed of delivery, and the emotional tone that the words call for. After the first reading, discuss all your observations and recommendations. Then practice reading the scene again, using those suggestions as guidelines. Finally, present your scene to the class. To simulate a radio play, position yourselves at the back of the room so other class members will only hear you and not see you.

# WRITE THE DIALOGUE FOR AN EMERGENCY PHONE CALL

In this unit you have analyzed what makes a radio drama an effective type of play. In this exercise you will use what you have learned in the lessons to write the dialogue for an emergency phone call.

Follow these steps to complete your dialogue. If you have questions about the writing process, refer to Using the Writing Process (page 300).

- First, assemble and review all the writing you did for this unit: *1)* a list of possible emergency situations, *2)* sentences describing the two speakers in the phone call, *3)* a paragraph describing the emergency and the first few sentences of the phone call, and *4)* a list of sound effects that can be heard and an explanation of why those sounds were chosen.
- Decide on the two people who will be speaking and the emergency they will be discussing. Then write the dialogue for a phone call between these two people. Try to make the dialogue last at least three minutes.
- Begin the dialogue with the first ring of the phone. Make sure the words the speakers say match each one's age, gender, and personality. Include stage directions that tell how readers should say each line. Use the format of the plays in this book. Try to build suspense with the pacing of the dialogue and the reactions of the speakers to whatever events take place. Use sound effects to effectively set the mood and advance the plot. Let the conversation end with some resolution of the original problem.
- Proofread your dialogue for spelling, grammar, punctuation, capitalization, and formatting errors. Make a final copy of the dialogue and ask a classmate to join you in reading it aloud to an audience. Let your voices reflect your characters' emotions.
- After your reading, save the final copy of your dialogue in your writing portfolio.

# The Teleplay

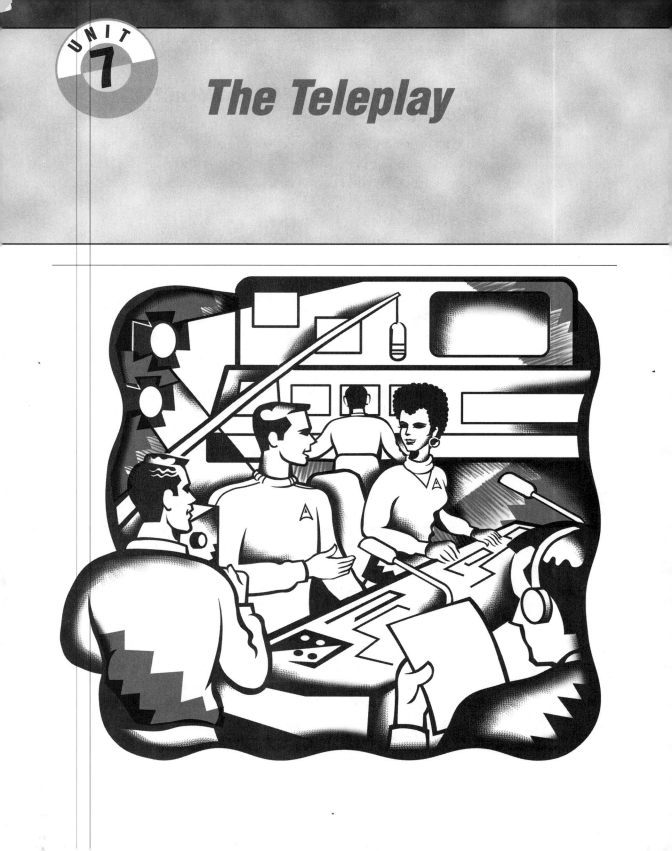

# The Trouble with Tribbles

◉

by David Gerrold

## INTRODUCTION

*The Trouble with Tribbles* is widely recognized as the single most popular episode of the original *Star Trek* series (1966–1969). It was broadcast during the series' second season and was brought back almost 30 years later when clips from the original were integrated with new footage for the episode *Trials and Tribble-ations* (1996) in the successor series *Star Trek: Deep Space Nine*. This script builds on the original situation created by *Star Trek*'s executive producer, Gene Roddenberry.

Some 200 years into the future, the starship *Enterprise* roams the universe to seek out new life forms and protect the interests of the Federation, which governs Earth and its allies. Its multi-racial crew is captained by James T. Kirk, a human from Kansas. His second-in-command is the relentlessly logical Mr. Spock, who is half human and half Vulcan. The crew also includes the ship's doctor, Leonard McCoy; chief communications officer Uhura; chief engineer Montgomery Scott (Scotty); and Ensign Pavel Chekov. Opposing the Federation is the war-loving and powerful Klingon Empire.

Some high-tech pieces of equipment on the *Enterprise* are view screens, which are used as communications devices or—as in the first scene—to locate the ship and other objects in space; a large screen on the bridge, which serves as either a window on space or a wall-size display screen; and palm-size communicators for simple audio messages. Other terms invented for the series that appear in the script are the following:

*transporter*—a device that sends travelers, particle by particle, to or from locations outside the ship. It then recombines the particles when they reach their destination. To travel via transporter is to "beam" down, up, or over.

*phaser*—a hand weapon.

*food processor*—a device that produces food and drink instantly in response to spoken orders.

*sensor*—an instrument for sensing things—for example, to determine the presence of life in an area or to analyze the chemistry of a thing. The *tri-corder* is a special kind of sensor.

*quadrant*—a section of the galaxy.

*Warp Factor*—a speed setting for the ship's engines.

**ABOUT THE AUTHOR**

Jarrold David Friedman has been writing science fiction since 1967 under the name David Gerrold. He was born in Chicago, Illinois, in 1944 and attended the University of Southern California and California State University at Northridge. Probably his best-known work is his first sale: the teleplay *The Trouble with Tribbles*, which was nominated for the Hugo Award for science fiction writing. Gerrold has received other nominations for the Hugo and for the Nebula, another science fiction award, and in 1995 he won both awards for *The Martian Child*, his semi-autobiographical novel about a science fiction writer who unknowingly adopts an alien. The novel was inspired by his own adoption of a son in 1992.

Gerrold is a very prolific writer. In addition to many science fiction teleplays and novels, he has written short stories, stage shows, computer software, and nonfiction. He also has taught screenwriting at Pepperdine University for fifteen years.

Gerrold said that as a student he had read all the science fiction literature there was, and when *Star Trek* came along he decided to submit a script. The series was eager for writers who had a grasp of science fiction. So beginning with the concept and characters developed by *Star Trek*'s creator, Gene Roddenberry, Gerrold wrote *The Trouble with Tribbles*.

Gerrold defines the essence of science fiction as the exploration of ideas. In his writing, he is interested in characters who grow beyond their apparent limitations. He has compared a story to a box of Cracker Jacks, saying that there is a prize in every story. "That prize is that piece of truth that the author believed in." Gerrold says he tries to maintain this standard in everything he writes, even for fun, as with *The Trouble with Tribbles*.

**ABOUT THE LESSONS**

The thing that sets *The Trouble with Tribbles* apart from all the other plays in this book is that it was written as a television play, or *teleplay*. The lessons following the teleplay will focus on how elements found in all plays are influenced by the special characteristics of television production. When a teleplay is filmed, the working script must include elaborate directions for every shot: how many people are in the shot, how close the camera is, at what angle it points, whether there is special lighting, and so on.

As you read *The Trouble with Tribbles*, these two terms for camera shots may be unfamiliar:

*fade in*—cause an image to gradually appear and fill a previously blank screen.

*fade out*—cause an image to gradually disappear from the screen, leaving the screen blank for a few seconds.

## WRITING: OUTLINING A TELEPLAY

In this unit you will look at some of the opportunities and limitations that are involved in writing for television. At the end of the unit you will write an outline and passages of dialogue and stage directions for a television script. The script outline will be for a half-hour teleplay based on a science fiction or fantasy theme. You can prepare for this project by considering possible settings, characters, and conflicts. Follow these steps:

- Do you choose to read or watch things that are based on science fiction concepts, or do you prefer to read or watch fantasy? Review your choices and decide which type of fiction you will be more comfortable writing.
- List typical story lines or themes that you have noticed in the type of fiction you chose. For example, in science fiction, time travel is always popular, as are saving Earth from alien invasions and saving aliens from Earth's errors. In fantasy, changing bodies or lives with another person and acquiring magical powers are popular. Try to list at least three more story lines or themes that you have seen used in science fiction or fantasy stories, books, plays, movies, and television programs.
- Next, decide if your characters will be human or if they will come from such groups as aliens, nymphs, or gnomes. Begin listing possible names for characters, along with brief descriptions. Make sure your characters are appropriate for the particular type of literature you have chosen.

**AS YOU READ**

In *The Trouble with Tribbles*, playwright David Gerrold effec-tively joins the usual elements of a play with the specific requirements of the television format. Thinking about the fol-lowing questions as you read will help you recognize a few of Gerrold's methods:

- How do the time requirements of television affect the struc-ture of the play?
- How do television production techniques affect the story line and the arrangement of scenes?
- How does the use of a camera affect the development of the characters?

# The Trouble with Tribbles

◠

by David Gerrold

*The program opens with a stock shot of the spaceship* Enterprise *flying through space. Fade-out.*

**TEASER:** *Briefing room.* **Kirk**, **Spock**, *and* **Chekov** *are seated around the table.* **Chekov** *is on the hot seat. As a young ensign, he is here to learn, and the Captain and the First Officer are now examining him to find out just how much he has learned. It is a lecture with questions, and it is obvious that* **Chekov** *hates it.*

**Spock.** *(consulting tri-screen on table)* Deep space station K–7 is now in sensor range, Captain.

**Kirk.** Good. Mr. Chekov, this flight is supposed to give you both experience and knowledge. How close will we pass to the nearest Klingon outpost on our present course?

**Chekov.** One parsec, sir. Close enough to smell them.

**Spock.** That is not logical, Ensign. Odors cannot travel through the vacuum of space.

**Chekov.** I was making a little joke, sir.

**Spock.** It was extremely little, Ensign.

**Kirk.** Immediate past history of this quadrant, Mister Spock?

**Spock.** Under dispute between the two parties since initial contact. The battle of Donatu Five took place near here 23 solar years ago . . . inconclusive.

**Kirk.** Analysis of the disputed area.

**Spock.** Undeveloped. Sherman's Planet claimed by both sides, our Federation and the Klingon Empire. Of course, we have the better claim.

**Chekov.** The area was first mapped by the famous Russian astronomer Ivan Burkoff almost two hun . . .

**Kirk.** John Burke, Ensign.

**Chekov.** Burke, sir? I don't think so. I'm sure it was . . .

**Spock.** John Burke was the chief astronomer at the Royal Academy in old Britain at the time.

**Chekov.** Royal Academy? Oh. Oh, well!

**Kirk.**    Is the rest of your history that faulty, Ensign? Key point of dispute.

**Chekov.**    Under the terms of the Organian Peace Treaty, one side or the other must prove that they can develop the planet most efficiently.

**Kirk.**    And unfortunately, the Klingons, though they are brutal and aggressive, are quite efficient.

**Chekov.**    I remember once when Peter the Great had a problem like that. He . . .

**Uhura's Voice.**    (*urgently interrupting*) Captain!

**Kirk.**    (*on the intercom*) Kirk here.

**Uhura.**    (*her face appearing on the viewing screen*) Captain, I'm picking up a subspace distress call—*priority channel!* It's from space station K-7!

**Chekov.**    (*to* **Spock**) Code one emergency? That's a disaster call.

**Spock.**    Quite.

**Kirk.**    Go to Warp Factor Six.

**Uhura's Voice.**    Aye aye, Captain. (**Kirk** *snaps off the intercom, already half out of his chair and on his way to the door.* **Spock** *and* **Chekov** *follow immediately. As they go out* **Uhura's Voice** *is amplified; loudspeaker*) All hands . . . this is a red alert. Man your battle stations. Repeat . . . this is a red alert. Man your battle stations. Repeat . . . this is a red alert. Man your battle stations.

## ACT ONE

**FADE IN:** *Space station hangs against a backdrop of stars, slowly growing in size as the* Enterprise *approaches.*

**Kirk.**    Captain's log; Stardate 4523.3. Deep space station K-7 has issued a priority-one call. More than an emergency, it signals near or total disaster. We can only assume the Klingons have attacked the station. We are going in armed for battle.

**SCENE 1:** *Bridge. Everyone on the bridge stares tensely, watching the screen showing the space station.*

**Chekov.**    Main phasers armed and ready. (*looks up at* **Kirk**) There's nothing. Just the station, sir.

**Kirk.**    (*stepping down, peering over* **Chekov**'s *shoulder*) A priority-one distress call and they're sitting there absolutely peaceful? Lieutenant Uhura, break subspace silence.

**Uhura.**    Aye aye, Captain.

**Kirk.**    Space station K-7, this is Captain Kirk of the *Enterprise*. What is your emergency?

**Lurry's Voice.**    Captain Kirk, this is Commander Lurry. I must apologize for the distress call. I—

**Kirk.**    Commander Lurry, you have issued a priority-one distress signal! State the nature of your emergency!

**Lurry.**    Uh, perhaps you had better beam over, I—uh—I'll try to explain . . .

**Kirk.**    You'll try to explain? You'd better be prepared to do more than that. Kirk out. (*starting toward door*) Mr. Chekov, maintain battle readiness. Uhura, have the transporter room stand by. Mr. Spock, I'll need your help . . . (**Kirk** *waits for* **Spock** *to join him at the elevator. They step into it.*)

**SCENE 2:** *Lurry's office on the space station.* **Lurry**, **Baris**, *and* **Darvin**; **Kirk** *and* **Spock** *materialize.* **Kirk** *is furious as he begins talking to* **Lurry** *as soon as materialization is complete.*

**Kirk.**    Commander Lurry, if there is no emergency, why did you order a priority-one distress call?!

**Baris.**    *I* ordered it, Captain!

**Lurry.**    Captain Kirk, this is Nilz Baris; he's out from Earth to take charge of the Development Project for Sherman's Planet.

**Kirk.**    And that gives you the authority to put a whole quadrant on a defense alert?

**Darvin.**  (*stiff and stuffy*) Mr. Baris is the Federation Under Secretary in Charge of Agricultural Affairs in this quadrant!

**Baris.**  This is my assistant, Arne Darvin. Now, Captain, I want all available security guards. I want them posted around the storage compartments.

**Kirk.**  (*angry, puzzled*) Storage compartments? What storage compartment?

**Darvin.**  The storage compartments with the quadro-triticale.

**Kirk.**  The what? What is . . . (*stumbling over the word [pronounced "quadro-triti-cay-lee"]*) . . . quadro-triticale? (*Darvin sniffs audibly at* **Kirk**'s *ignorance. He pulls a sample of the grain out of a container. He hands it to* **Baris**, *who hands it to* **Kirk**. **Kirk** *glances at it only briefly, then hands it to a curious* **Spock**. **Spock** *examines it.*) Wheat. So what?

**Baris.**  Quadro-triticale is not wheat, Captain! I wouldn't expect you or your First Officer to know about such things, but—

**Spock.**  (*quietly watching all this*) Quadro-triticale is a high-yield grain, a four-lobed hybrid of wheat and rye, a perennial, also, if I'm not mistaken. The root grain, triticale, can trace its ancestry all the way back to Twentieth-Century Canada, when—

**Kirk.**  (*making no effort to conceal his amusement*) I think you've made your point, Mr. Spock. (**Spock** *pauses and looks at* **Kirk**. *He gives* **Kirk** *the familiar* **Spock** *stare. He was just getting to the interesting part.*)

**Lurry.**  (*interrupting*) Captain, quadro-triticale is the only Earth grain that will grow on Sherman's Planet. We have several tons of it here on the station, and it's very important that that grain reach Sherman's Planet safely. Mr. Baris thinks that Klingon agents may try to sabotage it.

**Kirk.**  (*irked—to* **Baris**) You issued a priority-one distress call because of a couple of tons of—wheat?!

**Darvin.**   Quadro-triticale. (**Kirk** *starts to look at* **Darvin**, *but decides he is not worth it.*)

**Baris.**   (*coming in fast*) Of course, I—

**Kirk.**   (*his patience exhausted*) Mr. Baris, you summoned the *Enterprise* here without an emergency! Now, you'll take responsibility for it! Misuse of the priority-one channel is a Federation offense!

**Baris.**   I did not misuse the priority-one channel! I want that grain protected!

**Lurry.**   Captain Kirk, couldn't you at least post a couple of guards? We do get a large number of ships passing through.

**Spock.**   It would be a logical precaution, Captain. The Sherman's Planet affair is of extreme importance to the Federation.

(**Kirk** *looks at* **Spock** *as if to say* "Blast your logic!" *However,* **Spock** *is usually correct, so . . .*)

**Kirk.**   (*chagrined; taking out his communicator*) Kirk to *Enterprise*.

**Uhura's Voice.**   *Enterprise* here.

**Kirk.**   Secure from general quarters. Beam over *two* and *only* two security guards. Have them report to Commander Lurry. Also, authorize shore leave for all off-duty personnel.

**Uhura.**   Yes, Captain.

**Kirk.**   Kirk out. (*He puts away the communicator.* **Baris** *is upset, because* **Kirk** *has only authorized two guards.*)

**Baris.**   Kirk! Starfleet Command is going to hear about *this*. A mere two men!

**Kirk.**   (*looks at* **Baris** *for a long moment*) I have never questioned either the orders or the intelligence of any representative of the Federation . . . (*pause, looking at* **Baris**) . . . until now. (*Leaving a speechless* **Baris** *and* **Darvin**, **Kirk** *exits, followed by* **Spock**.)

**SCENE 3:** *Bar/store. Like a Western general store, this is a combination of two or more functions. Primarily it is a bar with a few tables and a bar against one wall, but a few extra props behind the bar should suggest that* **Trader** *also runs a general-store type of establishment.* **Kirk** *and* **Spock** *are at the bar, just putting down empty glasses.* **Kirk** *is shaking his head as he puts down the glass, looks at the wheat he holds in his hand.*

**Kirk.**　Summoned a starship on a priority A-1 channel to guard some storage compartments. Storage compartments of *wheat!*

**Spock.**　Still, Captain, it is a logical precaution. The Klingons would not like to see us successfully develop Sherman's Planet. *(He and* **Kirk** *are crossing toward the door on his last line.* **Uhura** *and* **Chekov** *enter, followed separately by* **Cyrano Jones.** **Uhura** *and* **Chekov** *wait to meet the* **Captain,** *but* **Jones** *crosses past them to the bar beyond where he will engage the* **Trader.**)

**Kirk.**　*(to* **Uhura** *and* **Chekov**) I see you didn't waste any time going off duty.

**Uhura.**　How often do we get shore leave?

**Chekov.**　She wanted to shop and I wanted to help her.

**Kirk.**　Mister Chekov. *(holds out wheat)* What do you make of this?

**Chekov.**　*(takes it eagerly)* Quadro-triticale! I've read about this, but I've never seen any of it till now!

**Kirk.**　Mister Spock, does everyone know about this grain but me?

**Chekov.**　Not everyone, Captain. It's a Russian invention. *(***Kirk** *gives up, shot down in flames by nationalism again. As he and* **Spock** *start to exit,* **Uhura** *and* **Chekov** *move toward the bar.* **Cyrano Jones** *is arguing with the* **Trader.** *He has a great amount of merchandise on the counter. Obviously, he has been trying to sell it to* **Trader,** *and* **Trader** *has obviously been very stubborn.)*

**Trader.**   No! I don't want any. I told you before, and I'm telling you again. (**Chekov** *and* **Uhura** *approach and wait for* **Trader**'s *attention*) I don't want any Spican Flame Gems. I already have enough Spican Flame Gems to last me a lifetime. (**Cyrano** *shrugs. He starts to open his carry-all sack to put them away.*)

**Cyrano.**   (*pityingly*) How sad for you, my friend . . . (*hopefully*) You won't find a finer stone anywhere. Ah, but I have something better . . . (*picking a vial[1] off the counter*) Surely you want some Antaran Glow Water.

**Trader.**   (*deadly monotone*) I use it to polish the flame gems. (*By this time* **Chekov** *and* **Uhura** *are watching interestedly.* **Cyrano** *sweeps most of his other stuff back into his sack.*)

**Cyrano.**   (*sighing*) You are a most difficult man to reach. (*Picking up something off the counter. It is a green-gold ball of fluff, a tribble.*) Surely, you want . . .

**Trader.**   (*although he is interested*) . . . not at that price.

**Uhura.**   (*catching sight of the tribble*) Oooooooh, what is it? Is it alive? (*taking the tribble*) May I hold him? Ooooh, he's adorable! (*to* **Cyrano**) What is it?

**Cyrano.**   What is it? Why, little darlin', it's a tribble.

**Uhura.**   (*softly*) A tribble?

**Cyrano.**   It's only the sweetest little creature known to man, exceptin' of course, yourself.

**Uhura.**   (*laughing; she is not taken in by the flattery*) Oh! Oh! It's purring! (*The tribble in the lieutenant's hands purrs and throbs. It is a ball of green-gold fluff about the size of a large bean bag. Its purr is soft and high-pitched like a dove's cooing.*)

**Cyrano.**   Ah, little lady, he's just sayin' that he likes you.

**Uhura.**   He's adorable. Are you selling them?

---

[1]small bottle or vessel

**Trader.** That's what we're trying to decide right now. (*He glares at* **Cyrano**.)

**Cyrano.** (*to* **Trader**) My friend, ten credits apiece is a very reasonable price. You can see for yourself how much the lovely little lady here appreciates fine things.

**Trader.** A credit apiece.

**Chekov.** (*asking* **Cyrano**, *as he takes the tribble from* **Uhura**; *he has put his grain on the counter; some spills out*) He won't bite, will he?

**Cyrano.** (*making a great show of ignoring* **Trader**) Sir! There is a law against transporting harmful animals from one planet to another, or weren't you aware of that? Besides, tribbles have no teeth.

**Trader.** (*trying to attract* **Cyrano**'s *attention*) All right. I'll double my offer. Two credits.

**Cyrano.** (*taking the tribble from* **Chekov** *and plopping it on the counter in front of* **Trader**) Twice nothing is still nothing.

**Trader.** (*eyeing the tribble*) Is he clean?

**Cyrano.** (*eyeing* **Trader**) He's as clean as you are. I daresay a good deal cleaner . . . (*While they have been talking, the tribble has been inching along on the counter, toward the grain. It now reaches it.*)

**Uhura.** If you don't want him, I'll take him. I think he's cute. (**Cyrano** *and* **Trader** *both notice this.* **Trader** *is annoyed.* **Cyrano** *beams.*)

**Trader.** (*to* **Cyrano**) All right. Four.

**Cyrano.** Is that an offer or a joke? (*And meanwhile, the tribble begins munching on* **Chekov**'s *grain.*)

**Trader.** That's my offer.

**Cyrano.** (*starting to leave*) Well, I can see that you're not interested. (*He reaches for the tribble.* **Trader** *stops him.*)

**Trader.** All right . . . five.

**Cyrano.** (*returning quickly now that* **Trader** *is talking money*) My friend, I'll tell you what I'll do for you. I can see that you're an honest man. I'll lower my price to eight and a half.

**Trader.**  You're talking yourself out of a deal. Six. Not a cent more.

**Cyrano.**  Seven and a half. (*no response*) Seven. (*still no response*) All right, you robber. Six. (*The tribble is happily munching on the grain; i.e., the grain is disappearing under it as the tribble throbs and croons contentedly.*)

**Trader.**  When can I have them?

**Cyrano.**  Right away. (*He starts pulling tribbles out of his sack.*)

**Uhura.**  (*to **Trader***) How much are you selling them for?

**Trader.**  (*already counting his profits*) Well, let me see now . . . six credits . . . figure a reasonable markup for a reasonable profit . . . ten percent markup . . . ten credits . . .

**Cyrano.**  (*under his breath*) Thief!

**Trader.**  In fact, I'll sell you this one.

**Chekov.**  Hey! He's eating my grain! (*quickly moves to rescue what is left of the grain; fortunately tribbles are slow eaters*)

**Trader.**  (*picking up the tribble*) That will be ten credits.

**Cyrano.**  (*taking the tribble from **Trader**, indignantly*) Sir! That happens to be my sample. And it is mine to do with as I please, and I please to give it to the pretty little lady here.

**Uhura.**  Oh, I couldn't.

**Cyrano.**  I insist.

**Trader.**  That's right. Ruin the market.

**Cyrano.**  Hah! Once the pretty little lady here starts to show this little precious around, you won't be able to keep up with 'em. (*He gallantly hands the tribble to **Uhura**.*)


**SCENE 4:** *Briefing room. **Kirk** and **Spock** are having a cup of coffee when a wall panel or desk panel "bleeps."*

**Kirk.**  Kirk here.

**Uhura's Voice.**    Message from Starfleet, Captain. Priority channel. Admiral Komack speaking.

**Kirk.**    Transfer it in here, Lieutenant. (*The screen on the table lights.* **Admiral Komack** *appears, seated at his desk.*)

**Komack.**    Captain Kirk.

**Kirk's Voice.**    Here, sir.

**Komack.**    Captain, it is not necessary to remind you of the importance to the Federation of Sherman's Planet. The key to our winning of this planet is the grain, quadro-triticale. The shipment of it must be protected. Effective immediately, you will render any aid and assistance which Under Secretary Baris may require. The safety of the grain and the project is your responsibility. Starfleet out.

**Kirk.**    Now that's just lovely.

**Spock.**    But not entirely unexpected.

**Uhura's Voice.**    Captain Kirk! Captain Kirk!

**Kirk.**    Kirk here. What's the matter, Lieutenant?

**Uhura's Voice.**    Sensors are picking up a Klingon battle cruiser, rapidly closing on the station!

**Kirk.**    Contact Commander Lurry. We're on our way. (**Kirk** *and* **Spock** *race for the door, not even waiting for* **Uhura**'s *acknowledgment.*)

**SCENE  5:** Enterprise—*bridge.* **Kirk** *enters the bridge, followed by* **Spock**.

**Kirk.**    (*to* **Chekov**) What's that Klingon ship doing now?

**Chekov.**    Nothing, Captain. He's just sitting there, a hundred kilometers off K-7.

**Uhura.**    I have Commander Lurry.

**Kirk.**    Put him on visual, Lieutenant. (*continuing*) Commander Lurry, there is a Klingon warship hanging one hundred kilometers off your station . . .

**Lurry**.   (*appearing on viewscreen in his office*) I do not think that the Klingons are planning to attack us.

**Kirk**.   Why not? (*Viewscreen reveals the Klingon Commander,* **Koloth***, and his aide,* **Korax***, also in the office.*)

**Lurry**.   Because at this moment, the captain of the Klingon ship is sitting here in my office.

**Kirk**.   (*covering his shock*) We're beaming over. (*He and* **Spock** *start to leave the bridge.*)


## ACT TWO

**FADE IN:** *Exterior of space station.*

**Kirk**.   Captain's log, Stardate 4524.2. A Klingon warship is hovering only a hundred kilometers off deep space station K-7, while its Captain waits in the station commander's office. Their intentions are unknown.


**SCENE 1:** *Interior of space station—***Lurry***'s office.* **Kirk**, **Spock**, **Lurry**, **Koloth**, *and two Klingon* **Aides** *are present.* **Koloth** *is the Klingon commander and like the last Klingon commander that we saw, he is evil-looking.*

**Koloth**.   My dear Captain Kirk, let me assure you that my intentions *are* peaceful. As I have already told Commander Lurry, the purpose of my presence here is to invoke[2] shore leave rights. (**Kirk** *and* **Spock** *exchange glances.*)

**Kirk**.   Shore leave?

**Koloth**.   Captain, Klingons are not as luxury-minded as Earthers. We do not equip *our* ships with nonessentials. We have been in space for five months and what we choose as recreation is our own business. (*pause*) Under the terms of the Organian Peace Treaty, you cannot refuse us.

---

[2]call on, ask for, or put to use

**Kirk.**    The decision is not mine to make. Commander Lurry is in charge of the station.

**Lurry.**    *(aside to **Kirk**)* Kirk, I don't want them here, but I have no authority to refuse.

**Kirk.**    I have some authority to act, and I'm going to use it. *(to **Koloth**)* All right, you can give your men shore leave, but no more than twelve at a time. And I promise you this, Koloth, for every one of your men on this station, I'll have at least one security guard. There won't be any trouble.

**Koloth.**    Captain Kirk, no formal declaration of hostility has been made between our two respective governments. So, of course, the nature of our relationship *will* be a peaceful one.

**Kirk.**    Let us *both* take steps to make sure that it stays that way. *(The Klingon bows stiffly, politely. He turns on his heel and exits. **Korax** follows. **Kirk**, **Lurry**, and **Spock** exchange a worried glance.)*

**SCENE 2:** *Recreation room of the* Enterprise. **Kirk** *and* **Spock** *enter. There are a few* **Crewmen** *in the room.* **Scotty** *is at one table, reading. The other people in the room are in a knot around the other table.* **Kirk** *moves over to* **Scotty**. **Spock** *moves toward the knot of people.* **Kirk** *moves up and peers at the title of the tape that* **Scotty** *is reading. It is a page reflected on a screen.*

**Kirk.**    Another technical journal?

**Scott.**    Aye, why shouldn't I?

**Kirk.**    Mr. Scott, don't you ever relax?

**Scott.**    *(puzzled)* But I am relaxing.

*(**Kirk** nods and moves over toward the group of people.* **McCoy** *and* **Uhura** *are in the foreground of a knot of people. On the table is one larger tribble and at least ten smaller ones. They are playing with them.)*

**McCoy.**    How long have you had that thing, Lieutenant?

**Uhura.**   Only since yesterday. This morning, I found that he—I mean *she* had had babies.

**McCoy.**   I'd say you got a bargain. (*He picks up one of the tribbles and examines it curiously.* **Spock** *does likewise.*) . . . hmm . . .

**Spock.**   Fascinating.

**Kirk.**   Lieutenant Uhura, are you running a nursery?

**Uhura.**   I hadn't intended to but the tribble had other plans.

(**Spock** *absent-mindedly begins stroking his tribble.*)

**Kirk.**   You got this at the space station?

   (**Uhura** *nods.*)

**Spock.**   A most curious creature, Captain. Its trilling seems to have a tranquilizing effect on the human nervous system. Fortunately, I am, of course, immune to its effect.

   (**Kirk** *grins at him, turns to leave.* **Spock** *comes out of it, realizing he is petting the tribble almost hypnotically, puts it down. He follows* **Kirk** *out.*)

**McCoy.**   (*to* **Uhura**) Lieutenant, do you mind if I take one of these things down to the lab to find out what makes it tick?

**Uhura.**   It's all right with me, but if you're planning to dissect it, I don't want to hear about it.

**McCoy.**   Lieutenant, I won't hurt a hair on his head. Wherever that is. (*exits with a medium-sized tribble*)

**Ensign Freeman.**   Say, Lieutenant, if you're giving them away, could I have one too?

**Uhura.**   Sure, why not? They seem to be old enough.

   (*The crewman takes one eagerly; others also help themselves.*)


**SCENE 3:** *Corridor.* **Kirk** *and* **Spock** *round a bend.*

**Chekov's Voice.**   (*filtered*) Bridge to Captain Kirk.

**Kirk.**   (*goes to button*) Kirk here.

**Chekov's Voice.**  Mr. Baris is waiting on Channel E to speak to you.

**Kirk.**  Pipe it down here, Mister Chekov.

**Chekov's Voice.**  Aye, sir. Mr. Baris is coming on.

**Kirk.**  Kirk here. What is it, Baris?

**Baris.**  Kirk! This station is swarming with Klingons!

**Kirk.**  I was not aware that twelve Klingons were a "swarm," Mr. Baris.

**Baris.**  (*quieter*) Captain Kirk. There are Klingon soldiers on this station. I want you to keep that grain safe.

**Kirk.**  I have guards around your grain. I have guards on the Klingons! Those guards are there only because Starfleet wants them there! As for what *you* want . . . (*angry pause*) It has been noted and logged. Kirk out. (**Kirk** *savagely slams off the button. He turns and starts away down the corridor.*)

**Spock.**  Captain, may I ask where you'll be?

**Kirk.**  Sickbay. With a headache!

**SCENE 4:** *McCoy's lab.* **Bones (Dr. McCoy)** *is analyzing a sample of something as* **Kirk** *enters. In the foreground is a box of tribbles.*

**Kirk.**  When you get a chance, Bones, I'd like something for a headache.

**McCoy.**  (*looking at* **Kirk**) Let me guess . . . the Klingons? Baris?

**Kirk.**  Both. (**McCoy** *nods as* **Kirk** *moves to look at the box of tribbles. Looking at tribbles*) How many did Uhura give you?

**McCoy.**  (*taking pills from cabinet*) Just one.

**Kirk.**  You've got eleven here.

**McCoy.**  Oh, you noticed that. (*He returns to* **Kirk** *with a couple of pills. Continuing, handing* **Kirk** *tablets*) Here. This ought to take care of it.

**Kirk.**  (*holding the tablets but concerned with the tribbles*) Bones?

**McCoy.**  I'm still trying to figure it out myself. I can tell you this much: almost fifty percent of the creature's metabo-lism[3] is geared to reproduction. Do you know what you get if you feed a tribble too much?

**Kirk.**   A fat tribble?

**McCoy.**   (*slightly irked at being a straight man*) No. You get a whole bunch of hungry little tribbles.

**Kirk.**   (*swallowing pills*) Well, Bones, I suggest you open a mater-nity ward. (*Exits.* **McCoy** *looks at the tribbles and grimaces.*)


**SCENE 5:** *Transporter room. A small knot of men are waiting to beam over to the space station for shore leave.* **Chekov** *is one of them.* **Mr. Scott** *is at the console[4] with a technician.* **Kirk** *is speaking to him.*

**Kirk.**   I want all men who are going on shore leave to stay in groups. Avoid any trouble with the Klingons.

**Scott.**   Aye, Captain, I'll tell them before they go.

**Kirk.**   Mr. Scott, aren't you going on shore leave?

**Scott.** (*puzzled slightly*) No, sir.

**Kirk.**   Mr. Scott, I *want* you to go on shore leave. I want you to make *sure* there will be no trouble with the Klingons.

**Scott.**   But, Captain—

**Kirk.**   And Scotty . . . (**Scott** *looks up.*) enjoy yourself.
   (**Scott** *moves to the transport platform.*)


**SCENE 6:** *Interior of bar/store on space station. As the three Earthmen,* **Scott**, **Chekov**, *and* **Freeman**, *are sitting down, they notice a group of three or four* **Klingons** *at another table in bar, but they make a point of ignoring them.* **Cyrano Jones** *enters the bar. Spotting the Earthmen at their table, he moves toward them.*)

---

[3]the chemical and physical processes always going on in a living organism. Metabolism helps organisms grow and stay alive
[4]an instrument panel containing controls, as for operating aircraft.

**Cyrano.**    Ah, friends, can I interest you in a tribble? (*He is holding one at* **Mr. Scott***'s shoulder.* **Scotty** *turns and looks straight into the tribble's absence of a face. He shudders.*)

**Scott.**    No thank you.

**Cyrano.**    (*looking around*) Perhaps one of you other gents? (*No response.* **Cyrano** *shrugs, walking away, cooing at his tribble. In background,* **Waitress** *approaches the Earthmen.* **Cyrano** *approaches the Klingon table. He goes to* **Korax***, one of the Klingon aides of* **Koloth***.*) Friend Klingon, may I offer you a charmin' little tribble? (*He offers the tribble.* **Korax** *stares at it. The tribble reacts to the Klingon. It rears back with an angry spitting hiss. The Klingon reacts just as violently to the tribble. They hate and fear little fuzzy things.*)

**Korax.**    Get it away from me!

**Cyrano.**    (*to tribble*) Stop that! (*to* **Korax**) I can't understand. I apologize for his bad manners. He's never done that before!

**Korax.**    Take it away! Get out of here with that parasite.

**Cyrano.**    It's only a friendly little—

**Korax.**    (*loudly*) Take it away! (**Cyrano** *approaches* **Trader** *and puts the tribble on the counter. The* **Waitress** *is taking down a pitcher, preparatory to using it.*)

**Cyrano.**    Sir! Would you be willin' to engage in another little transaction? One of my little tribbles in exchange for a spot of . . . (*As he says this,* **Trader** *looks at him, and turns the pitcher upside down. Two or three tribbles tumble out onto the counter in front of* **Cyrano***.* **Cyrano** *looks at them and his voice trails off. As* **Trader** *moves away,* **Cyrano** *shakes his head at the tribbles.*) Tsk, tsk, tsk.

(*The* **Waitress** *moves across the room to the Earthmen's table with a tray of drinks. She begins setting them down. In front of* **Mr. Scott***, she puts a small bottle of Scotch and a glass. In front of* **Chekov***, she puts a small bottle of vodka and a glass. The other* **Crewmen** *get nondescript[5] drinks.*)

---

[5]not easy to describe or classify due to a lack of recognizable qualities

**Scott.**  (*examines* **Chekov**'s *drink, then looks up deadpan, but teasing*) When are you going off your milk diet, lad?

**Chekov.**  (*indignant*) This is vodka.

**Scott.**  Where I come from, that's soda pop. (*indicates own glass*) Now this is a drink for a *man*.

**Chekov.**  Scotch? (**Scott** *nods.*) A little old lady from Leningrad invented it.

(**Scott** *raises an eyebrow at this. He watches as* **Chekov** *downs his drink in one quick gulp. He shudders and downs his Scotch. The Klingons are laughing and joking among themselves.* **Korax** *suddenly rises and goes to* **Cyrano** *at the bar.* **Cyrano** *is contemplating an empty glass that the bartender has left on the bar.* **Korax** *steps up and pours something into it from his own bottle.* **Cyrano** *looks up. There are tribbles on the bar.*)

**Korax.**  (*loudly*) The Earthers like those fuzzy things, don't they? (*He points at tribbles on the bar, but they hiss and shrink away.*) Frankly, I never liked Earthers. They remind me of Regulan Blood Worms.

**Chekov.**  That Cossack!

**Scott.**  Easy, lad. You've got to learn to be forgiving.

**Korax.**  (*moving toward the Earthmen*) No, I just remembered. There is one Earthman who doesn't remind me of a Regulan Blood Worm. That's Kirk. A Regulan Blood Worm is soft and shapeless, but Kirk isn't soft. (**Chekov** *is seething.* **Korax** *is being sarcastic.*) Kirk may be a swaggering, overbearing, tin-plated dictator with delusions[6] of godhood, but he's not soft. (**Chekov** *tries to stand, but* **Scott** *holds him down with a hand on his shoulder.*)

**Scott.**  (*gently*) Take it easy, lad. Everybody's entitled to an opinion.

**Korax.**  That's right. And if I think that Kirk is a Denebian Slime Devil, well, that's my opinion too. (*He smiles.* **Chekov**

---

[6]false belief or opinion

*makes for the Klingon, only* **Scott** *has hold of* **Chekov**'s *arm and jerks him quickly and awkwardly back down into his chair. The Klingon laughs.)*

**Scott.**    Don't do it, mister! That's an order!

**Chekov.**    But you heard what he called the captain!

**Scott.**    It's not worth it, lad! It's not worth fightin' for. We're big enough to take a few insults. Drink your drink. *(He starts to pour* **Chekov** *another drink, but the vodka bottle is empty. So he pours the ensign a drink of Scotch instead.* **Chekov** *downs it without looking at it. His attention is still on* **Korax**. *After a bit, he does a take and looks at* **Scott** *with a peculiar expression on his face.)*

**Korax.**    *(laughing)* Of course, I'd say that Captain Kirk deserves his ship. We like the *Enterprise*. We really do. *(to* **Scott***)* That sagging old rust bucket is designed like a garbage scow! Half the quadrant knows it; that's why they're learning to speak Klingonese! *(He laughs as do his fellow Klingons.)*

**Chekov.**    Mr. Scott!

**Scott.**    *(deceptively pleasant)* Laddy, don't you think you should rephrase that?

**Korax.**    You're right, I should. I didn't mean that the *Enterprise* should be *hauling* garbage. I meant that it should be *hauled away AS garbage!*

*(Something snaps. Without a word,* **Scott** *stands up and belts the Klingon across the chops. The Klingon is hurled clear across the room and onto the table of his friends. It collapses onto the floor with him in the center of it. The Klingons rise and face the Earthmen. The Earthmen face the Klingons. At the bar,* **Cyrano** *looks up. The attendant starts to move to the wall panel. The Klingons and the Earthmen attack each other with a ferocity that is unparalleled in barroom brawls.* **Cyrano** *watches calmly.* **Trader** *is at the wall panel yammering into it, but the noise of the fight keeps us from hearing what he has to say. Casually,* **Cyrano**

*helps himself to a bottle and pours himself a drink. Then he walks out. As* **Cyrano** *strolls out of the bar, a squad of security men tear past him, running toward it.* **Cyrano** *watches them, toasts them with a bottle, and then strolls gaily off.)*

## ACT THREE

**FADE IN:** *Exterior of* Enterprise.

**Kirk's Voice.** Captain's log, Stardate 4525.6. A small disturbance between the Klingon crew and members of the *Enterprise* crew has broken out aboard Space Station K-7. I am forced to cancel shore leave for both ships.

**SCENE 1:** Enterprise—*briefing room.* **Kirk** *is addressing the whole line of transgressors.[7] A few tribbles are in evidence.*

**Kirk.** I want to know who started it. *(There is no response.)* I'm waiting. *(He waits.)* Freeman, who started it?

**Freeman.** . . . Uh . . . I don't know, sir.

**Kirk.** All right. Chekov. (**Chekov** *stares resolutely ahead. He is not in the best of condition, the effect of the fight and the vodka.)* Chekov, I know you, you started it, didn't you?

**Chekov.** No, sir. I didn't.

**Kirk.** Who did?

**Chekov.** Uh . . . I don't know, sir.

**Kirk.** You don't know. *(Stepping back and surveying all of the men.* **Scott** *is at the end of the line, next to* **Chekov**.*)* I want to know who threw the first punch. *(He waits.)* All right. You are all confined to quarters until I find out who started it. That's all. Dismissed. Not you, Mr. Scott. Mr. Scott, you were supposed to prevent trouble.

**Scott.** Aye, Captain.

**Kirk.** Who threw the first punch, Scotty? Scotty . . .

---

[7]one who breaks a rule or law

**Scott.**   Uh . . . I did, Captain.

**Kirk.**   (*momentarily startled*) You did? Mr. Scott? What caused it, Scotty?

**Scott.**   (*stiffly*) They insulted us, sir.

**Kirk.**   It must have been some insult, Mr. Scott.

**Scott.**   Aye, it was.

**Kirk.**   You threw the first punch?

**Scott.**   Aye. Chekov wanted to, but I held him back.

**Kirk.**   Why did Chekov want to fight?

**Scott.**   Uh—the Klingons . . . is this off the record, Captain?

**Kirk.**   (*stiffly*) No, this is not off the record.

**Scott.**   Well, Captain, the Klingons called you a . . . (*pauses to remember*) . . . tin-plated, overbearing, swaggering dictator with delusions of godhood.

**Kirk.**   (*intrigued in spite of himself*) Was that all?

**Scott.**   No, sir. They also compared you to the Denebian Slime Devil.

**Kirk.**   I see.

**Scott.**   And then they said that you were a—

**Kirk.**   I get the picture, Mr. Scott.

**Scott.**   Yes, sir.

**Kirk.**   And after they said all this, that's when you started the fight?

**Scott.**   No, sir.

**Kirk.**   (*startled*) No?

**Scott.**   No, sir—I didn't. You told us to avoid trouble.

**Kirk.**   Oh.

**Scott.**   And I didn't see that it was worth fightin' about. After all, we're big enough to take a few insults. Aren't we?

**Kirk.**   (*nodding slowly*) Mr. Scott, just what was it they said that made the fight break out?

**Scott.**   They called the *Enterprise* a garbage scow, sir.

**Kirk.**   I see. And that's when you hit the Klingon?

**Scott.**   Yes, sir.

**Kirk.**   (*comparing the two insults*) You hit the Klingon because he insulted the *Enterprise*? Not because he . . . ?

**Scott.**   Well, Captain, this was a matter of pride!

**Kirk.**   (*pauses*) That's all, Scotty. Oh, and Scotty . . . you're restricted until further notice.

**Scott.**   Yes, sir. Thank you, sir. (*pauses*) It'll give me a chance to catch up on my technical journals. (**Scott** *exits.* **Kirk** *stares after him regretfully.* **Scott** *is a good officer.* **Kirk** *does not like to have to discipline him.* **Kirk** *is also slightly amused at the whole incident.*)

**SCENE 2:** *McCoy's lab.* **Spock** *and* **McCoy** *are present. There are a number of tribbles in evidence on the counter, some of them feeding at a small dish.* **McCoy** *is examining one.* **Spock** *is regarding them with a jaundiced eye.* **McCoy** *glances sharply at him.*

**McCoy.**   What's the matter, Spock?

**Spock.**   There is something disquieting about these creatures.

**McCoy.**   Oh? Don't tell me you've got a feeling, Spock.

**Spock.**   Of course not, Doctor. They remind me somewhat of the lilies of the field. They toil not, neither do they spin, but they seem to eat a great deal. I see no practical use for them.

**McCoy.**   Does everything have to have a practical use for you? They're nice. They're furry and soft. They make a pleasant sound.

**Spock.**   So would an ermine violin, Doctor, but I see no advantage in one.

**McCoy.**   It is a human characteristic to be fond of lower animals, especially if they are attractive in some way.

**Spock.**   I am aware of human characteristics, Doctor. I am frequently inundated[8] by them. However, I have trained myself to put up with practically anything.

**McCoy.**    Spock, I don't know much about tribbles, yet, but I've found out one thing about them. I like them better than I do you.

**Spock.**    They do, indeed, have at least one redeeming factor. (*pointed, at* **McCoy**) They do not talk too much. If you will excuse me, sir. (**Spock** *leaves.* **McCoy** *glares after him.*)

**SCENE 3:** *Bridge.* **Kirk** *is stepping out of bridge elevator. He is gently kicking some tribbles out of the way. He goes to his chair, still preoccupied[9] with something. Almost without noticing it, he has to scoop three or four off his chair before he can sit down. He sits in the chair, absent-mindedly stroking a tribble that is perched on the chair arm. Suddenly he realizes there are tribbles all over the bridge.* **Kirk** *brushes the tribble away and activates his intercom.*

**Kirk.**    Dr. McCoy, get up here, right away. (*Gets out of his chair and makes a circuit of the bridge starting with* **Lieutenant Uhura** *and circling around counter-clockwise. He brushes tribbles off consoles, out of chairs, down from shelves, etc.*) Lieutenant Uhura, how did all of these tribbles get into the bridge?

**Uhura.**    I don't know, Captain. They seem to be all over the ship. (**Kirk** *steps down into the center of the bridge and moves over to the central console. He brushes a tribble off it. He crosses to the other side, as* **Bones** *enters.*)

**McCoy.**    You wanted to see me, Jim?

**Kirk.**    Yes, I did. (*He holds up a tribble.*)

**McCoy.**    Don't look at *me.* It's the tribbles who are breeding. If we don't get them off the ship we'll be hip deep in them!

**Kirk.**    Explain yourself, Doctor.

---

[8]flooded
[9]absorbed in one's thoughts

**McCoy.**   The nearest thing I can figure out is that they're born pregnant. It seems to be a great time-saver.

**Kirk.**   *(sourly)* Really?

**McCoy.**   From all I can find out, they seem to be bisexual, reproducing at will. And they have a lot of will.

**Spock**.   *(moving closer)* Captain, for once I am forced to agree with Doctor McCoy, though his way of putting it is most imprecise. They are consuming our supplies and returning nothing. I am running computations on their rate of reproduction, and although all of the figures are not yet in, I must confess I am somewhat alarmed by the direction they are taking.

**Uhura.**   They do give us something, Mr. Spock. Their love. (*on* **Spock**'s *raised eyebrows*) Cyrano Jones says that a tribble is the only love money can buy. (**Spock** *gives her the stare.* **Kirk**, *amused, steps in.*)

**Kirk.**   Lieutenant, too much of anything, even love, is not necessarily a good thing. *(pause)* Have a maintenance crew start clearing the whole ship. Then contact Commander Lurry. Tell him I'm beaming over. Ask him to find Cyrano Jones.

(**Uhura** *nods and turns to her console.* **Kirk** *and* **Spock** *start for the elevator, but pause long enough to remove some of the tribbles that have crawled back up onto the consoles.*)

**SCENE 4:** *Lurry's office.* **Lurry** *is standing.* **Cyrano Jones** *is sitting in a chair.* **Kirk** *is staring at him.* **Spock** *is standing thoughtfully.*

**Cyrano.**   Captain Kirk, I am mystified at your tone of voice. I have done nothing to warrant such severe treatment.

**Kirk.**   Really?

**Spock.**   Surely you realized what would happen if you transferred the tribbles from their predator-filled environment into an environment in which their natural multiplicative proclivities[10] would have no restraining factors.

**Cyrano.**    Yes, I . . . would you mind trying that on me again?

**Spock.**    By removing them from their natural habitat, you have, so to speak, removed the cork and let the genie escape.

**Cyrano.**    If you mean do I know they breed fast, of course I do. That's how I maintain my stock. But breeding animals is not against regulations, only breeding dangerous ones. Tribbles are not dangerous.

**Kirk.**    Just incredibly prolific.[11]

**Cyrano.**    Precisely. And at six credits a head, that is, a body, it mounts up. I'm a businessman, after all. Now, if you'll excuse me. (*He rises. Absent-mindedly he hands* **Kirk** *the tribble.*)

**Kirk.**    You ought to sell a manual of instructions with these things.

**Cyrano.**    If I did, Captain, what would happen to the search for knowledge? Pardon me. I must be tending to my ship. (*As he exits,* **Baris** *and* **Darvin** *enter.*)

**Kirk.**    (*under his breath*) Oh, fine.

**Darvin.**    Go ahead, sir. Tell him.

**Baris.**    Captain Kirk, I consider your security measures a disgrace. In my opinion, you have taken this entire, very important project far too lightly.

**Kirk.**    I regard the project as extremely important, Mr. Baris. It is you I regard lightly.

**Baris.**    (*dangerous*) I shall report fully to the proper authorities that you have given free and complete access to this station to a man who is quite probably a Klingon agent.

---

[10]natural tendency
[11]fruitful; productive

**Kirk.** *(staring hard at him)* That is a very serious charge, Mr. Baris. To whom do you refer?

**Baris.** That man who just walked out of here. Cyrano Jones!

**Kirk.** *(amused)* A Klingon agent?

**Baris.** You heard me.

**Kirk.** Oh, I heard you all right.

**Spock.** He just couldn't believe his ears.

**Kirk.** *(a pause, then to **Baris**)* What evidence do you have against Cyrano Jones?

**Baris.** *(drawing himself up to his full height)* My assistant here spent some time keeping Mr. Jones under surveillance.[12] His actions have been, ah, most suspicious. I believe he was involved in that little altercation between your men and the—

**Kirk.** Go on. What else do you have?

**Darvin.** Captain, I checked his ship's log. He was within the Klingon sphere of influence less than four months ago.

**Baris.** The man is an independent scout. It's quite possible that he's also a Klingon spy.

**Spock.** We have checked on the background of Mr. Jones. He is a licensed asteroid locater and prospector. He has never broken the law . . . at least not severely . . . and he has, for the past seven years, obtained a marginal living by engaging in the buying and selling of rare merchandise, including, unfortunately, tribbles.

**Baris.** He's after my grain! He's out to sabotage the entire project.

**Kirk.** You have no proof of that.

**Darvin.** You can't deny he has disrupted this station!

**Kirk.** People have disrupted Space Stations before without being Klingons. *(meaningful look at the two)* They need

---

[12]a watch kept over someone, especially a suspect

only have some influence. Unfortunately, disrupting a space station is not an offense. If you'll excuse me, I have a ship to take care of. Mister Spock? (**Kirk** *starts to leave, realizes that he is still holding* **Cyrano**'s *tribble. He shrugs, looks around and puts it in an ashtray. They exit.*)

**SCENE 5:** *Recreation room.* **Kirk** *goes to a wall panel.* **Spock** *and* **Scott** *are also there.*

**Kirk.**    Chicken sandwich, coffee. (*Almost immediately, the wall panel "bleeps."* **Kirk** *goes over to the wall. A panel slides open. He stares.* **Kirk**'s *sandwich is covered with tribbles, throbbing and purring.*) Mister Spock.

**Spock.**    (*approaches—he peers at it curiously*) Most interesting.

**Kirk.**    (*Reacting. Up till now, they have only been a nuisance, now they are definitely out of hand.*) Mister Spock, I want these creatures off my ship. I don't care if it takes every man we've got. I want them off!

**Scott.**    (*approaches, takes a look*) Aye, they've gotten into the machinery all right. They've probably gotten into all of the other food processors, too.

**Kirk.**    How?

**Scott.**    Probably through one of the air vents. (*points to a duct*)

**Spock.**    (*alarmed*) Captain, there are vents like that in the space station.

**Kirk.**    And the storage compartments. (*stepping to a wall panel*) This is Kirk. Contact Commander Lurry and Nilz Baris. Have them meet us near the warehouse. We're beaming over. (**Kirk** *and* **Spock** *exchange a glance. They run out.*)

**SCENE 6:** *Transporter room.* **Kirk** *and* **Spock** *enter, dash up to the platform, kicking tribbles out of the way.*

**Kirk.**    Energize. (*The* **Crewman** *slides the lever upward.*)

**SCENE 7:** *Space-station corridor—storage compartment.* **Kirk** *and* **Spock** *and a half dozen tribbles materialize.* **Lurry** *and* **Baris,** *but not* **Darvin,** *come running to meet them.*

**Lurry.** What's wrong?

**Kirk.** *(glancing around)* Plenty, if what I think has happened, has happened. (**Kirk** *turns to the storage-compartment door. There are two* **Guards** *standing by it. There are lots of tribbles in the corridor.)*

**Spock.** Guard, is this door secure?

**Guard.** Yes, sir. Nothing could get in.

**Kirk.** I hope so. Open the door. *(The* **Guard** *moves to the wall panel and touches a magnetic key to a panel. At first the door doesn't open. Continuing; impatient)* Open it! *(The* **Guard** *fiddles with the key.* **Kirk** *watches, waits; finally he steps up and pushes the* **Guard** *aside and pushes the door.)*

**Guard.** It's not working, sir. It seems to be— *(What it seems to be, we will never know, because at that moment, the door slides open with a WHOOSH!!! This is immediately followed by a silent FWOMP!! Hundreds and hundreds and hundreds of tribbles come tumbling out of the door, cascading down around* **Kirk,** *tumbling and seething and mewling and writhing and throbbing and mewling and trilling and purring and . . . )*

## ACT FOUR

**SCENE 1:** *Space station—corridor outside storage compartment, including door.* **Kirk** *is standing in the middle of a mountain of tribbles. More and more keep tumbling out, fat and sassy and lethargic.*

**Spock.** *(examining a tribble)* It seems to be gorged.

**Baris.** Gorged! On my grain! Kirk! I'll hold you responsible! *(despairingly at the grain)* There must be thousands.

**Kirk.** Hundreds of thousands.

**Spock.** One million, seven hundred and seventy-one thousand, five hundred and sixty-one. That's assuming one tribble multiplying with an average litter of ten, producing a new generation every twelve hours over a period of three days.

**Kirk.** That's assuming that one got in here three days ago.

**Spock.** *Also* allowing for the amount of grain consumed and the volume of the storage compartment.

**Baris.** Kirk! You should have known! You're responsible for turning the Development Project into a total disaster!

**Kirk.** (*slowly*) Mr. Baris—

**Baris.** Kirk, I'm through being intimidated! You've insulted me, ignored me, walked all over me! You've abused your authority and rejected my requests! And this . . . this . . . (*indicating the tribbles*) . . . is the result!! I'm going to hold you responsible. (**Kirk,** *thoroughly angry, but thoroughly cool, reaches out, grabs* **Baris** *by the coat front.*)

**Kirk.** Baris, shut up. Or *I* will hold *you* in irons. (**McCoy** *approaches.* **Kirk** *releases* **Baris,** *who hauls himself together.*)

**McCoy.** Jim, I think I've got it. All we have to do is stop feeding them. Once they stop eating, they'll stop breeding.

**Kirk.** Now he tells me. (**McCoy** *looks at the tribbles on the corridor floor and realizes that his advice is a little late.* **Spock** *is also looking at the tribbles on the floor. He is kneeling curiously.*)

**Spock.** Captain, this is most odd. This tribble is dead . . . (*He begins examining others.*) So are these. (**McCoy** *and the others begin examining the tribbles more carefully.*)

**McCoy.** This one is alive—a lot of them are still alive, but they won't be for long.

**Spock.** A logical assumption is that there is something in the grain.

**Kirk.** Bones, I want a complete analysis of the tribbles, the grain, everything. I want to know what killed them.

**McCoy.** I still haven't figured out what keeps them alive. (**Kirk** *just glares at him.*) I'll let you know as soon as I find anything. (*His arms laden with tribbles, he moves off.*)

**Baris.** Kirk, that won't do you any good. The project is ruined. Starfleet will hear of this disaster. There'll be a board of inquiry, and they'll roast you alive, Kirk. I'm going to be there to enjoy every minute of it.

**Kirk.** All right. But until that board of inquiry convenes, I'm still a captain. We have two things to do. First, find Cyrano Jones. (*pauses, glances at door.*) Second, close that door.

**SCENE 2: Lurry**'s *office. The last few preparations are being made. Two* **Crewmen** *escort* **Cyrano Jones** *into the room, then begin removing excess tribbles.* **Kirk** *and* **Spock** *and* **Lurry** *are discussing something.* **Baris** *is waiting at the door, looking for* **Darvin**. **Koloth** *enters, followed by* **Korax**.

**Kirk.** What do you want?

**Koloth.** An official apology, Kirk, addressed to the High Klingon Command. I want you to take responsibility for your persecution of Klingon nationals in this quadrant.

**Kirk.** An apology?

**Koloth.** You have harassed my men, treated us like criminals. You have been most uncourteous, Kirk. And if you wish to avoid a diplomatic crisis . . .

**Baris.** You can't let him, Kirk! That'll give them the wedge they need to claim Sherman's Planet!

**Spock.** I believe more than the word of an aggrieved[13] Klingon commander will be necessary for that, Mr. Baris.

**Koloth.** (*glaring at* **Spock**) As far as Sherman's Planet is concerned, Captain Kirk has just given it to us.

**Kirk.** We'll see about that, Captain. But before any official action is taken, I want to find out just what happened here. Who put the tribbles in the quadro-triticale, and what was in the grain that killed them?

**Koloth.** (*interrupting*) Captain Kirk, before you go on, I have a

---

[13]offended

request. Can you get those things out of here? (**Koloth** *points uncomfortably at the tribbles that* **Cyrano** *is holding in his lap and stroking.* **Kirk** *gestures to a* **Crewman**. *The man takes the tribbles and moves to the door just as* **Darvin** *enters. The tribbles hiss and spit at* **Darvin**. **Cyrano** *looks surprised.* **Kirk** *and* **Spock** *react.* **Spock**'s *eyebrows shoot up.*)

**Spock.**   Remarkable.

**Kirk.**   Jones, I thought tribbles liked everybody.

**Cyrano.**   Why, they do, Captain. I can't understand it. Last time I saw them act like that was in the bar.

**Kirk.**   What was in the bar?

**Cyrano.**   Klingons, sir. Him for one. (*He points at* **Korax**. **Kirk** *steps over, picks up a nice big fat tribble. He moves to* **Korax**, *extends the tribble. The tribble hisses and reacts.*)

**Kirk.**   You're right, Jones. (*He repeats the act with* **Koloth**, *who shrinks away. They obviously hate the tribbles, and the tribble rears back and hisses.* **Bones** *enters with a tri-corder in time to hear.*) They don't like Klingons. (*He moves to* **Spock**. *The tribble purrs loudly.*) They do like Vulcans. I never thought you had it in you, Spock.

**Spock.**   Obviously the tribble is an extremely perceptive creature.

**Kirk.**   (*Takes the tribble to* **Baris**. *The tribble purrs loudly.*) He even likes you, Baris. I guess there's no accounting for taste. (*He moves back to* **Darvin**, *extends the tribble.* **Darvin** *shrinks, the tribble rears back and hisses violently.*) But he doesn't like you, Darvin. I wonder why. Bones . . . (*gestures to* **McCoy**)

**McCoy.**   (*curious, unbuckles his medical tri-corder. He runs a sensor over* **Darvin**, *looks at the reading; looks again, runs the sensor over* **Darvin** *again. He is puzzled. He repeats the performance.*) Jim . . . (*checking a reading*) His heartbeat is all wrong. His body temperature is . . . Jim, this man is a Klingon!

**Baris.**   Klingon!? (**Kirk** *looks at* **Baris**. *Two* **Crewmen** *move up on either side of* **Darvin**.)

**Kirk.**   What do you think Starfleet will have to say about this, Mr. Baris? (*to* **Bones**) What did you find out about the grain?

**McCoy.**   Oh. It was poisoned.

**Baris.**   Poisoned?!!

**McCoy.**   It's been impregnated with a virus. The virus turns into an inert material in the bloodstream. The more the organism eats, the more inert matter is built up. After two or three days, it would reach a point where they couldn't take in enough nourishment to survive.

**Kirk.**   You mean they starved to death? A whole storage compartment full of grain and they starved to death?

**McCoy.**   That's essentially it.

**Kirk.**   (*looking at* **Darvin**) You going to talk?

**Darvin.**   I have nothing to say. (**Kirk** *picks up a couple of tribbles. He walks up to* **Darvin**, *about to shove them in his face. The tribbles hiss.*) All right. I poisoned the grain. Take it away!

**Kirk.**   Then the tribbles didn't have anything to do with it?

**Darvin.**   I don't know. I never saw one before in my life!! I hope I never see one of those horrible fuzzy things again! (**Kirk** *gestures. Two* **Crewmen** *drag* **Darvin** *away.* **Kirk** *catches sight of* **Koloth**, *who has been standing rather quietly, for a Klingon.*)

**Kirk.**   Captain Koloth, about that apology. You have six hours to get your ship out of Federation territory! (**Koloth** *says nothing, leaves stiffly. The tribbles hiss at him.*) You know, I could almost learn to like tribbles.

**Cyrano.**   Ah then, Captain Kirk, I suppose that I may be free to go.

**Kirk.**   Not yet. First I've got something to show you.

**SCENE 3:** *Store/bar.* **Kirk**, **Spock**, *and* **Jones** *enter.* **Trader** *is sitting in the door in the middle of a pile of tribbles. There are tribbles galore. It looks like a snowfall of fur. He has been inundated. He* *is close to tears, because there are too many even to try sweeping them out of his store. He sits there with his head in his hands.*

**Cyrano.**    Uh . . .

**Kirk.**    Mr. Jones, do you know what the penalty is for transporting an animal that is proven harmful to human life?

**Cyrano.**    But one little tribble isn't harmful. (**Kirk** *stares at him.*) Gentlemen, you wouldn't do a thing like that to me, now would you?

**Spock.**    The penalty is twenty years in a rehabilitation colony.

**Cyrano.**    Ah now, Captain Kirk, Friend Kirk. Surely we can come to some form of mutual understanding. After all, my little tribbles did put you wise to the poisoned grain and they did help you to find the Klingon agent. We must have saved a lot of lives that way.

**Kirk.**    Perhaps, there is one thing.

**Cyrano.**    (*eagerly*) Yes?!

**Kirk.**    If you can remove every tribble from the space station, I'll have Commander Lurry return your ship to you.

**Cyrano.**    (*gasping*) Remove every tribble? That'll take years.

**Spock.**    Seventeen point nine, to be exact.

**Cyrano.**    Seventeen point nine years?

**Kirk.**    Think of it as job security.

**Cyrano.**    Ahh, Captain, you are a hard man. (*looks at a tribble*) I'll do it. (*sighs, and begins picking up tribbles*)

**SCENE 4:** *Bridge.* **Kirk** *and* **Spock** *enter.*

**Kirk.**    I'm glad Starfleet was able to divert that freighter. Sherman's Planet will get their quadro-triticale only a few weeks late. (**Kirk** *steps down and takes his place in his chair. He glances around. The bridge is strangely free of tribbles.* **Scott** *and* **McCoy** *are on the bridge, and* **Kirk** *is speaking to them.*) I don't see any tribbles in here. . . .

**McCoy.**    You won't find a tribble on the whole ship.

**Kirk.**    How did you do that, Bones?

**McCoy.** (*suddenly modest*) I can't take the credit for another man's work. Scotty did it.

**Kirk.** Where are they, Mr. Scott?

**Scott.** Oh, but Captain, it was Mr. Spock's recommendation.

**Spock.** Based on computer analysis, of course, taking into consideration the elements of . . .

**Kirk.** Gentlemen, if I may be so bold as to interrupt this meeting of your mutual-admiration society, I'd like to know just what you did with the tribbles.

**McCoy.** Tell him, Spock.

**Spock.** It *was* Mr. Scott who did the actual engineering.

**Kirk.** (*firmly*) Scott, how did you get rid of the tribbles?

**Scott.** I used the transporter, Captain.

**Kirk.** You used the transporter?

**Scott.** Aye.

**Kirk.** (*curious*) Where did you transport them to, Scotty? (**Scott** *coughs into his hand.* **McCoy** *looks off into the distance.* **Spock** *blinks and manages a patently blank, innocent stare.* ) Scotty, you didn't just transport them out into space, did you?

**Scott.** (*slightly offended*) Sir! That'd be inhuman!

**Kirk.** Mr. Scott, what did you do with them?

**Scott.** (*realizes he is going to have to tell it sooner or later*) I gave them a good home, sir.

**Kirk.** Where?

**Scott.** I gave them to the Klingons, sir.

**Kirk.** You gave them to the . . .

**Scott.** Aye, sir. Just before they went into warp I transported the whole kit and kaboodle into their engine room where they'll be no tribble at all.

(*All react as the joke sinks in. Curtain.*)

THE END

## REVIEWING AND INTERPRETING

Record your answers to these questions in your personal literature notebook. Follow the directions for each part.

*REVIEWING*

Try to complete each of these sentences without looking back at the play.

*Recalling Facts*

**1.** Besides the fact that they seem to have no faces, a disturbing characteristic of tribbles is their
   a. ability to reproduce with great speed.
   b. high-pitched whine.
   c. popularity with Klingons.
   d. musty smell.

*Understanding Main Ideas*

**2.** The only thing that provokes Engineer Scott to fight is
   a. cruelty to defenseless people or animals.
   b. an insult to himself or one of his friends.
   c. an insult to the captain of his ship.
   d. an insult to his ship.

*Recognizing Literary Elements (Character)*

**3.** An action of Cyrano Jones's that suggests he is a bit dishonest is his
   a. bargaining with Trader.
   b. giving a tribble to Uhura.
   c. trying to sell merchandise to Klingons.
   d. walking off with Trader's liquor during the brawl.

*Identifying Cause and Effect*

**4.** The officers of the *Enterprise* realize that there's something suspicious about Arne Darvin because
   a. tribbles hiss at him.
   b. he supports Baris in everything Baris says.
   c. he doesn't get along with the officers.
   d. he accuses Cyrano Jones of wrongdoing.

*Identifying Sequence*

**5.** After a storage bin full of tribbles empties on Kirk, McCoy finds that
   a. feeding tribbles makes them reproduce.
   b. tribbles are born pregnant.
   c. tribbles are bisexual and reproduce at will.
   d. most of those tribbles are dead or dying.

**INTERPRETING**   To complete these sentences, you may look back at the play if you'd like.

*Making Inferences*

**6.** Although Cyrano Jones says he is giving his sample tribble to Uhura so that she can show it around the ship and build up demand, his real reason is to
   a. thank her for convincing Trader that tribbles are a desirable item.
   b. punish Trader for being such a tough customer.
   c. make sure that Uhura will support Jones in any future problems.
   d. get as many tribbles out of his own ship as possible.

*Predicting Outcomes*

**7.** The crew of the Klingon ship that received tribbles from the *Enterprise* probably will
   a. file an official complaint with the Federation.
   b. suffer great discomfort until the tribbles are removed.
   c. be grateful for the gift, although they might never admit it.
   d. return to attack the *Enterprise*.

*Making Generalizations*

**8.** The discussion immediately before the barroom brawl would support all of the following generalizations *except* the idea that
   a. Klingons don't know how to have fun except in a fight.
   b. *Enterprise* crew members dislike their captain.
   c. *Enterprise* crew members dislike Klingons.
   d. anyone looking for a fight can usually find one.

*Analyzing*

**9.** Captain Kirk's frustration that he is apparently the only officer who has not heard of quadro-triticale indicates that
   a.  Kirk is not intelligent enough to lead the *Enterprise*.
   b.  there is a terrible rivalry between Kirk and his officers.
   c.  agriculture and grains are popular topics in the era depicted in this play.
   d.  Kirk prides himself on being well informed.

*Understanding*
*Literary Elements*
*(Conflict)*

**10.** The conflict between Kirk on one side and Baris and Darvin on the other reaches its turning point when
   a.  Baris blames Kirk for the tribbles' getting into the grain.
   b.  Kirk threatens to put Baris in irons.
   c.  a tribble hisses and spits at Darvin.
   d.  McCoy discovers that Darvin is a Klingon in disguise.

Now check your answers with your teacher. Study the questions you answered incorrectly. What types of questions were they? Talk with your teacher about ways to work on those skills.

# The Teleplay

In the early days of television, performances were live. Actors had to hurry from set to set to perform their scenes. There were abrupt jumps from scene to scene and no second chances to redo or hide mistakes. But even then, television had changed the nature of the play. The camera could focus on a detail in the scenery, on an individual's face, or on a simple hand movement. What the camera could bring to the audience's eyes became as important to a plot as what the microphone brought to their ears. As soon as television programs started being prerecorded, however, the teleplay was freed from the physical limitations of scene changes. In addition, postproduction work could correct mistakes, provide smooth transitions, and add special effects.

It's not surprising, then, that writing for television requires special skills. A writer must be aware of the particular characteristics and needs of television production in order to write an effective teleplay. In these lessons, you will examine one of the most successful teleplays ever shown on commercial television, *The Trouble with Tribbles*. You will look at some of the methods that David Gerrold, its writer, uses to make it so effective:

1. Gerrold adjusts the pacing of plot developments to take advantage of the time requirements of commercial television.

2. He takes advantage of techniques made possible by television production in developing the plot.

3. He uses close-up camera shots to help develop the characters.

## LESSON ① TIME AND PLOT STRUCTURE

As you have seen in the stage plays in this book, plays vary in length. Many are only one act long, with only two or three scenes in the act. Others run two, three, or five acts long,

with over a dozen scenes. There are no particular time stan-
dards beyond the commonsense realizations that people want
a fair return on the money they spend on a ticket, and they
cannot sit still for more than about an hour at a time. Within
those broad guidelines, a playwright is free to structure a play
as he or she chooses. On commercial television, however,
time rules. A complete teleplay must fit within a multiple of
30 minutes, and it must allow for breaks at regular intervals
for commercials.

The freedom of the television audience is another important influence on plot development in a teleplay. Once the-
atergoers have spent money on tickets and taken their seats,
they usually are reluctant to leave the theater. Even when
they aren't thrilled by what happens before the first intermission, they generally stick around for more—and they frequently end up enjoying the play more by the end.

Television viewers, however, have no such commitment.
They must be convinced in the first minute or so of the program that the show is worth watching. Otherwise, in the
commercial break that follows the first scene, called the
*teaser,* viewers will switch channels and find something more
appealing to watch. The same danger exists at each of the
later commercial interruptions. This puts pressure on a playwright to begin strong and to make sure the high points of the
plot coincide with the commercial breaks.

How does David Gerrold meet this challenge? How does
he develop the elements of a good teleplay within these time
requirements? Review the teaser of *The Trouble with Tribbles*
on page 251. Notice how this brief scene firmly establishes
the following:

*Setting*—Spock's opening statement, accompanied by a camera
shot that includes the tri-screen, lets viewers know that the
first setting is a ship in space. This alone suggests a time in the
future, and the discussion about Ivan Burkoff vs. John Burke
suggests a particular time: two hundred years in the future.

*Characters*—The discussion among the three men and the scene-ending message from Uhura quickly introduce four important characters and indicate their relationships. *Conflict*—Spock's two-sentence analysis of the disputed area identifies a background conflict between two super-powers, the Federation and the Klingon Empire. Uhura's message jump-starts an immediate crisis.

Equally importantly, this scene immediately establishes a mood that sets this science fiction story apart from the stereotypical science fiction tale. Within the first half-dozen speeches, the viewer discovers that this play does not take itself too seriously:

**Spock.** (*consulting tri-screen on table*) Deep space station K-7 is now in sensor range, Captain.

**Kirk.** Good. Mr. Chekov, this flight is supposed to give you both experience and knowledge. How close will we pass to the nearest Klingon outpost on our present course?

**Chekov.** One parsec, sir. Close enough to smell them.

**Spock.** That is not logical, Ensign. Odors cannot travel through the vacuum of space.

**Chekov.** I was making a little joke, sir.

**Spock.** It was extremely little, Ensign.

The lighthearted mood is reinforced by Chekov's claim about English astronomer John Burke being a Russian named Ivan Burkoff, as well as his casual reference to Peter the Great. The switch to a warlike mood then, with Uhura's interruption, is all the more effective. Even viewers who are not fans of science fiction will be interested in seeing how the humor of the teaser will affect the solution of the problem.

Skim the rest of the play, giving special attention to the last scene in Act One and the last scene in Act Two. Notice how each act ends with a crisis that is a natural development of the story but is also effectively situated before a commercial break.

EXERCISE ①

Reread Act Two, Scene 6 (pages 265–269). Then use what you have learned in this lesson to answer these questions:

**1.** Identify at least three conflicts in this scene. Which of them builds to a scene-ending crisis?

**2.** What line or lines does Chekov speak that build on his dialogue in the teaser? How is the humorous mood further developed by Scott's reactions to Korax's insults? How does the last paragraph of stage directions carry the lightness into the fight scene?

Now check your answers with your teacher. Review this part of the lesson if you don't understand why an answer was incorrect.

WRITING ON YOUR OWN ①

This exercise should give you a solid foundation for the writing exercises that follow. Still, if you find your first plans and story line unworkable, start over. Follow these steps:

- At the top of your paper, write whether you will deal with science fiction or fantasy. Then write three headings: *Setting, Conflict,* and *Major Characters.* Using your notes from the first writing exercise, choose a story line. Feel free to adapt ideas from stories you have read or watched. Then settle on a setting and a conflict that grows out of the story line you chose. Under the first two headings, write a short description of your setting and a two- or three-sentence summary of the conflict.
- Under the third heading, list three or more characters. After each character's name, write a sentence that describes the quality or qualities for which the character will be known.
- Begin to plan the scenes of your half-hour play. Using the first half of *The Trouble with Tribbles* as a guide to what can

fit into 30 minutes of air time, list 10 to 15 possible scenes. What crisis in the plot might fall at the midpoint, just before the commercial break, which would pull viewers back for the second half? Arrange your plot developments so as to place an exciting moment at the midpoint.

## LESSON ② PRODUCTION TECHNIQUES AND STAGING

When it became possible to prerecord, or film television shows before their broadcast, many new opportunities arose. Scenes could be shot in whatever sequence was easiest. If an actor made a mistake, a scene could be re-shot. Afterward, film editors could superimpose visual effects over action or add background music or sound effects to different scenes. Additional scenery also could be shot to establish new settings or provide smooth transitions. Finally, after all the scenes were shot and perfected individually, they were pieced together in the right order. You will now look at how David Gerrold makes use of special effects and other TV techniques to build the action and develop the plot of *The Trouble with Tribbles*.

By the end of the first act of the play—roughly 12 minutes of performance time—six scenes have taken place in the briefing room, the bridge, Lurry's office on the space station, the bar/store, the briefing room, and the bridge. In live theater, such short scenes can be presented by having lights come up on different areas of the stage or by having actors stand in front of the curtain for transitions. On television, however, each scene can be presented on different sets, with appropriate scenery and props. The stage directions for *The Trouble with Tribbles* combine the actors' movements with television filming techniques to move smoothly from one scene to the next.

For example, here is the beginning of Act One. Can you identify two techniques that the script calls for which would be impossible to do on a stage?

**FADE IN:** *Space station hangs against a backdrop of stars, slowly growing in size as the* Enterprise *approaches.*

**Kirk.**    Captain's log; Stardate 4523.3. Deep space station K-7 has issued a priority-one call. More than an emergency, it signals near or total disaster. We can only assume the Klingons have attacked the station. We are going in armed for battle.

**SCENE 1:** *Bridge. Everyone on the bridge stares tensely, watching the screen showing the space station.*

The fade-in on the *Enterprise*, created by trick photography, forms a transition from the commercial break into the story. The voice-over of the Captain dictating his log is a second TV technique regularly used on *Star Trek*. These two steps overcome the disruption the commercial break creates between the teaser and the body of the play. They bring to mind the situation at the end of the teaser and carry the viewer into the next scene at the level of anticipation set up by the teaser.

The transition from Scene 1 to Scene 2 is basically a *fast cut*. However, the dialogue and stage directions at the end of Scene 1 and the special effects at the beginning of Scene 2 bridge the jump between scenes so well that Kirk's first lines in Lurry's office seem almost like a continuation of his earlier lines:

**Kirk.**    You'll try to explain? You'd better be prepared to do more than that. Kirk out. (*starting toward door*) Mr. Chekov, maintain battle readiness. Uhura, have the transporter room stand by. Mr. Spock, I'll need your help . . . (**Kirk** *waits for* **Spock** *to join him at the elevator. They step into it.*)

**SCENE 2:** *Lurry's office on the space station.* **Lurry**, **Baris**, *and* **Darvin**; **Kirk** *and* **Spock** *materialize.* **Kirk** *is furious as he* *begins talking to* **Lurry** *as soon as materialization is complete.*

**Kirk.**　Commander Lurry, if there is no emergency, why did you order a priority-one distress call?!

Besides using production methods to carry the plot forward at a fast pace, Gerrold calls on television techniques, too, to give life to the title creatures in *The Trouble with Tribbles*. Although the following stage direction does not specify camera shots, it is clear that a close-up is required.

> *(The tribble in the lieutenant's hands purrs and throbs. It is a ball of green-gold fluff about the size of a large bean bag. Its purr is soft and high-pitched like a dove's cooing.)*

The throbbing motion of the tribble could be produced by some machinery inside the beanbag-like prop, or it could be added by postproduction special effects. On stage, such a small object would be difficult if not impossible to see. The tribble's soft sounds, likely to be produced by an offstage instrument, would be either not noticed or not connected to the tiny object in the lieutenant's hand. Without the availability of television techniques, Gerrold could not have used tribbles effectively, and this plot would not have been possible.

EXERCISE ②

Read Act One, Scene 3, from Trader's question "Is he clean?" to the end of the scene (pages 256–259). Then use what you have learned to answer these questions:

1. Where is the tribble that Trader and Cyrano Jones are discussing? What is it doing during the discussion? How is the television audience made aware of what the two characters don't notice?

**2.** Which character finally sees what the tribble is doing? What part of his reaction would be unclear without the aid of close-ups and postproduction tricks?

**3.** In his final speech, Cyrano promises that concerning the tribbles, ". . . you won't be able to keep up with 'em." How does his promise foretell the developments in Act Two?

Now check your answers with your teacher. Review this part of the lesson if you don't understand why an answer was incorrect.

## WRITING ON YOUR OWN ②

To take full advantage of the television medium, your script should call for effects not possible on a stage. In this exercise you will describe an element of your play that requires television production techniques. Follow these steps:

- Think about how you can use camera shots and postproduction tricks to tell your story more effectively. For example, is one of your characters visible only under certain conditions? To understand the plot, must the audience see objects or actions not easily presented on a stage? Select a special effect vital to the plot that can be developed best with television techniques. Briefly explain in what way the special effect is necessary to the teleplay.
- Describe the special effect so that a production crew would know what is needed. For example, if a character needs to be invisible at times, explain what would need to happen to indicate the character's presence. Also explain what visual or sound effects, if any, should be used when the character becomes visible.
- On your developing outline of the scenes, note the scenes in which this special effect will be needed.

## LESSON ③   TV TECHNIQUES AND CHARACTER DEVELOPMENT

Most dramatic characters are created for a single play. The writer creates them to make a specific contribution to a particular plot, and he or she has complete control over their behavior. This is true of individual plays that are written for television and also of plays that are written for the stage. Television series, however, present a different situation.

In a television series such as *Star Trek*, there are continuing characters who appear from episode to episode. The writer of any single episode, therefore, does not have complete control over these characters. For example, in *The Trouble with Tribbles*, David Gerrold could not introduce a personality trait that would conflict with a continuing character's established nature because his episode would not fit in with the rest of the series. And yet Gerrold had to develop each character almost as if he or she were new because, for viewers seeing *Star Trek* for the first time, the characters really are new. So for an episode to stand on its own successfully, there must be enough character development that viewers can understand and appreciate the continuing characters without ever seeing any other episode in the series. The fact that *The Trouble with Tribbles* includes this character development is one of the reasons why the episode appeals to an audience that extends beyond regular *Star Trek* viewers.

In presenting the crew members of the *Enterprise*, Gerrold emphasizes established qualities that contribute to the particular conflict in *The Trouble with Tribbles*. Mr. Spock, for example, has a major role in almost every episode of the series. He is only half-human and is embarrassed by any emotional responses his human attributes provoke. His Vulcan half looks down on any illogical actions or thoughts. To present Spock, Gerrold uses the usual methods of characterization in a play—dialogue from and about the character and actions by the character. To these methods he adds one that is effective only on film: facial expressions. Look, for example, at his stage directions for this passage involving Spock.

**Baris.**   Quadro-triticale is not wheat, Captain! I wouldn't expect you or your First Officer to know about such things, but—

**Spock.**   (*quietly watching all this*) Quadro-triticale is a high-yield grain, a four-lobed hybrid of wheat and rye, a perennial, also, if I'm not mistaken. The root grain, triticale, can trace its ancestry all the way back to Twentieth-Century Canada, when—

**Kirk.**   (*making no effort to conceal his amusement*) I think you've made your point, Mr. Spock. (**Spock** *pauses and looks at* **Kirk**. *He gives* **Kirk** *the familiar* **Spock** *stare. He was just getting to the interesting part.*)

**Lurry.**   (*interrupting*) Captain, quadro-triticale is the only Earth grain that will grow on Sherman's Planet.

Spock's encyclopedic knowledge is established by this dialogue, as he identifies the nature and history of quadro-triticale. His social ineptness is just as quickly established by the close-up on his reaction to Kirk's interruption. His facial expression works well in this play, and it also meshes nicely with the personality established in the *Star Trek* series.

## EXERCISE ③

Read this passage. Then use what you have learned to answer the questions that follow it.

**Lurry.**   Captain Kirk, couldn't you at least post a couple of guards? We do get a large number of ships passing through.

**Spock.**   It would be a logical precaution, Captain. The Sherman's Planet affair is of extreme importance to the Federation.

(**Kirk** *looks at* **Spock** *as if to say* "*Blast your logic!*" *However,* **Spock** *is usually correct, so . . .*)

**Kirk.**   (*chagrined; taking out his communicator*) Kirk to *Enterprise*.

**Uhura's Voice.** *Enterprise* here.

**Kirk.** Secure from general quarters. Beam over *two* and *only* two security guards. Have them report to Commander Lurry.

1. When Lurry makes his request, Kirk is angry enough to reject it without hesitation. However, Spock supports the request before Kirk can react. From the stage direction following Spock's statement, how would you expect Kirk's expression and manner to change? Describe two or more stage directions that reflect his gradual change of mind.

2. Taken together with the passage quoted in the lesson right before this exercise, what does the viewer learn of Kirk's relationship with Spock?

Now check your answers with your teacher. Review this part of the lesson if you don't understand why an answer was incorrect.

WRITING ON YOUR OWN ③

In this exercise you will make use of close-up shots to develop a character. Follow these steps:

- Review the outline you have developed so far for your half-hour play. In which situation might a character's facial expression tell more than dialogue would? Choose a scene in which a close-up on a character will reveal something about the character.
- Now set the scene for the close-up. Summarize the plot developments immediately leading up to the close-up or use a combination of background explanation and dialogue.
- Write stage directions that tell the actor what expressions to assume or what actions to take. Give the camera operator an idea of how to focus the shot. Make sure that what viewers learn about the character comes strictly from the close-up.

## DISCUSSION GUIDES

1. There are many who believe that a Federation-style govern-ment would be undesirable on Earth because the United States would have to give up its own government in the process. Others believe that only a world government would be able to find fair solutions to world problems. Where do you stand on this issue? Prepare a one- to three-minute state-ment explaining your view and present it to the rest of the class.

2. Is the United States doing enough to unlock the mysteries of space? Should it be researching the possible colonization of space? Should it be spending more on space travel, or is it already spending more of its budget on the space program than is justified, considering other current problems? Choose one side of this issue and prepare arguments supporting it. Join two classmates who share your views and debate a team that holds the opposite opinion. Take a poll of class-mates both before and after the debate to find out if the debate changes anyone's mind.

3. Join other members of your class to videotape your own pro-duction of *The Trouble with Tribbles*, taping either selected scenes or the complete teleplay. You may enjoy trying to duplicate some of the scenery, costumes, make-up, and spe-cial effects, but consider them optional. Give more attention to determining the best possible camera shots, including close-ups, that help develop character and plot. If you have access to editing equipment, you can shoot scenes out of order. Otherwise, shoot the scenes in the order in which they should occur. At the end of production, show the tape to your class.

# WRITE A TELEPLAY OUTLINE AND TEASER

In this unit you have examined how the special techniques of television production can be used with traditional methods to develop the plot and characters of a teleplay. In the writing exercises, you have explored how to use these techniques in an original teleplay. Now you will use what you have learned to write an outline of scenes and a teaser for a half-hour teleplay.

Follow these steps to complete your outline and teaser. If you have questions about the writing process, refer to Using the Writing Process, which begins on the next page.

- Assemble and review the writing you did for the exercises in this unit: *1)* summaries of themes or story lines for your chosen type of fiction and some character descriptions, *2)* a description of certain special effects critical to the development of your plot, *3)* stage directions for a close-up that reveals a particular character, *4)* notes for a scene-by-scene outline of a teleplay on a fantasy or science fiction theme.
- Revise your outline to reflect the concepts you have learned about in the course of this unit. The outline should indicate major plot developments in the scenes and whether techniques unique to film production are used in the scenes.
- Then write a teaser that lasts no longer than a minute and a half when performed. Begin by identifying the setting and the characters who will be onscreen. Include all special effects and transitions, dialogue, and stage directions for actors' movements and important camera shots.
- Read your teaser to a few classmates. Then ask them if they would wait through the commercial and watch the rest of the show or change the channel after the teaser. Be sure they give reasons for their decisions. If necessary, use their comments to revise your teaser.
- Proofread your teaser and script outline for spelling, grammar, punctuation, capitalization, and formatting errors. Then make a final copy and place it in your portfolio.

# USING THE WRITING PROCESS

This reference section explains the major steps in the writing process. It will help you complete the writing exercises in this book. Read the information carefully so you can understand the process thoroughly. Whenever you need a quick review of important things to think about when you write, refer to the handy checklist on page 306.

Most tasks worth doing have several steps. For example, houses can be built only after the builder follows a number of complicated, logical steps. Moviemakers must go through a series of steps before releasing a film. Even a task as simple as making a peanut butter and jelly sandwich requires that the sandwich maker perform specific steps in order. So it should be no surprise that anyone who wants to write a good story, play, poem, report, or article must follow certain steps too. Taken together, the steps a writer follows are called the *writing process*. This writing process is divided into three main stages: prewriting, writing, and revising. Each stage is important for good writing.

STAGE 1: **Prewriting**
Prewriting consists of all the preparation you do before you put a single word down on paper. There are many decisions that you must make in order to make your writing as interesting, logical, and easy to read as possible. Here are the steps you should take before you begin to write:

1. **Decide on your audience.** Who will read your writing? Will your audience be your teacher? Will it be readers of the school newspaper? Or will your audience be family or friends? Your writing will change, depending on who you think your audience will be.

2. **Decide on your purpose.** Why are you writing? Do you want to teach your audience something? Do you want to entertain

them? Do you want to change someone's mind about an issue? Think about your purpose before you begin to write.

3. **Think about possible topics.** What are some topics that interest you? Make a list of topics that you are familiar with and might like to write about. Make another list of topics that interest you and that you want to learn about.

One technique that helps some writers at this stage is *brainstorming.* When you brainstorm, you let your mind wander freely. Without judging your ideas first, scribble them down as they come to you—even if they seem silly or far-fetched. Good ideas often develop from unusual thoughts.

If you're having trouble coming up with ideas by yourself, brainstorm with a partner or a group of classmates. Jot down everyone's ideas as they say them. Brainstorming alone or with others should give you a long list of possible writing topics.

4. **Choose and narrow your topic.** Once you have chosen a topic, you will probably find that it is impossible to cover every aspect of it in one piece of writing. Say, for example, you have chosen to write about the possibility of life on other planets. In a single piece of writing, you could not possibly include everything that has been researched about extraterrestrial life. Therefore you must choose one or two aspects to focus on, such as alleged sightings in the United States or worldwide organizations that study extraterrestrial life. Otherwise you might overload your writing with too many ideas. Concentrate on telling about a few things thoroughly and well.

5. **Research your topic.** You probably have had experience using an encyclopedia, the library, or the Internet to look up information for factual reports. But even when you write fictional stories, you often need to do some research. In a story set during the Civil War, for example, your characters wouldn't use pocket cameras or wear suits of armor. In

order to make your story as accurate and believable as possible, you would have to research how Americans lived and dressed during the years of the Civil War.

To conduct your research, you may want to use books, magazines, newspapers, reference works, or electronic sources, such as the Internet. Some topics may require you to interview knowledgeable people. For realistic stories set in the present time, you may find that the best research is simple observation of everyday life. Thorough research will help ensure that your facts and details are accurate.

6. **Organize your research.** Once you have the facts, ideas, and details you need to decide how to arrange them. Which order will you choose? No matter what you are writing, it is always helpful to begin with a written plan. If you are writing a story, you probably will tell it in time order. Make a list of the major story events, arranged from first to last.

Arranging details in time order is not the only way to organize information, however. Some writers start by making *lists* (informal outlines) of the facts and ideas they have gathered. Then they rearrange the items on their lists until they have the order that will work well in their writing.

Other writers make formal *outlines,* designating the most important ideas with roman numerals (I, II, III, IV, and so on) and related details with letters and numerals (A, B, C; 1, 2, 3; a, b, c; and so on). An outline is a more formal version of a list, and like the items in a list, the items in an outline can be rearranged until you decide on a logical order. Both outlines and lists help you organize and group your ideas.

*Mapping* or *clustering* is another helpful technique used by many writers. With this method, you write a main idea in the center of a cluster and then surround it with facts and ideas connected to that idea. Following is an example of a cluster map:

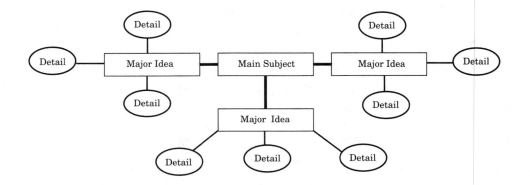

## STAGE 2: Writing

1. **Get started.** Begin your writing with an introductory sentence or paragraph. A good introduction can become a guide for the rest of your piece. For ideas on good opening sentences, take a look at some of your favorite stories or magazine articles.

   Your introduction should give your audience a hint about what is coming next. If you are writing a story, your introduction should set the tone and mood. It should reveal the narrator's point of view; and it may introduce the main characters, the setting, and your purpose for writing. Do the best you can with your introduction, but remember that if you wish to, you can always change it later.

2. **Keep writing.** Get your thoughts down as quickly as possible, referring to your prewriting notes to keep you on track. Later, when you are done with this *rough draft,* you will have a chance to revise and polish your work to make it as clear and accurate as possible. For right now, however, don't stop for spelling, grammar, or exact wording problems. Come as close as you can to what you want to say, but don't let yourself get bogged down in details.

## STAGE 3: Revising

Now you're ready to revise your work. Careful revision includes editing and reorganizing that can make a big difference in the final product. You may wish to get feedback from your classmates or your teacher about how to revise your work.

1. **Revise and edit your work.** When you are revising and editing, ask yourself these questions:
   - Did I follow my prewriting plan? Reread your entire first draft. Compare it to your original plan. Did you skip anything important? If you added an idea, did it work logically with the rest of your plan? Even if you decide that your prewriting plan is no longer what you want, it may include ideas you don't want to lose.
   - Is my writing clear and logical? Does one idea follow the other in a sensible order? Do you want to change the order or add ideas to make the organization clearer?
   - Is my language clear and interesting? Have you chosen exact verbs, nouns, and adjectives? For example, have you used forms of the verb *to be (is, are, being, become)* more often than you should? If so, replace them or change your sentence to make them unnecessary. Include precise action words such as *raced, hiked, zoomed,* and *hurried* in place of the overused verb *went.* Instead of using vague nouns such as *water* and *green,* choose exact ones such as *cascade* or *pond* and *lime.* Replace common adjectives such as *beautiful* and *nice* with precise ones such as *elegant, gorgeous,* and *lovely.*
   - Is my writing clear and to the point? Take out words that repeat the same ideas. For example, don't use both *liberty* and *freedom.* These words are synonyms. Choose one word or the other.

2. **Proofread for errors in spelling, grammar, capitalization, and punctuation.** Anyone reading your writing will notice such

errors immediately. These errors can confuse your readers or make them lose interest in what they are reading.

If you are in doubt about the spelling of a word, look it up or ask someone for help. If you are unsure about your grammar, read your writing aloud and listen carefully. Does anything sound wrong? Check with a friend or classmate if you need a second opinion—or refer to a grammar handbook.

Make sure every group of words is a complete sentence. Are any of your sentences run-ons? Do proper nouns begin with capital letters? Is the first word of every sentence capitalized? Do all your sentences have the correct end marks? Should you add any other punctuation to your writing to make your ideas even clearer? If your writing includes dialogue, have you used quotation marks correctly?

3. **Make a clean final draft to share.** After you are satisfied with your writing, it is time to share it with your audience. If you are lucky enough to be composing on a computer, you can print out a final copy easily, after running a spell-check. If you are writing your final draft by hand, make sure your handwriting is clear and easy to read. Leave margins on either side of the page. You may want to skip every other line. Make your writing look inviting to your readers. After all, you put a lot of work into this piece. It's important that someone read and enjoy it.

# A WRITING CHECKLIST

Ask yourself these questions before beginning a writing assignment:

- Have I chosen a topic that is both interesting and manageable? Should I narrow it so I can cover it in the space that I have?
- Do I have a clear prewriting plan?
- What should I do to gather my facts and ideas? read? interview? observe?
- How will I organize my ideas? a list? an outline? a cluster map?
- Do I have an opening sentence or paragraph that will pull my readers in?
- Do I need to add more information? Switch the order of paragraphs? Take out unnecessary information?

Ask yourself these questions after completing a writing assignment:

- Did I use my prewriting plan?
- Is the organization of my writing clear? Should I move, add, or delete any paragraphs or sentences to make the ideas flow more logically?
- Do all the sentences in one paragraph relate to one idea?
- Have I used active, precise words? Is my language interesting? Do the words say what I mean to say?
- Are all the words spelled correctly?
- Have I used correct grammar, capitalization, punctuation, and formatting?
- Is my final draft legible, clean, and attractive?

# GLOSSARY OF LITERARY TERMS

This glossary includes definitions for important literary terms that are introduced in this book. Boldfaced words within the definitions are other terms that appear in the glossary.

**act**   a major section of a play. An act can be further divided into several smaller sections called **scenes**.

**aside**   a **monologue** in which a character directs his or her speech to the audience instead of to other characters on stage.

**cast of characters**   a list of all the **characters** who appear in a play. A play's characters are usually listed in the order in which they appear on stage.

**center stage**   the middle of a stage.

**characterization**   the methods by which a writer develops a particular character's personality. Four common methods of characterization are 1) giving a physical description of a character, 2) showing the character's actions, 3) revealing the character's thoughts and words, and 4) revealing how others feel about the character.

**characters**   the people who act and speak in a play. The word *character* also refers to the personalities of those individuals. Characters in a play are portrayed by actors. Characters can be **dynamic** or **static**.

**climax**   the point of highest tension or greatest interest in a story or play. The climax is usually the turning point in the **plot**. From that point, the probable outcome of the story or play becomes clear.

**comedy**   a play that causes laughter and ends happily.

**conflict**   a struggle or tension between opposing forces that is central to a **plot**.

**dialogue**    all the words spoken by the actors in a play. Dialogue helps move the **plot** along and also reveals the personalities of the **characters**.

**downstage**    the area of a stage that is nearest the audience.

**drama**    a kind of literature designed for the theater and meant to be performed in front of an audience. Actors take the roles of the **characters**, perform the assigned actions, and speak the written words.

**dynamic character**    a character who changes from the beginning to the end of a story or play.

**exaggeration**    an intentional overstatement of facts or events so that their meanings are intensified. Exaggeration often produces humorous results.

**exposition**    the part of a **plot** in which the playwright introduces the **characters** and **conflicts** and provides whatever background information is necessary. The exposition often presents information about the **setting** also.

**falling action**    the part of a **plot** in which the tension eases and the action begins to slow down. The falling action leads to the **resolution**.

**introduction**    *see* **exposition**.

**monologue**    whatever a character says that is not part of a back-and-forth conversation, including a **speech**, a **soliloquy**, and an **aside**.

**mood**    the general feeling or atmosphere of a play.

**narration**    the kind of writing that gives the events and actions of the story.

**narrator**    the person who is telling a story. The narrator speaks directly to the audience.

**pace**    the overall rate of speed at which the speeches and actions of a play are performed.

**play**    a literary work that tells a story through the characters' words and actions. A play is meant to be performed in front of an audience.

**plot**   the sequence of events in a piece of writing. A plot usually has five sections: **exposition** or **introduction, rising action, climax, falling action,** and **resolution.**

**props**   the movable articles used in a play, other than costumes and **scenery**. The word *props* is a shortened version of *properties*.

**radio play**   play written expressly to be performed on the radio. The radio play relies on voices, **sound effects,** and music to tell its story.

**resolution**   the last part of a **plot**; the conclusion of a play. The resolution contains the outcome of the **conflict.**

**rising action**   the part of a **plot** in which the tension builds and complications develop. During the rising action, the **conflict** increases and the action moves toward the **climax.**

**scene**   a section of a play that occurs in one place and at one time. A new scene begins each time there is a change in place or time. In many plays, several scenes make up a single **act.**

**scenery**   the backdrop on a stage that identifies a play's **setting,** or time and place.

**set**   a combination of **scenery** and **props** that establish the **setting** and its **mood.**

**setting**   the time and place of the action of a story or play. Many playwrights establish the setting of a play through **stage directions** in the **exposition.**

**soliloquy**   a **monologue** in which a character speaks his or her thoughts aloud while alone on stage.

**sound effects**   the sounds called for in the script of a play, radio or television program, or motion picture.

**speech**   an extended **monologue** delivered by one character.

A speech is heard but uninterrupted by the other character or characters on stage.

**stage directions**    any information that is intended for the director, the actors, or the readers of a play. Stage directions are separate from the **dialogue** and are often printed in *italics*.

**stage left**    the part of a stage that is on the left from the actors' point of view. The audience sees it as the right side of the stage.

**stage right**    the part of a stage that is on the right from the actors' point of view. The audience sees it as the left side of the stage.

**staging**    everything that an audience sees and hears during a play. Staging covers decisions about costumes, **scenery, props,** actors' movements on stage, and **sound effects**.

**static character**    a character who remains the same from the beginning to the end of a story or play.

**storyboard**    a series of pictures depicting the important events in a plot. Storyboards are often used by movie directors for reference throughout the filming of a screenplay.

**style**    the distinctive way in which something is said or written.

**suspense**    the interest, excitement, and anticipation that the reader or the audience feels about what will happen next in a play.

**synopsis**    brief summary.

**teaser**    the first scene of a **teleplay.**

**teleplay**    play written expressly to be performed on television.

**tempo**    speed with which words are spoken or actions are performed on stage.

**theme**    the underlying message or central idea of a piece of writing.

**tone**    a writer's attitude toward his or her subject.

**upstage**    the area of a stage that is farthest from the audience.